Why and How to Teach Music Composition:

A New Horizon for Music Education

Why and How to Teach Music Composition:

A New Horizon for Music Education

Edited by Maud Hickey

Based on a Northwestern University
Music Education Leadership Seminar

The National Association for Music Education

Production Editor: Teresa K. Preston

Contents

The Role of the Teacher

Preface
The Northwestern University
Music Education Leadership Seminars

Imagine having the opportunity to spend five uninterrupted days with a small core of colleagues who have the same research interest as you and have devoted a considerable amount of time and energy to this research. While in the past you've not had more than a passing 10-minute conversation (if any) with some of these scholars, these 5 days offer time that is completely dedicated to brainstorming, discussing, questioning, and challenging ideas in the field. Such a "think tank" atmosphere is a rare commodity in the music education field because of our tendency (and the necessity) to spend much of our time and energy in "mixed company" forums. Yet this luxurious scenario is desperately needed in order to help focus, as well as advance, research in music education. The vision to develop such a thought-provoking gathering comes from, and was realized by, Bennett Reimer through the Northwestern University Music Education Leadership Seminars (NUMELS). Reimer describes his conception of these seminars in the preface to the first NUMELS book, *Performing with Understanding: The Challenge of the National Standards for Music Education:* "The Northwestern University Music Education Leadership Seminars (NUMELS) are conceived as a means of elevating all aspects of the music education profession by providing intensive learning experiences for its top-level leaders, thinkers, and activists" (Reimer, 2000, p. vii).

In 1996, the first NUMELS focused on "Performance in the Context of National Standards for Music Education" and resulted in the book *Performing with Understanding* (2000, Reimer, ed., MENC). The 1998 NUMELS was on "Issues of Multiculturalism in Music Education" and resulted in *World Musics and Music Education: Facing the Issues* (2002, Reimer, ed., MENC). The topic for the 2002 NUMELS was popular music.

The topic of this book, *Why and How to Teach Music Composition: A New Horizon for Music Education,* was the focus of the 2000 NUMELS. The authors gathered on the campus of Northwestern University in Evanston, Illinois, to share research, question each other, and discuss the ideas most relevant to the field of teaching music composition to children. Near the end of our days together, we began to focus on the topics that would help shape this book. As a result, readers will see purposely rich and diverse views on topics that are pertinent to teaching music composition to children—a subject in need of resources and one that has recently been of great interest to the music education community. The eleven chapters are organized into sections on philosophy, creativity, the developing composer, contexts, and the role of the teacher in teaching music composition. They offer philosophical, theoretical, and practical advice for researchers and practitioners alike. And, as in the first two NUMELS books, the chapters are written by internationally known researchers on this topic.

Bennett Reimer deserves to be commended for his vision and follow-through that led to the NUMELS events. Bernard Dobroski, dean of the Northwestern University School of Music, warrants deepest gratitude for providing tremendous financial and personal support that made the 2000 NUMELS not only fruitful, but truly enjoyable for those involved. Finally, much thanks goes to Teresa Preston, associate editor at MENC: The National Association for Music Education, whose prodding as well as quick turnaround time helped to bring this book to publication in a timely manner.

—Maud Hickey

Philosophy

1

Freedoms and Constraints: Constructing Musical Worlds through the Dialogue of Composition

Margaret S. Barrett

During the twentieth century, a growing interest in the function of creativity in learning led to the championing of creative experience in arts education (Abbs, 1987) and the development of music curricula that incorporate composition and creative experience. National documents in such countries as Australia (Curriculum Corporation, 1994), England (Department for Education and Employment: QCA, 2000), and the United States (Consortium of National Arts Education Associations, 1994) advocate composition as a component of a complete music education. Attendant to these developments, music education researchers have focused on issues surrounding composition and creative experiences in children's music education, including the study of the processes and products of composition and improvisation and the social and cultural contexts in which these occur. Yet as a community, we still know very little about the role of musical composition and creative experiences in the lives of children. While

many believe that musical composition and creative experiences are beneficial for children, the theoretical foundations for this belief remain largely unexamined. The study of musical composition and creativity and their function in children's musical development continues to provide fertile ground for music researchers and practitioners alike.

In this chapter, I shall explore issues surrounding the role of musical composition and creativity in music education and propose a view of composition as a meaning-making process that is fundamental to the intellectual, social, and emotional life of children. In preparing this chapter, I have drawn on Wallas's (1926) model of the process of creativity. In this model, Wallas identifies four discrete stages in the creative process: (1) *preparation,* the gathering of relevant information and materials; (2) *incubation,* the unconscious reflection on the problem; (3) *illumination,* the identification of a possible solution; and (4) *verification,* the formulation, testing, and refinement of the solution. Through this structure, I shall attempt to explore some of the freedoms and constraints involved in the study of composition and creativity in music education.

Preparation: Questioning Some Assumptions

My initial preparations for this chapter were guided by a series of questions through which I hoped to gather relevant information on the topic. The first of these questions—*What do we mean by composition?* and *What do we mean by creativity?*—focus on how the terms *composition* and *creativity* are used in music education. One striking issue that emerges from the literature is the way these terms tend to be used interchangeably. Any discussion of musical composition and creativity must include some clarification of these terms and their use in the context of music education.[1]

The conflation of the terms *composition* and *creativity* suggests that all composition is creative and that all creative experience in music education involves composition; both assumptions are profoundly misleading. While composition and improvisation[2] have traditionally been viewed as the province of creative activity in music and music education, these are not necessarily the only processes through which creative activity is evidenced. Within Western music education, processes such as arranging, conducting, and performing may be viewed as equally creative enterprises (Elliott, 1995; Webster, 1992). When we move beyond the ways in which musical experience is construed within Western settings to those of other cultures, activities such as audience-listening are also viewed as inherently "creative" (Racy, 1998). Further, the notion that all composition experience is creative

fails to recognize the potential influence of context and task on the compositional process and its emergent products. The completion of a composition exercise that is designed to demonstrate the learner's understanding of a specific technique may result in a work that is technically proficient but lacking evidence of creativity, however it is defined.

In seeking possible answers to the concerns outlined above, it is helpful to examine the literature on creativity in general. In defining creativity, many writers identify the dual features of *novelty* and *usefulness* as the distinguishing features of creative endeavor (Amabile, 1996; Csikszentmihalyi, 1996; Gardner, 1993). Specifically, creativity is defined as "the ability to produce work that is both novel (i.e., original, unexpected) and appropriate (i.e., useful, adaptive concerning task constraints)" (Sternberg & Lubart, 1999, p. 3). The complementarity of these features is emphasized by Amabile and Tighe (1993), who suggest that "a product or response cannot merely be different for the sake of difference; it must also be appropriate, correct, useful, valuable, or expressive of meaning" (p. 9).

The identification of these features raises questions concerning the nature of novelty and usefulness. In his systems theory of creativity, Csikszentmihalyi (1999) describes creativity as a "novel variation" in a domain of practice that is judged by knowledgeable others to be suitably "useful" for inclusion in the domain (p. 315). This view implies that the individual must possess considerable knowledge and skill in a domain of practice in order to develop a creative product—knowledge and skill that is rarely possessed by a school-aged child. A number of writers avoid the suggestion that children are incapable of creative achievement by asserting that creativity occurs at a range of levels (Amabile, 1983). Boden puts forward the notion that creativity may occur at an individual or psychological level *(P* creativity), where the product or idea is novel to the individual mind that created it, or at a historical level *(H* creativity), where the product or idea is novel both to the individual mind and in the context of the "whole of human history" (1991, p. 32; 1994, p. 76). In a similar move, Gardner (1993) puts forward the notion of *little-C* and *big-C* creativity. For Gardner, the latter is characterized in the works of individuals such as Sigmund Freud, Martha Graham, and Pablo Picasso, whereas the former may be evidenced in the ways that individuals approach everyday activity in novel ways.

From the above, it could be argued that while children's composition endeavors may not always yield a product that would be judged as a worthy addition to a society's cultural capital (a big-C contribution), through the notion of little-C creativity, children may be viewed as capable of producing creative compositions. However, the relegation of children's musical composition to the category of little-C creativity is troubling. Implicit in the notion of big-C and little-C creativity is a hierarchical difference that treats little-C creativity as a lowly counterpart to big-C creativity. I suggest that children's musical compositions and creative experiences are not ersatz versions of adults' experiences of similar activities. Rather, I suggest that the function of composition and creative

experience in the lives of children differs from that of adults in crucial ways.

Such reflections lead to a second set of questions: *What are we trying to achieve in the teaching of composition?* and *What are the beliefs that we hold about the role of composition in the teaching and learning process?* A number of reasons have been put forward for the incorporation of musical composition and creative experience in the school curriculum:

- the desire of progressive educationists in the latter half of the twentieth century to *provide creative experience for all students*
- the view that experience in composition would introduce children to the materials and techniques of contemporary music
- the view that composition experience underpins the development of musical thinking and understanding
- the desire to more effectively teach composition as a musical process in order to develop the "next generation of composers" (Jones, 1986, p. 63).[3]

Inherent in each of these views is a different conception of the child as composer and the nature and function of composition in the child's life and musical education. In each of these views, engagement in musical composition is subject to differing degrees of "freedoms and constraints." As Bruner (1996) comments, "Any choice of pedagogy implies a conception of the learner. … Pedagogy is never innocent. It is a medium that carries its own message"(p. 63). The progressivists viewed creative experience as a means of promoting self-expression and individual growth. This was achieved through activities that emphasized expressive freedom, unhampered by technical constraints and any reference to the socio-cultural contexts of the art form. Abbs (1987) comments in a critique of the movement:

> The accent on self-expression left the mastery of technique unaccented, even mute. For the progressives if the work was some-how expressive of self then, by definition, it became laudatory, whatever the artistic merit. ... Many children in "free" art lessons may have expressed themselves only too well but produced, for want of technique and initiation into the symbolic medium, artistic non-entities. (p. 44)

By contrast, those who believed that composition is taught in school primarily to develop the next generation of composers were less concerned with the development of the self and more concerned with a rigorous introduction to the technical demands of the art form. This approach may be viewed as so bound by constraints as to stifle individual expression.

Between these two extremes lie the view of composition as instrumental in developing an understanding of stylistic changes in contemporary music and the view that composition is a powerful means to promoting musical thinking and understanding. This latter view has been perhaps the more influential in recent curriculum developments (Paynter, 1982, 1992), reflecting a belief that children should engage in all the processes of music—including generating, perceiving, and performing music.

This linking of music education with musical worlds beyond those of the school leads to another question: *What is the continuing role and function of composition in the lives of children?* A growing body of research probes the ways children compose and the nature of their compositions, but there has been less emphasis on exploring the function of composition in children's lives. In recent years, descriptive studies of children's conceptions and practice of music (Campbell, 1998), musical improvisation (Kannellopoulos, 1999), and improvisation and composition (Burnard, 2000) have provided valuable insights into the ways children conceive of music. However, theoretical views of the function of composition in the lives of children are yet to be explored.[4]

In the following section, I shall explore the notion that the process of composing is essentially a *meaning-making* enterprise. It is a culturally mediated form of meaning-making and is most effectively described as a dialogue between the child as musician and composer, the emerging musical work, the culture that has produced the composer and the emerging work (these may be products of different cultures), and the immediate setting in which the transaction takes place (most often, the school classroom). If education, and by extension music education, is the development of children's capacity both to construct meaning from encounters with their worlds and to construct their worlds in meaningful ways, then a view of composition as a form of meaning-making seems a worthy enterprise.

In a thoughtful exploration of the philosophical foundations for music education research, Reimer (1992) comments that "freedom without structure is anarchic, and music education research has suffered from an excess of disorder because its structure has been insufficient to give meaning to freedom of choice" (p. 25). In advocating a more coherent structure for music education research, Reimer suggests that music education researchers and practitioners have much to gain from examining the theoretical and methodological developments in domains other than music education. In formulating a view of composition as a form of meaning-making, I shall draw on cultural psychology (Bruner, 1990, 1996; Cole, 1996), social constructivism (Vygotsky, 1934/1986, 1978), situated learning (Wertsch, 1991), and dialogic inquiry (Bakhtin, 1981). These mutually informing theories may be described as part of the sociocultural turn in the study of human behavior. In a complementary move, I shall conclude with a discussion of Greene's (1995) work in educational philosophy, with a particular emphasis on the role of imaginative reflection.

Incubation: Some Reflections around a Theoretical Framework

Cultural Psychology

Cultural psychology is described as "the study of the culture's role in the mental life of human beings" (Cole, 1996, p. 1), a study that recognizes that when examining human development we must also consider surrounding social and cultural practices. Cultural psychology seeks to reunify the study of culture and the mind in order to facilitate a culturally informed theory of the mind. This approach may be contrasted with approaches to the study of the human mind and behavior that "treated culture as an independent variable and mind as a dependent variable, [and] broke apart the

unity of culture and mind and ordered them temporally—culture is stimulus, mind [is] response" (Cole, 1996, p. 327).

Cultural psychology admits that higher mental processes, such as language and music, are both formed by, and formative of, culture; this assertion is evidenced in the ways in which these processes differ from society to society. Such an admission involves recognizing the ways in which our thinking is shaped, not only by our encounters with others in the world but also by the social practices and objects that constitute our worlds. Practices, conventions, artifacts, rites, and rituals that have been developed by others are a powerful means through which we understand the world. Cole (1996) suggests that culture is a "medium," a "system of artifacts" (cultural models, scripts, tools, and symbols) that is contextually embedded, and that mind is a "process of mediating behaviour through artifacts" (pp. 143–44). Bruner (1996) puts this more simply, stating that "culture is a toolkit of techniques and procedures for understanding and managing your world" (p. 98).

Social Constructivism

Cole acknowledges his debt to the Russian school of psychology, particularly as exemplified in the work of Vygotsky (1934/1986) and Vygotsky and Luria (1930/1993). Vygotsky's social constructivism suggests that human learning is inherently social in nature. Through *interpsychological processes*—i.e., the interactions between people and the attendant cultural artifacts or "mediational tools" (Wertsch, 1991)—*intrapsychological processes*— i.e., the complex processes that occur within the child's mind—are developed. For Vygotsky, the higher mental functions are a result of mediated activity where the mediating agents are psychological tools and interpersonal relations. Vygotsky's work signaled a move away from a singular focus on the individual toward a multifaceted focus on the social group and its cultural-historical context. This new focus acknowledges the crucial role of the *sociocultural* and *material* worlds in the construction and demonstration of knowledge.

Situated Learning

Inherent in a view of a culture as a system of artifacts is the recognition of the ways in which values and identity are embedded in such objects, rituals, and events (Goodnow, 1990). As we engage with these artifacts in the process of acquiring knowledge and skill, we consciously and unconsciously foster beliefs, values, and attitudes concerning the use of that skill or knowledge in relation to other cultural practices. In acknowledging the ways in which beliefs, values, and attitudes are embedded in culture, it is also crucial to recognize the ways in which they act as constraints on our thinking. By their very nature, cultural models, scripts, tools, and symbol systems—such as language and music—eliminate in advance a number of possible behaviors and interpretations, and, in the process, we internalize a number of "cultural constraints" (Hatano, Inagaki, & Oura, 1993). Indeed, any sociocultural context constrains and affords certain ways of behaving.

In applying these ideas to music education, I suggest that there are ways of reading meaning into musical practices that privilege one perspective over another. Within the music classroom, the cultural models, musical scripts, and tools that we provide inevitably encourage particular ways of engaging with music experience, constructing musical meanings, and articulating and communicating those meanings. It is crucial that music educators be aware of the ways in which specific practices and conventions, and the traditions from which they emerge, become the *cultural benchmark* against which other constructions and ways of communicating meaning are judged—and are often found deficient. The notion of an official sanction suggests that other constructions and presentations of meaning may be less authoritative and less likely to be encountered in the school setting, disenfranchising those students to whom the cultural benchmark is not familiar. For students whose primary means of musical engagement occurs through the practices of cultures that are not endorsed by the school "authority," the music classroom may be an inhospitable and unrewarding environment.

The concept of *scaffolding* (Bruner, 1975; Wood, Bruner, & Ross, 1976) emphasizes the construction of knowledge through activity embedded in social interaction. In this view of learning, the child is an active, knowledgeable participant in the learning process—not a passive recipient of the thoughts of others. Such learning takes place in the *zone of proximal development* (ZPD), which Vygotsky describes as "the distance between the actual developmental level as determined by independent problem solving and the level of potential development as determined through problem solving under adult guidance or in collaboration with more capable peers" (as cited in Bruner, 1986, p. 73).

In acknowledging the social nature of learning, consideration needs to be made of two facets: (1) the role of socioemotional aspects in the development of mind (Markus & Kitayama, 1991; Rogoff, Mistry, Goncu, & Mosier, 1993) and (2) the conscious and unconscious transmission of values and attitudes. Emotions are "intrinsically social" (Sloboda & Juslin, 2001, p. 86), subject to developmental change (Ekman & Davidson, 1994), and involve some form of "cognitive appraisal" (Scherer, 1999). Consequently, any learning experience necessarily engages the emotions in some way. On this latter point, Kruger and Tomasello (1996) comment:

> In cultural learning children learn not just about the affordances of the inanimate environment but also something about the intentional states of adults— what they intend to do in performing certain actions or, perhaps, the strategy they are using or the thoughts they are thinking. In cultural learning the child does not learn from the adult's actions, but the child learns through the adult's perspective in a truly intersubjective fashion. It is also important in our definition of cultural learning that on many occasions children internalize adult's intentional attitudes from such encounters and make them their own. (p. 371)

Through the concept of a cultural tool kit (Bruner, 1990) or mediational tools (Wertsch, 1991), it is possible to recognize that learning is inherently social, even when it occurs in the absence of others. This notion may be related to Vygotsky's (1934/1986) view of egocentric, or inner, speech. For Vygotsky, inner speech is a powerful instrument in the development of thought, "an instrument of thought in the proper sense—in seeking and planning the solution of a problem" (1934/1986, p. 31). Vygotsky proposes that internally directed egocentric speech—as opposed to externally directed communicative speech—occurs when the child "transfers social collaborative forms of behaviour to the sphere of inner-personal psychic functions" (p. 35). Inner speech is the integral component of the child's activity, serving "as a mediator in purposive activity and in planning complex actions" (p. 39). In short, through the intermediary of inner speech, when children engage with the system of artifacts and mediational tools that constitute culture, things do shape mind (p. 39).

Dialogic Inquiry

The characterization of inner speech as a form of internal collaboration with oneself (Vygotsky, 1934/1986) has led some to describe it as *dialogic* and to link the concept of inner speech and the development of thought to Bakhtin's notion of dialogism or *dialogicality* (Wertsch, 1991). Dialogicality refers to "the ways in which one speaker's concrete utterances come into contact with ... the utterances of another" (Wertsch, 1991, p. 54), acknowledging that an "utterance" is distinguished not by the meanings of the words used but by the ways in which words are used in particular contexts. Central to the idea of dialogicality is the notion that meaning is constructed in collaboration with others and with available mediational tools. Writing of the ways meaning is constructed in language, Bakhtin (1981) comments:

Language is not a neutral medium that passes freely and easily into the private property of the speaker's intentions; it is populated—overpopulated—with the intentions of others. Expropriating it, forcing it to submit to one's own intentions and accents, is a difficult and complicated process. (p. 294)

This view of the construction of meaning as an act of *expropriation* (dispossession) that precedes the act of *appropriation* (taking to oneself) highlights the active struggle to construct meaning. Appropriation becomes a form of socially formulated, context-dependent, goal-directed, and tool-mediated action.

Illumination: Toward a View of Composition as a Dialogue of Meaning-Making

Through the multifaceted lens afforded us by the theoretical frameworks of cultural psychology, social constructivism, situated learning, and dialogic inquiry, we are able to acknowledge the role of history, culture, and context—both social and material—in the development of children's musical understanding and the ways in which they interact with their worlds. Drawing on these theoretical positions, I propose a view of composition that revolves around the development of children's capacity both to construct meaning from encountering their worlds and to construct their worlds in meaningful ways.

I suggest that composition is a form of dialogical meaning-making through which children expropriate the surface features and deep structures of the music they encounter in order to appropriate and

submit them to their "own intentions and accents" (Bakhtin, 1981, p. 294). Through composition and attendant musical processes, children are able to construct knowledge of themselves (self-identity), as well as their culture (group-identity). This occurs through a dialogic process that is both an "internal collaboration with oneself" (Vygotsky, 1934/1986, p. 35) and a collaboration with one's material and social worlds. From a cultural psychology view, an original composition is inevitably a reflection of and response to the social and cultural contexts in which a composer works. These contexts reflect particular sociohistorical traditions, and, to this extent, composition can become an act of developing both self-knowledge and cultural knowledge. Later in this chapter, I shall explore this view of composition through the analysis of the musical discourse of two 10-year-old children.

Verification: Composition as a Meaning-Making Process

My interest in the nature of children's musical thinking has led me to explore children's aesthetic decision making and musical thinking as composers (Barrett, 1996); children's aesthetic decision making and musical thinking as critics of compositions (Barrett, 2000/2001); and children's musical thinking as users of invented notation (Barrett, 1997; 1999; 2000; 2001). This research has entailed working with children in naturalistic settings, public schools where musical teaching and learning occur. The term *naturalistic* refers to those settings where the researcher must adjust to the vagaries of the school, acknowledging all the "constraints" and interpretations of "freedom" such settings impose, as opposed to those settings in which some features are manipulated to accommodate the needs of the researcher and the experiment. As children compose and improvise, they are actively constructing their own musical world while expropriating and appropriating salient features of their musical worlds both within and beyond the school. Children's demonstration of musical understanding as they generate music can reveal the ways in which they negotiate their musical cultures.

In an ongoing investigation of children's aesthetic decision making and musical thinking as composers and critics (Barrett, 2000/2001), I have been observing 70 children aged 5–12 years as they participate with their peers in a weekly 30-minute music lesson conducted by a specialist teacher in a large suburban public primary school. The music program includes composition, critical listening, vocal and instrumental performance, and limited instruction in formal notation. The specialist music teacher's pedagogical approach is eclectic and shows the influences of Kodály, Orff, and the "composition" movement exemplified by Paynter (1982, 1992). The time devoted to each of these aspects is limited because of such constraints as the time allocated for the children's weekly lesson, the average class size of 28 children, the limited instrumental resources, and the usual interruptions of a public school timetable (e.g., sports days, assemblies, and preparations for presentation of musical items for special events). In addition to the classroom program, the school offers an instrumental program to children in grades three and above.

Data generated through the project include observations of the children's music classes; recordings of children's original compositions and notations; children's written reflections on composition, performance, and listening experiences; and transcripts of interviews conducted with children on the completion of composition and critical-listening experiences. For the purposes of this chapter, I shall focus on the musical "discourse" of two 10-year-old grade-four children engaged in a music project that revolves around Oscar Wilde's story *The Selfish Giant* (1888/1978).

On finding that the children's general classroom teacher had selected *The Selfish Giant* as a text for classroom reading and discussion, the music teacher decided to use this as the basis for a composition task over the ensuing 4 weeks. Earlier in the year, the children had completed one other composition task, focused on "musical contrasts." An additional impetus for using the story as a composition stimulus was the recent acquisition of a recording of Graham Koehne's ballet suite *The Selfish Giant* (1996). These serendipitous events led to the formulation of a project that involved a solo composition task requiring children to respond to the story through composition and a critical-listening task that focused on Koehne's work. The children listened to Koehne's work in the music classroom after completing their own compositions. This class discussion focused on the ways in which the emotions in the story were explored through instrumentation (strings and woodwind), tempo, and dynamic change. At the completion of the composition component of the project and prior to the group-listening experience, I conducted individual interviews with children from the class in which we listened to both their own compositions and that of Koehne and discussed their responses as composers and critical listeners. The discussion of each work was interspersed with repeated hearings of the relevant recording.

Jenna

Jenna was 10 years old and in grade four at the time of the project. Her professed musical listening encompassed the Spice Girls, Hanson, Savage Garden, and Celine Dion—to which she listened "every morning and night"—and "the stuff we hear in school." The latter referred to the easy-listening classics the classroom teacher used as background to visual-art activities and relaxation exercises, as well as the works presented through the music specialist program. At the time of the project, Jenna had been taking flute lessons through the school program for 6 weeks, and she was enthusiastic about these lessons. The 30-minute lessons took place during the school day and were conducted in groups of six. Students were able to borrow

school instruments on a daily basis, and Jenna had established a pattern of taking a flute home twice a week and occasionally practicing during lunch or recess when an instrument was available. This was Jenna's first instrumental experience beyond that of the music specialist program, and no one in her family played a musical instrument.

For the composition task, Jenna composed a short work for metallophone. The transcription of this work (Figure 1) seeks to capture the dynamic of the performance of the work rather than interpret Jenna's intentions within a frame of traditional notation. When performing the work for the recording, Jenna held her notation tightly in her left hand while playing with the mallet in her right hand. Throughout the performance, she referred back and forth between the notation and the instrument, suggesting that she was focused on producing an accurate rendition of her work. The composition is rhythmically static and melodically centered in C major. The latter may be seen as both a product of her chosen instrument (metallophone

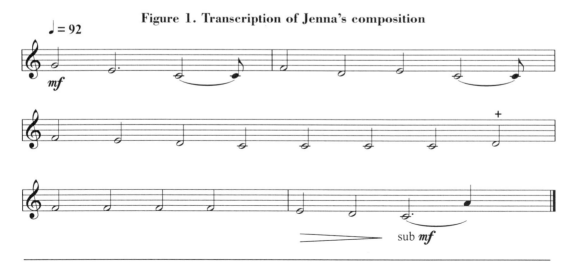

Figure 1. Transcription of Jenna's composition

tuned to the C major diatonic scale) and a reflection of Jenna's early experiences of flute tuition. There are strong similarities between bars one and two of the work and the introductory exercises that Jenna had encountered in her group flute lessons.

Jenna's detailed notation (Figure 2) reveals her thinking in structural terms, her reflections on the story, the stimulus for the composition, and her musical and emotional intent in composing the work. She divided the work into three distinct sections: beginning (bars 1 and 2); middle (bar 3); and end (bar 4). These divisions were signaled in the performance of the work through slight augmentation of the final durations in the beginning and middle sections and a surprise ending in the final section. This structural approach may be related to Jenna's previous experience of composing around musical contrasts, a task in which the children were advised to "think about how you will start, what will happen next, and how you will end." It is clear from Jenna's notation that each section relates to a particular moment in the story. However, while aspects of the composition may be viewed as literal depictions of the action (for example, the Giant walking in sections two and three may be indicated by the use of repeated notes), it is interesting to note Jenna's emotional intentions through an indication above the notation of mood states and musical effect: sad/calm; quiet/soft; slow/relaxing.

Jenna and I met to talk about both her composition and Koehne's composition approximately 10 days after the completion of the recording phase of the project. As our conversation began ("M" represents me, and "J" represents Jenna), it was Jenna's

new experience of handling and learning an instrument that shaped how she responded as a listener and critic to both her own composition and that of Koehne:

> M: Jenna, we have just listened to your piece of music. Can you tell me what you were thinking when you listened to that?
> J: Oh, well, I was feeling sort of nervous because I thought I'd sort of muck up. My face I think went pretty red, and I got all hot and sweaty. I felt like I was going to muck up, and I thought I was. Everyone watching is sort of nerve racking, and I was shaking.
> M: So you were thinking about what it was like to perform that piece of music for the recording? Were you thinking anything about the music itself?
> J: Well, I thought it went the way I wanted it to with my music. I didn't do anything like the letters, the keys I wasn't supposed to on my sheet. So I did it properly, how I had planned to.
> M: Ok. Now if you had to describe that to somebody who hadn't heard it, didn't know how that piece of music went, what would you tell them?
> J: I'd just say, well, I had a bit of a sheet of paper and I just had to copy off that, and I didn't muck up or anything—I was close to it. I looked at my sheet and concentrated. I just pretended there was no one else around watching me so I wouldn't muck up but, yeah, I got it the way I wanted it to.

In this initial questioning, Jenna focused on her experience as a performer of her own music, despite attempts to prompt her

Figure 2. Jenna's original notation

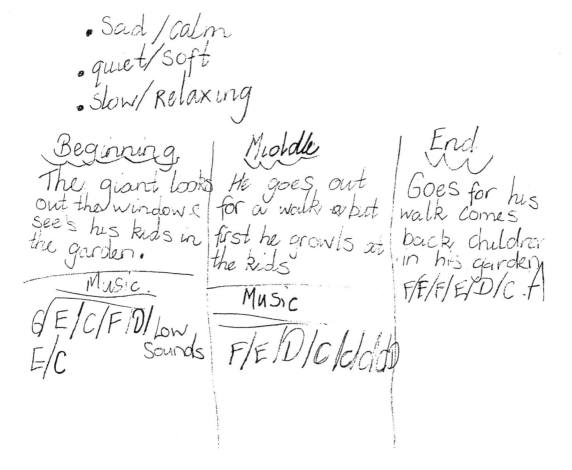

to think about the music itself through the request to describe the composition for another. This focus on aspects of the performance—including nervousness, accuracy, and faithfulness to her notation—and the judgment that she "got it the way I wanted to" reflect a view of composition that is tied to Jenna's new experience as an instrumentalist and her developing understanding of the function of notation. In subsequent questioning, Jenna commented:

> **J:** Well, at the start it was sort of really quiet, and in the middle it got louder, and in the end bit it got quieter, and the last letter that I did I had to make it go loud—which was an A, I think. When I hit that, I had to stop it echoing.
>
> **M:** Ok, so that gives us an idea that it went from quiet to loud, and then you have that stopping the echoing right at the very end. Can you remember how you went about making that piece of music?
>
> **J:** I had sort of a little bit of trouble; I couldn't think what I could do. I was just doing in the middle; I was like, um, it was sort of like a growling bit, like the Giant was growling. At the end it was like they're making up sort of thing. At the very end, the last letter was meant to be a big yell and then stop. At the start he went for a walk, like a nice calm thing; in the middle it went sort of loud; and at the end it was sort of like a calm thing as well.
>
> **M:** Ok, how does listening to that piece of music make you feel?
>
> **J:** Oh, well, when I play it, it feels like it's not the same as I wanted it to be, but once I listened to it, it's sort of like the same as I wanted it. I really needed to listen to it.
>
> **M:** And what feelings does it give?
>
> **J:** Well, because I didn't muck up, I feel sort of good about myself. I sort of get a bit red as well listening to it.
>
> **M:** You imagine somebody else who hadn't made it just listening to it as listeners; what sort of feelings do you think they would have?
>
> **J:** Oh, they would be just sitting there concentrating and they'd sort of picture what you, *I* was like, and like picture if it was calm.

Although Jenna was able to discuss the structure of her composition and the aural effects of the work, her experience as a performer resurfaced when she was asked to comment on her feelings as a listener to her own work. It was only through the lens of the other listener that Jenna was able to return to a focus on the musical effect of the work.

In trying to probe Jenna's response to her work as a critical listener, I asked her if the work reminded her of anything else. In her answer, Jenna made reference to a range of other music encountered both within and beyond school, including pop songs. However, Jenna made an important distinction between these other musical models that highlights her view of her composition as primarily instrumental, with the intention of generating an atmosphere of calm and quiet, of relaxation:

> **J:** Sort of at the start it sort of sounded like "Twinkle Twinkle Little Star," 'cause it was nice and calm and quiet and that song is calm and quiet, but in the middle it sounded like a pop song because it

was so loud and fast, and at the end it sounded like a sort of a pop and a slow song, and then the last bit sounded like just a big boom, of sorts.

M: So it reminds you of other pieces of music?

J: Yeah. Well, it's sort of like no one— when someone plays that sort of thing, no one should just sing to it; it should be a relaxing sort of thing like just a playing thing.

Subsequently, we listened to an excerpt of Koehne's ballet suite of *The Selfish Giant*.[5] Jenna's responses reflect a movement between a view of herself as a critical listener who is able to comment on the emotive effect of the music, a view of herself as a performer-listener focused on issues of performance, and a view of herself as a composer making similar decisions to those evident in Koehne's work. In the latter section of this excerpt, prompted by my questions concerning how she would go about composing such a work, Jenna's view of composition in this context is clearly shaped by her experience and perceptions of the demands of performance:

> **M:** Just listening to that, can you tell me what you were thinking?
>
> **J:** I'm still very relaxed. They sort of keep going. I had to sort of stop and find the letters, 'cause they're very talented, and I've just sort of begun doing it, and they've been doing it for years. They've even got a CD out.
>
> **M:** So you were thinking about how the music was being played?
>
> **J:** (Jenna nods confirmation.) I was feeling very relaxed and calm.

> **M:** So if you had to describe that to somebody else, what would you say?
>
> **J:** Well, I'd say like they are very talented, and like I had to stop and find the letters, but they just don't have to look down; they are playing like the clarinet or something they just have to—they know where the keys are so that they can just do it. Like, I have to look down and make sure I get the right key. I usually have to stop and find the key—I can't just go and keep going.
>
> **M:** What would you tell them about the music itself?
>
> **J:** Well, the one that you just played like the CD, that was sort of fast and slow. It wasn't fast fast, but it was medium sort of thing, and mine was sort of like slow, and, um, the CD that you played again, that was like slow at the start. It was sort of just really slow and then in the middle and in the end it got sort of medium sort of thing, not fast but medium.
>
> **M:** How would you go about making music like that?
>
> **J:** I'd have a lot of trouble; it would probably take me a couple of months to do it because I'd have to really, really practice, and like if I did it with the flute I'd have to take it home like every day so I could just get it right, and it would be pretty hard.
>
> **M:** What is the first thing you think you would have to do to make the music?
>
> **J:** Well, find out, make sure you know where the keys are, and just get your piece of music ready, and just concentrate and watch it. So, you'd really have to be looking at the music the most. Like the first thing you'd do is practice where the keys are, and the second bit

you'd have to just watch the music. Like I can watch the music, but I have to watch where my fingers go. With D and C, I usually do, but when it goes up further I don't.

In the excerpt below, I returned to the issue of emotional response, asking Jenna what feelings listening to the music generated. Her response draws on both the establishment of an appropriate public context for the music (a funeral) and a more personal context through her reference to "dreaming of stuff in your head":

> **J:** At first, music—it sometimes, it would be a good song for a funeral because it was nice and slow. I felt really kind of relaxed, like if I had problems they'd just sort of float away. It just made me all calm.
> **M:** What is it in the music that makes you feel calm and relaxed?
> **J:** Nice and quiet, not really loud, nice and slow, and it was like not fast. If it was fast, it would make me feel pfft—all giddy.
> **M:** Ok, does the music remind you of anything? Does it make you think of anything outside of it?
> **J:** It sort of feels like it's in a church somehow. It doesn't really feel like you are outside with all the kids and yeah! It just feels like you're somewhere by yourself with no one else in, just like a nice little quiet spot.
> **M:** What is it in the music that helps give that feeling?
> **J:** 'Cause it's not fast and loud and all those sort of things that make it yuck. It just makes you feel like you're dreaming

of stuff in your head. Yeah, it's nice and quiet, so you think you're just like in somewhere really quiet.

Daniel

Daniel was also 10 years old at the time of the project and a member of the same class as Jenna. Unlike Jenna, Daniel "did not listen to much," although he owned one Backstreet Boys CD. Daniel's family was musically active in that his mother and father played recorder together, the latter "by ear," and his elder brother was learning to play violin. Daniel also played the recorder "at home, but only sometimes by myself." At the time of the project, Daniel had begun learning guitar 6 weeks earlier through the school program and participated in a weekly 30-minute group lesson. Daniel's parents had bought him a guitar, and he had managed to acquire some facility, possessing a repertoire of eight chords.

Figure 3 is a transcription of Daniel's composition for guitar. The work commences with picking the open strings of the instrument in ascending and descending order, punctuated by strumming across the open strings. This is repeated at the end of the work. The middle section of the work consists of a chord pattern that moves through G, Em, A, D, A, E, D^7, G, and is then repeated. Daniel's notation (Figure 4) consists of written instructions that have been scored through with the chord sequence described above written below (with substitution of A^7 for A). Beneath these is the statement "Play range of notes because it makes me happy." When performing his composition for the recording, Daniel did not refer to his notation, appearing to rely entirely on his memory of the work.

Figure 3. Transcription of Daniel's composition

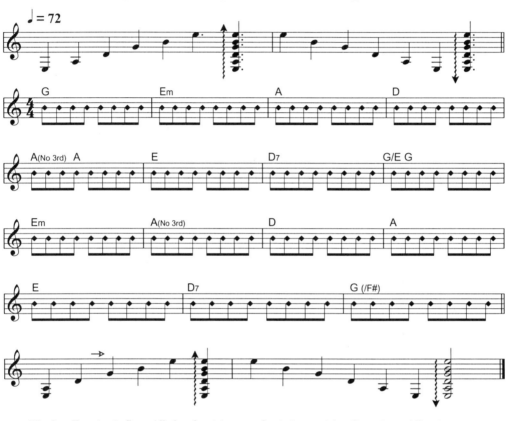

The low E string is flat. All chord voicings are basic 1st position fingerings. All strings are played. (D chords include low A and E.) All strums are down-strokes.

Our conversation ("M" represents me, and "D" represents Daniel) commenced as follows:

M: Daniel, can you tell me what you were thinking as you were listening to it?
D: Well, I made a bit of a mistake at the end where I had to strum each string separately except I got two at a time where I was just meant to get one, so that was sort of embarrassing, but other-wise I was pretty pleased with it.
M: So, as you were listening through it, you were thinking mainly about the per-formance of it?
D: Yeah, it sounded a bit different to what I thought it would like on the day I played it.
M: Ok, how does it sound different?
D: Well, it sounds a lot stronger and just different to what I had expected it to.
M: When you say stronger, what do you

Figure 4. Daniel's original notation

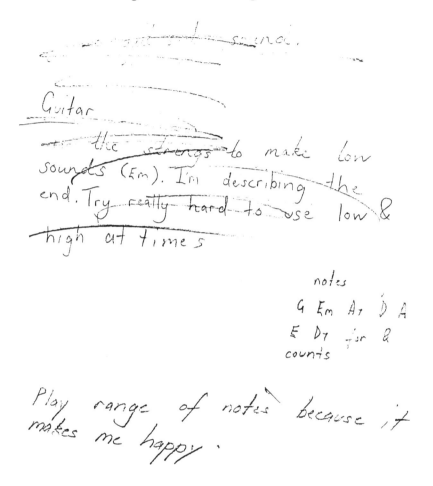

mean?

D: Like louder and it had a more—a bigger beat type of.

M: Ok, now if you were going to describe that piece of music to somebody—say you had to go back and describe it to Mrs. [teacher's name] in a couple of minutes' time, what would you tell her about it?

D: Well, I played a range of notes and so I wanted each note to sound different,

so it would sound mixed up and they would just sound different. Like, I played my G and my A minor and my A^7 and my D, then my A, then my E, then my D^7. Then I repeated that again, and I liked that type of tune because I fiddled around with it all the time.

M: So that was something you had been working on at home, quite a bit by yourself as well?

D: MMM-hmm.

M: Ok, what about the opening and closing bits of it?

D: I thought it might sound all right to start it off like that and end it like that.

As with Jenna, Daniel's initial focus was on the quality and accuracy of his performance of the work. However, it is interesting to note the different role that notation plays in Daniel's experience. His notation is far less detailed than Jenna's. Additionally, Daniel did not refer to his notation in performance or in subsequent discussion. This may reflect the differing approaches to notation in the teaching of the flute and the guitar in the school. In the former, all learning is notation based, but in the latter, notation plays little part in the initial teaching and learning process.

Daniel then went on to explain his intentions to make his work "sound different," and he described the structure of the work, a structure with which he is familiar from "fiddling around with it all the time." Daniel expanded on this in his explanations of how he went about making his composition:

D: Well, it's quite funny because at home when I started learning it, I started fiddling around with tunes like that, and I tried the range of notes except I cut out the A minor and the G^7, and I thought the way I put it together sounded really good, so I thought I'd play it in the recording thing.

D: Well, like I said before, I just fiddle around with chords and strings, and so that kind of gave me the idea and like, at the, when we were learning about it in guitar lessons, we were told to like switch to different chords, like we play in E minor and then E^7, and then it got harder as we went along, and sometimes some of the things we played sounded good to me, and I added a few extra chords in so I thought it sounded all right.

Daniels' composition is both formed by and formative of his experience as a beginning guitarist. This is evidenced in his expropriation of the conventions offered within the guitar lessons and his subsequent appropriation of these conventions in his own constructions of musical meaning. While Daniel's descriptions of his work appear to be technically oriented, it is interesting to note the ways in which he related his work to *The Selfish Giant*:

D: Well, I thought at the end, kind of because it makes that lower sound, and it was a bit sadder, but, it kind of makes you happy as well 'cause the Giant went up to heaven, I think it was, so that's the bit I like, kind of.

Daniel's decision to compose for the instrument that he was learning, rather than one of the classroom percussion instruments, also reflects his captivation by this instrument and its importance in his life. This became more evident in our conversation about the feelings evoked by listening to his composition:

M: Ok, listening to it, how does the music make you feel?

D: Kind of a bit happy, and like you want to, like you're thinking about something and it's a nice thought and everything.

M: Can you tell me what it is in the music that gives that feeling of happiness and thinking?

D: The sound and the way it works.

M: What sort of sound is that?

D: Well, it's a kind of a lower sound except I can like, it kind of—well, when I play I kind of think about something and I can't really describe this now. Yeah, but I normally play the recorder or the guitar when I'm feeling bad or I want to think about something. I play different sounds that make me happy and sad and things.

M: So, you know which sounds make you happy?

D: Yeah.

M: You said earlier the way it's put together as well?

D: Yeah, I like it because the sound, that kind of makes—like it's, I like it that way, it's probably the music I like. And, yeah, I think it's just the different notes. Say if I played a D then a D⁷ that would sound a bit—'cause they sound pretty much the same, I wouldn't really like putting them at the same time. And like, if you played the—yeah, I guess it's just where you position your fingers, I guess, on the string.

Daniel was clearly struggling to articulate his thoughts and feelings; however, he provides us with an insight into the function of playing and composing in his life. For Daniel, the process of playing and putting together "different sounds that make me happy and sad and things" is a process of meaning-making as he struggles with instances of "feeling bad" or wanting to "think about something."

While Jenna's response to Koehne's work was primarily as a performer, Daniel's initial response focused on feelings and associations with particular settings and effects. In further discussion, Daniel commented on the instrumentation and musical aspects, such as tempo, and the musical effect these provide:

M: Now Daniel, can you tell me what you were thinking when you were listening to that piece of music?

D: Well, it's definitely more realistic than mine and it comes into the—it makes you feel happy, and, well, what I was thinking would be like I was standing somewhere nice, like looking across at the sea or something and there was wind blowing in my face, something like that and the horizon was there and everything, and it sounded really nice and not necessarily happy but calm.

M: Ok, you said it sounded more realistic than yours, can you tell me a bit more about that?

D: Well, thinking someone could play like that would probably want to change mine after hearing that 'cause it's got a range of different instruments I think, and it sounds good together and—yeah— it's got that calm bit in it and that kind of—yeah—kind of, I don't know. It makes you feel a bit different I guess.

M: Now, if you were describing this to somebody else, what would you tell them?

D: Well, it's a beautiful piece of music for one thing, and, like I said before, it has got that calm thing in it, and it kind of describes something that you're doing, I guess, and something that's really nice and, you know, really good and everything.

M: What would you tell them about how the piece of music begins and what happens next and so on?

D: Oh, well, it has got that like "ding-ing, ding-ing" [sings the opening ostinato phrase played by the strings] and that sounds good like that and it kind of … You know I'm not very good at describing things. Well, it's a beautiful piece of music, kind of, I'd describe it as—but I couldn't really describe it as an emotion to someone; I don't know; I'm not really used to it.

M: How would you describe the sounds?

D: Well, very light, and very slow at times and then fast and it's got a—it goes together well like that I reckon so, mmm.

Despite Daniels' protestation that he "couldn't really describe it as an emotion to someone," when asked to comment on the feelings evoked by listening to the music, he referred to the ways in which the music provides a medium for reflection and evokes an atmosphere of "calm." Daniel was also able to identify the ways in which the music evokes these feelings through instrumentation, dynamic effect, tempo, and use of ostinato:

> **D:** Um, probably what I said before, very calm and it does make you think at times and probably about in the past and things that have happened.
>
> **M:** Can you pinpoint what it is in the sounds that gives that feeling of calmness?
>
> **D:** Well, it was the way it was played for one, but it was the certain instrument

that played it—I'm not sure; I think it was the flute. That's a very nice quiet type of instrument, but I like that more than the louder instruments.

M: So, that helped give that feeling of calm. Is there anything else about the way that the music or the sounds were put together that helped give that feeling of calm?

D: Just probably the way it was played I guess.

M: How was that?

D: Very slowly and then it kind of like has got that "Ding, Ding, Ding" [sings the ostinato], and that kind of made it sound interesting, kind of.

M: Ok, now does the music remind you of anything? You said sometimes you get pictures in your mind?

D: Probably what I described before with the wind in my face and looking over at the sea and the horizon.

M: What is it in the music that gives that image?

D: Well, I think it is the calmness really because the sea is very calm and you're looking, you're in a really nice place.

M: Now would you change anything in this piece of music?

D: Not being a musical expert, I wouldn't, but I guess it would depend on what I thought of it, because [in] my opinion it is very good and nice and it sounds really good put together like that, but others would think differently I reckon, some others.

M: Well, let's just focus on you, not worry about them—so Daniel the music expert, what would you do?

D: Well, I wouldn't change it unless I thought something different like, if I thought it could sound any better I'd change it, but I think I don't want to change it because if you change it, it can wreck the whole effect. So, I don't think I'd change much if I knew what to do about them things.

Finally, in contrast to Jenna, when Daniel was invited to speculate on how he would go about composing this work, it was not issues of performance that dominated. Rather it was the notion of conveying a thought or image that directed his thinking:

D: I don't know really, um, well, I'd probably think about something nice and a view or something I'd like to see, and then in your mind think what it would sound like, and that's a bit of a hard thing to describe but think like, what type of music describes what type of thing, and I'd kind of put it together like that.

Conclusion

I have drawn extensively on Jenna's and Daniel's responses as composers and critical listeners to illustrate the ways in which they are both constructing meaning through their engagement with music as composers. This process reflects their experiences as composers, as critical listeners to both their own work and that of others, and as performers of their own work and that of others. These aspects are not separate but are intertwined in an ongoing dialogue between these roles—composer, performer, and critical listener—that is mediated by the students' experience of musical worlds and their developing psychological and cultural tool kits.

Through these tool kits of techniques and procedures for understanding and managing their musical worlds, Jenna and Daniel are engaged in an internal collaboration with themselves and an external collaboration with their material and social worlds. I suggest that both Jenna's and Daniel's compositions are responses to the social and cultural contexts in which they work and through which they generate meaning. This is evident in the ways both children draw on their knowledge and previous experiences as composers and their concurrent experiences as beginning instrumentalists. It is also evident in the ways they are able to link their own compositions to the stylistic traditions of other musical worlds. For example, Jenna's references to the connections between her work and the world of popular music illustrate her expropriation and appropriation of the materials and practices of this world. Her insights into the social practices of music, whereby Koehne's work is deemed suitable for performance at a funeral due to its calming qualities and is identified as personally relevant for reflection or "dreaming of stuff in your head," suggest a growing knowledge of self and culture. Daniel's descriptions of the function of playing and composing music in his life indicate the vital role of composition as a form of meaning-making in his emotional life.

While neither composition could be regarded as a significant contribution to the cultural capital, I suggest that the process of making and reflecting upon these compositions constitutes an essential component in these children's processes of meaning-making and "world-making" (Bruner, 1986). Musical meaning-making is an accomplishment of the child who—as musician and composer—is engaged in a dialogue with self and the emerging musical work, a dialogue that is mediated by the culture. This constant dialogue—between individual and society, process and product, intention and expression and between the roles of composer, critical listener, and performer—forms the heart of musical meaning-making.

Greene (1995) describes education as a process in which we foster the "active learner, here conceived as one awakened to pursue meaning and to endow a life story with meaning" (p. 132). I suggest that it is the active engagement in the processes of meaning-making as composers that assists Jenna and Daniel in endowing their life stories with meaning. For Greene, imagination plays a vital role in this process because

> imagination is what, above all, makes empathy possible … of all our cognitive capacities imagination is the one that permits us to give credence to alternative realities. It allows us to break with the taken for granted, to set aside familiar distinctions and definitions. (p. 3)

For both children, the imaginative act of composing has provided a means to explore alternative realities of thought and emotion and to relate these to their lives. Greene (1995) comments, "The role of the imagination is not to resolve, not to point the way, not to improve. It is to awaken, to disclose the ordinarily unseen, unheard, and unexpected" (p. 28). In providing children with opportunities to compose and to reflect on that experience, we provide them with the means to develop habits of mind that value curiosity, courage, openness, observation, interpretation, reflection, and risk taking, habits of mind that shape attention in different ways.

The dialogic process of meaning-making that is composition is bound by freedoms and constraints. These constraints include the musical problem that is assigned, the skills and knowledge the child brings to the task, the child's perceptions of the task, and the larger sociocultural context that constitutes the child's world. When we acknowledge these constraints, we may then begin to explore the freedoms of creative experience. Considering the implications of these constraints for education requires us to recognize the musical understandings, musical cultures, and communities of music practices that the child *and* the teacher bring to the teaching-learning encounter. Such recognition is crucial in shaping dialogic teacher-student relationships that are focused on mutual problem posing and that support risk taking in the pursuit of meaning-making. Freire (1968) suggests that a "problem-posing education bases itself on creativity and stimulates true reflection and action upon reality" (p. 71), and this is the foundation of meaning-making. I suggest that a view of composition in music education as a means of developing the individual's capacity to construct meaning from and through encounters with the world provides an avenue to explore what it is to be more human and to endow our life stories with meaning.[6]

Notes

1. For an extended discussion of these issues,

see Hickey in Chapter 2.

2. The distinction between composition and improvisation is one that is viewed in a range of ways. For some, *improvisation* is a form of "composition-in-action" (Davies, 1992; Marsh, 1995) that is largely indistinguishable from composition. Others view improvisation as a precursor to or preliminary stage of composition (Kratus, 1989), while an alternative view links improvisation to specific musical genres, such as jazz and blues. In a recent study, Burnard (2000) suggests that the relationship between composition and improvisation is threefold: (1) distinct and separate, (2) interrelated, and (3) indistinguishable (p. 21).

3. For further discussion of these viewpoints, see Barrett (1998).

4. As I put forward a view that is deeply embedded in culture, the proposal of an all-purpose universal theory is inappropriate. Rather, I suggest that this be viewed as a contribution to the development of a framework that assists us in dealing with children's compositions in increasingly thoughtful and sensitive ways.

5. The excerpt, "Interlude," is a "complete" 3-minute work for orchestra.

6. The research reported in this chapter was supported by a small ARC grant awarded by the University of Tasmania.

References

Abbs, P. (1987). *Living powers: The arts in education.* London: Falmer Press.

Amabile, T. M. (1983). *The social psychology of creativity.* New York: Springer-Verlag.

Amabile, T. M. (1996). *Creativity in context: Update to the social psychology of creativity.* Boulder, CO: Westview.

Amabile, T., & Tighe, E. (1993). Questions of creativity. In J. Brockman (Ed.), *Creativity* (pp. 7–270). New York: Simon & Schuster.

Bakhtin, M. M. (1981). Discourse in the novel (C. Emerson & M. Holquist, Trans.). In M. Holquist (Ed.), *The dialogic imagination: Four essays by M. M. Bakhtin* (pp. 259–422). Austin: University of Texas Press.

Barrett, M. (1996). Children's aesthetic decision-making: An analysis of children's musical discourse as composers. *International Journal of Music Education, 28,* 37–62.

Barrett, M. (1997). Invented notations: A view of young children's musical thinking. *Research Studies in Music Education, 8,* 2–14.

Barrett, M. (1998). Researching children's compositional processes and products: Connections to music education practice? In B. Sundin, G. E. McPherson, & G. Folkestad (Eds.), *Children composing* (pp. 10–34). Malmö, Sweden: Malmö Academy of Music, Lund University.

Barrett, M. (1999). Modal dissonance: An analysis of children's invented notations of known songs, original songs, and instrumental compositions. *Bulletin of the Council for Research in Music Education, 141,* 14–22.

Barrett, M. (2000). Windows, mirrors and reflections: A case study of adult constructions of children's musical thinking. *Bulletin of the Council for Research in Music Education, 145,* 1–19.

Barrett, M. (2000/2001). Perception, description and reflection: Young children's aesthetic decision-making as critics of their own and adult compositions. *Bulletin of the Council for Research in Music Education, 147,* 22–29.

Barrett, M. (2001). Constructing a view of children's meaning-making as notators: A case study of a five-year-old's descriptions and explanations of invented notations. *Research Studies in Music Education, 16,* 33–45.

Boden, M. A. (1991). *The creative mind.* New York: Basic Books.

Boden, M. A. (1994). What is creativity? In M. A. Boden (Ed.), *Dimensions of creativity* (pp. 75–118). Cambridge, MA: MIT Press.

Bruner, J. (1975). From communication to language: A psychological perspective. *Cognition, 3,* 255–87.

Bruner, J. (1986). *Actual minds, possible worlds.* Cambridge, MA: Harvard University Press.

Bruner, J. (1990). *Acts of meaning.* Cambridge, MA: Harvard University Press.

Bruner, J. (1996). *The culture of education.* Cambridge, MA: Harvard University Press.

Burnard, P. (2000). How children ascribe meaning to improvisation and composition. *Music Education Research, 2*(1), 7–23.

Campbell, P. S. (1998). *Songs in their heads.* New York: Oxford University Press.

Cole, M. (1996). *Cultural psychology. A once and future discipline.* Cambridge, MA: Bellknap Press of Harvard University Press.

Consortium of National Arts Education Associations. (1994). *National standards for arts education.* Reston, VA: MENC.

Csikszentmihalyi, M. (1996). *Creativity: Flow and the psychology of discovery and invention.* New York: HarperCollins.

Csikszentmihalyi, M. (1999). Implications of a systems perspective for the study of creativity. In R. J. Sternberg (Ed.), *Handbook of creativity* (pp. 313–35). Cambridge, England: Cambridge University Press.

Curriculum Corporation. (1994). *The arts: A statement for Australian schools.* Carlton, Victoria, Australia: Author.

Davies, C. (1992). Listen to my song: A study of songs invented by children aged 5–7 years. *British Journal of Music Education, 9*(1) 19–48.

Department for Education and Employment: QCA. (2000). *Music in the national curriculum for England: Key stages 1–3.* London: Qualifications and Curriculum Authority.

Ekman, P., & Davidson, R. J. (Eds.). (1994). *The nature of emotion: Fundamental questions.* New York: Oxford University Press.

Elliott, D. J. (1995). *Music matters: A new philosophy of music education.* New York: Oxford University Press.

Freire, P. (1968). *Pedagogy of the oppressed.* New York: Seabury Press.

Gardner, H. (1993). *Creating minds.* New York: Basic Books.

Goodnow, J. J. (1990). The socialization of cognition: What's involved? In J. S. Stigler, R. A. Schweder, & G. Herdt (Eds.), *Cultural psychology: Essays on comparative human development* (pp. 259–86). Cambridge, England: Cambridge University Press.

Greene, M. (1995). *Releasing the imagination: Essays on education, the arts, and social change.* San Francisco: Jossey-Bass.

Hatano, G., Inagaki, K., & Oura, Y. (1993). Changing conceptions of development and their implications for art education. *The Bulletin of the Faculty of Education, Chiba University, 41,* 137–53.

Jones, T. (1986). Education for creativity. *British Journal of Music Education, 3*(1), 63–78.

Kanellopoulos, P. A. (1999). Children's conception and practice of musical improvisation. *Psychology of Music, 27,* 175–91.

Koehne, G. (1996). *The selfish giant: Ballet music by Graham Koehne* [Recorded by Queensland Philharmonic Orchestra, conducted by Stephen Barlow]. Sydney: Tall Poppies Records.

Kratus, J. (1989). A time analysis of the compositional processes used by children ages 7–11. *Journal of Research in Music Education, 37,* 5–20.

Kruger, A. C., & Tomasello, M. (1996). Cultural learning and learning culture. In D. R. Olsen & N. Torrance (Eds.), *The handbook of education and human development: New models of learning, teaching and schooling* (pp. 369–86). Cambridge, MA: Blackwell.

Markus, H. R., & Kitayama, S. (1991). Culture and the self: Implications for cognition, emotion, and motivation. *Psychological Review, 98,* 224–53.

Marsh, K. (1995). Children's singing games: Composition in the playground? *Research*

Studies in Music Education, 4, 2–11.

Paynter, J. (1982). *Music in the secondary school curriculum.* Cambridge, England: Cambridge University Press.

Paynter, J. (1992). *Sound and structure.* Cambridge, England: Cambridge University Press.

Racy, A. J. (1998). Improvisation, ecstasy, and performance dynamics in Arabic music. In B. Nettl & M. Russell (Eds.), *In the course of performance: Studies in the world of musical improvisation* (pp. 95–112). Chicago: University of Chicago Press.

Reimer, B. (1992). Toward a philosophical foundation for music education research. In R. Colwell (Ed.), *Handbook of research on music teaching and learning* (pp. 21–37). New York: Schirmer Books.

Rogoff, B., Mistry, J., Goncu, A., & Mosier, C. (1993). Guided participation in cultural activity by toddlers and caregivers. *Monographs of the Society for Research in Child Development, 58*(8, Serial No. 236).

Scherer, K. R. (1999). Appraisal theories. In T. Dalgleish & M. Power (Eds.), *Handbook of cognition and emotion* (pp. 637–63). Chichester, England: Wiley.

Sloboda, J. A., & Juslin, P. N. (2001). Psychological perspectives on music and emotion. In P. N. Juslin & J. A. Sloboda (Eds), *Music and emotion: Theory and research* (pp. 71–105). Oxford, England: Oxford University Press.

Sternberg, R. J., & Lubart, T. I. (1999). The concept of creativity: Prospects and paradigms. In R. J. Sternberg (Ed.), *Handbook of creativity* (pp. 3–15). Cambridge, England: Cambridge University Press.

Vygotsky, L. (1978). *Mind in society.* (M. Cole et al., Eds.). Cambridge, MA: Harvard University Press.

Vygotsky, L. (1986). *Thought and language* (A. Kozulin, Rev. & Trans.). Cambridge, MA: MIT Press. (Original work published 1934)

Vygotsky, L. S., & Luria, A. R. (1993). *Studies on the history of behaviour: Ape, primitive, and child* (V. I. Golod & J. E. Knox, Eds. & Trans.). Hillsdale, NJ: Erlbaum. (Original work published 1930)

Wallas, G. (1926). *The art of thought.* London: Jonathan Cape.

Webster, P. (1992). Research on creative thinking in music: The assessment literature. In R. Colwell, (Ed.), *Handbook of research on music teaching and learning* (pp. 266–80). New York: Schirmer Books.

Wertsch, J. V. (1991). *Voices of the mind: A sociocultural approach to mediated action.* Cambridge, MA: Harvard University Press.

Wilde, O. (1978). *The selfish giant* (3rd ed.). Harmondsworth, England: Puffin. (Original work published 1888)

Wood, P., Bruner, J., & Ross, G. (1976). The role of tutoring in problem solving. *Journal of Child Psychology and Psychiatry, 17,* 89–100.

Margaret Barrett is senior lecturer in music education and director of research in the faculty of education at the University of Tasmania. She is a past president of the Australian Society for Music Education (1999–2001) and has contributed to a range of public policy forums in music and arts education. Her research interests encompass children's musical thinking as composers and notators, the interrogation of the meaning and value of the arts in children's lives, and the philosophy of music education. This research has been supported by nationally competitive grants from the Australian Research Council. Dr. Barrett has published extensively in journals in the fields of music and arts education.

Creativity

2

Creative Thinking in the Context of Music Composition

Maud Hickey

As a teacher and researcher, I have long been interested in creative thinking in children. In music, while creative thinking can be manifest in performance, it is probably best observed through music composition and improvisation. It is interesting to note that these two growing bodies of research—one on creative thinking in general, the other on music composition of children—have rarely met in the research literature or in the classroom. While there is a push for, and subsequent growth of, music composition and improvisation in music education, few of the pedagogical methods are informed by research on creative thinking. Except for the work of a few researchers such as Gardner (1993) and Simonton (1987, 1991, 1997, 1999), there is very little study of music composition and improvisation to inform the general creative-thinking literature. There is a need to combine these fields in order to learn more about both musical creative thinking and general creative thinking and to inform the pedagogy of music composition and improvisation in the music classroom.

The purpose of this chapter is to focus on the psychological construct of creativity and all of its components and how these

relate to teaching music composition to children. I will present evidence from research in creativity to support ways in which we can best nurture creative thinking in our music classrooms. I will begin by examining what we know about the person, process, product, and place of creativity and then move toward a more holistic view of creativity. I will also briefly investigate developmental trends in creativity, as well as in music research. I will conclude by suggesting a curricular model for music composition that will enhance the development of creative musical thinking.

A more complete understanding of creativity and all of its parts may help teachers nurture creative thinking in children through music composition. Simply having students go through the activities of composing and improvising does not necessarily mean we are encouraging quality creative musical thinking. And, conversely, musical creativity does not take place only through music composition or improvisation. How can we best encourage children to think creatively through music composition? What makes a musical child more or less creative? An understanding of concepts from the fields of music *and* creativity will aid in answering these important questions.

Creative Person, Process, Product, and Place

Creativity is a valued and encouraged trait, especially in the arts. However, the term *creativity* can be confusing because of its many possible meanings and the obvious subjectivity it carries. A common approach for examining creativity in the general literature is to view creativity from four perspectives: person, process, product, and place. The term *creative* is used to describe personality traits (person), thinking styles or behaviors (process), the characteristics of a product, and the place or environment in which an activity occurs (this environment can be viewed on a micro or macro level). I will review research that dissects each of these categories and illustrate how this information can be applied to composition in the music classroom.

Creative Person

A great deal of research on the creative person has been compiled by studying creative people in our society, past and present. Measurement tools for the creative personality are developed through the aggregation of the most common behavioral and personality traits of highly creative individuals (Plucker & Renzulli, 1999). Analyses of findings from several creative-personality measures resulted in what we may consider to be common characteristics of creative people. These characteristics include risk taking; a sense of humor; independence; curiosity; attraction to ambiguity, complexity, and novelty; an open mind; capacity for fantasy; and heightened perception (Davis, 1998; Feist,

1999). Potentially negative traits associated with the creative personality include aloofness, distractibility, compulsiveness, sloppiness, and rebelliousness (Davis, 1998).

It is clear that not all of the traits associated with creative people are conducive to maintaining quiet and orderly classrooms. At times, the personality characteristics of the class troublemaker might also characterize that student as the most creative. An awareness of the creative potential of disruptive students may help teachers deal better with their behavior. This is not to say that all troublemakers are creative. However, if students' behavior stems from their creative abilities, then the activities of troublemakers could become more positive and productive if their energy were channeled toward more creative music-making tasks and responsibilities. Of course, *all* children have potential for creative development, and an awareness of creative-personality characteristics can help teachers to support the most positive creative-personality traits in students. We can promote creative potential by offering music tasks or assignments that may require some risk taking or even silly behavior. Teachers should support risk taking and humor in the classroom (when appropriate, of course) and model desirable creative traits for their students.

Creative Process

The study of the creative process constitutes the largest body of research in creativity studies. This literature includes conceptual models, as well as efforts to quantify creative thinking through divergent-thinking tests. I will examine some of the models and theories of the creative-thinking process and apply these to pedagogy in the music composition classroom.

Conceptual Model. A longstanding model of the creative-thinking process, conceived by Wallas (1926), proposes four stages: *preparation,* in which the creative person begins thinking about and gathering materials or ideas for the creative product; *incubation,* which occurs while the person is away from the creative problem and ideas are assimilated into the subconscious; *illumination,* often described as the "aha!" effect, which is the time in which the solution comes to mind; and *verification,* which is the final stage when ideas come together and the final product is created. Though the Wallas model has proved more anecdotal than empirical, it nonetheless provides support to other stage models of the creative process and to the findings that this process requires time.

If we apply Wallas's stages to music, the creative thinker, in preparation, begins by asking "What do I want to compose? What instruments should I use? What style shall I incorporate into my composition?" These questions provide an important stimulus for students to explore and experiment with different musical parameters.

There is a need for incubation, or time away from a project, before finishing. Ideally, we should encourage *think time* by giving students opportunities not only to be away from their creative tasks but also to revise projects over time. Completing several brief music-composition exercises is simply not as conducive to the creative-thinking process as spending longer periods of time probing one musical project. Young students often reach the verification stage prematurely and do not want to go back

and think about revision or continued work on a project. As children gain more experience in composition, their tolerance for revision and patience toward longer projects should expand.

Divergent Thinking. The creative process has also been said to contain characteristics of fluency, flexibility, originality, and elaboration. Torrance's (1974, 1981) widely used standardized *Torrance Tests of Creative Thinking (TTCT)* measure these four divergent-thinking factors, which were first hypothesized by Guilford in 1950. The TTCT are paper-and-pencil tests provided in both verbal ("Thinking Creatively with Words") and figural ("Thinking Creatively with Pictures") versions. In each version, subjects are asked to guess causes or consequences, provide ideas for product improvement, or suggest unusual uses for a variety of items. Responses are scored for fluency, flexibility, originality, and elaboration. Fluency is determined by the sheer quantity of responses, flexibility by the number of different categories of responses, originality by the uniqueness of the response (relative to a set of responses), and elaboration by the details given in the response. Webster's (1994) *Measurement of Creative Thinking in Music-II (MCTM-II),* the most well-known measure of creative musical thinking, is modeled after the TTCT and measures divergent-thinking factors, and the convergent factor of musical syntax, through music improvisation tasks. While divergent-thinking factors have been the most common indicators of creative thinking, there has been recent criticism of these measurements (e.g., Amabile, 1996; Brown, 1989; Hocevar & Bachelor, 1989; Michael & Wright, 1989; Plucker & Renzulli, 1999).

Some alternative views will be discussed later in this chapter.

Problem Finding. Problem-finding behavior has been identified as important in the creative-thinking process and has been considered an indicative behavior of creative people. Problem-finding behavior includes manipulating, exploring, and selecting elements of a problem and shaping the parameters of the problem itself. The less that a task is defined, the more problem-finding behavior will be needed. A relationship between problem-finding behavior and creative output has been shown in visual art (e.g., Chand & Runco, 1993; Dillon, 1982; Getzels & Csikszentmihalyi, 1976; Runco, 1994; Sapp, 1997; Wakefield, 1985, 1991, 1994) and in music (Brinkman, 1999; Hickey, 1995b). These studies found that subjects who spent more time exploring materials before coming to create a product produced more creative products than subjects who spent less time exploring.

Too often, as teachers, we take over the problem-finding role and select all of the parameters for a given music-composition project in order to get to the product as quickly as possible. With the typical time constraints in music education today, this is not surprising. However, if the value of music composition lies, at least partly, in the idea that it may promote creative musical thinking, then time needs to be given to problem-finding and exploratory activities.

Related to problem-finding behavior, researchers have suggested that open-ended and heuristic (exploratory) tasks are more conducive to creative thinking than contrived and algorithmic tasks and that the successful manipulation of open-ended

tasks is indicative of creative thinking (Amabile, 1983; Getzels, 1964, 1975, 1982; Getzels & Csikszentmihalyi, 1976; Perkins, 1981; Torrance, 1963). The ability to deal with fewer parameters is a trait that will encourage creative thinking, and this ability should be developed in children who have difficulty coping in open-ended situations.

Creative-Thinking Process in the Music Classroom. It is clear that the process of creative thinking takes time and is messy, yet our controlled and hurry-up classroom culture is often the antithesis of this. It is important to encourage and facilitate more careful and thoughtful approaches to creative musical growth in the classroom by providing more time and opportunities for exploration of a variety of sounds and composition possibilities. Depth over breadth and quality over quantity should be the rule rather than the exception in music-composition exercises.

Supporting the creative-thinking process through music composition does not need to be entirely open and uncontrolled. We can offer guidance for exploration by asking students to spend time exploring different pitches, dynamics, tempos, and timbres. Ask students what their favorites are and why. Have them keep a log with descriptions of favorite sounds. Listen to recordings of a wide variety of music that uses traditional and nontraditional sound sources. The goal is to get students to become critical listeners who explore music creatively on their own.

Naturally, because of the different personalities and temperaments of children, students will have varying degrees of tolerance for the open creative process. However, too often it is assumed that students are only able to work within the strictest parameters and that giving fewer parameters means a loss of teacher control. Neither extreme is educational or conducive to creativity. Children need structure and discipline as well as the chance for freedom, spontaneity, and the exploration and manipulation of musical sounds. We need to provide varied opportunities for children in music-composition tasks if we want to encourage and nurture the most creative musical-thinking processes.

The Creative Product

The creative product is the tangible result of the creative-thinking process, and it is original to the creator. The most widely used, and perhaps standard, definition of a quality creative product is that it contains qualities that are unique as well as valuable or pleasing. A creative product is one that is both novel to its creator and appropriate or valuable in the context of a domain (Mayer, 1999). The context of the domain is relative to the social context and group from which a product emerges. In other words, a musical composition is creative relative to what other composers have done in that social context and time, be it the opera composers of the twentieth century or children in a third-grade classroom. Each context contains a different set of standards, yet each is a place in which more or less creative products can be made.

A novel or unique musical composition is one that is exceptional when compared to the norm. A fifth-grade child's composition may stand out because of the surprisingly unusual features for that age and experience level. However, a composition that is *only* unique—it contains a wide variety of unusual ideas but is not aesthetically appealing or interesting—would not be considered creative under this definition. A unique or original composition must also be interesting or aesthetically appealing, or it would simply be chaotic or nonsensical. The most successful compositions meet both criteria of originality and aesthetic appeal.

What does *pleasing* or *valuable* mean in music composition? These are the craftsmanship and musical-sensitivity qualities that we listen for in all music and become used to in our cultures—different cultures have different concepts of pleasing. A seemingly random array of notes without an interesting beginning or logical conclusion is not pleasing to Western-trained ears. Closely entwined with the idea of being aesthetically pleasing or interesting, and also important for novice composers, is the idea of *intent*. A composition may be unique only because of its unintentional and random wanderings. It helps the listener, at times, to know about a composer's intent and plan for a composition. Did the composer intend for the composition to sound as it sounds? Or is the composition a nonintentional and accidental scrambling of notes? Whether a music composition is planned is not always clear upon listening. In these cases, reflective thoughts from the composer can help determine the intentionality and purpose of the piece—especially in atonal or serial pieces—and, therefore, contribute to its aesthetic sense.

We need not dismiss nor discourage strange-sounding pieces by students, but we should instead provide time for reflection and explanation about music compositions.

For example, students can write ongoing reflective thoughts about their compositions in a journal. Asking "What is the plan for your composition?" at the start of an assignment and "What can you tell me about your composition?" at the end will help keep children focused on a composition goal and aid the listener in understanding these goals and subsequent products.

The Creative Place

The importance of the place in which creativity occurs has emerged recently as one of the most important factors in creative output. Of course, the creative environment must be flexible enough to support creative personalities and nurture the creative-thinking processes described above. While there are no theories of creativity based solely on the environment, more recent theories have put much greater emphasis on the importance of environment than in the past. The environment presents a rich and complex array of factors that are all integral to the creative process. The role the environment plays will be described later in the examination of more holistic approaches to creativity.

The Complexity of Creativity

Though it is somewhat helpful to dissect and understand the parts of creativity, a recent trend is to examine the complex interaction of these parts in a more holistic manner. Recent *multiple-systems* approaches to creativity support the notion that creativity is more complex than any behavioral or psychometric examination can reveal. While one might describe a person's cognitive processes or personality as more or less creative (perhaps based on the results of a creativity paper-and-pencil test), it is more informative to examine other variables that affect the personality, such as task motivation and social context, in order to have a complete understanding of creativity. While we may be able to view someone's personality as more or less creative or assign a prize to the most creative musical product, we cannot fully judge a person's creativity separate from the total system in which the person creates. In the following paragraphs, some of these models will be briefly explained, and their application to music composition illustrated.

Multiple-Systems Approaches

"Creativity is a process that can be observed only at the intersection where individuals, domains, and fields interact" (Csikszentmihalyi, 1999, p. 314). In holistic approaches to creativity, the focus is on the system in which creativity occurs amid a set of rules and practices that are transmitted by a domain and within a field that recognizes the rules of the cultural domain (Csikszentmihalyi, 1988, 1999; Feldman, Csikszentmihalyi, & Gardner, 1994; Gardner, 1993). A *domain* is a "formal body of knowledge such as in art or music" (Sternberg, Kaufman, & Pretz, 2001, p. 76), and the *field* is the society of individuals who are familiar with the "grammar of rules" for a particular domain (as bebop jazz is a field in the domain of music). The field changes over time, and some creative artists are not recognized until after their lifetime, when the domain has been transformed because of their creative endeavors.

Gruber and Wallace propose an *evolving-systems* approach in which the creative person is examined as a unique case study and is considered an evolving system (Gruber & Wallace, 1999; Wallace & Gruber, 1989). They posit that only a few obvious generalizations are possible about creative people overall:

> An evolving system does not operate as a linear sequence of cause-effect relationships but displays, at every point in its history, multicausal and reciprocally interactive relationships both among the internal elements of the system and between the organism and its external milieu. (Gruber & Wallace, 1999, p. 93)

Sternberg et al. (2001) propose a *propulsion model,* which includes eight types of creative contributions necessary to propel a field "from wherever the field is to wherever the creator believes the field should go" (p. 78). In all of these models, the field is crucial and ties together the many parts of creativity to present more realistic, albeit complex, views of creative people, processes, and products.

In these theories just briefly described, creativity is exclusively limited to the most gifted creators in any given time. The notion that only those who significantly change the field or domain are considered creative leaves the music classroom out of the picture.

An alternative view is that creativity is a normally distributed trait present in all humans. Like other capacities, it is distributed in varying degrees among the entire population of children and adults. All children have the capacity to think creatively and, as teachers, we have multiple opportunities to tap and nurture this potential.

Amabile's (1996) *Componential Model of Creativity* presents a holistic theory of creativity that acknowledges that creative cognition is part of all thinking in all people, including children. The society or culture in Amabile's scheme could include the typical music classroom, which consists of teachers, students, parents, and audience members; and the field could be as simple as music in the elementary classroom. In the section that follows, I will describe Amabile's scheme and apply its tenets to creative musical thinking in the context of musical composition with children.

The Componential Model of Creativity

Amabile's (1996) Componential Model of Creativity provides a comprehensive view of general creative thinking and is based upon results of studies with children and adults involving the creation of artistic products (e.g., poems, visual art, stories, and computer graphics). Amabile provides empirical support for her model through experimental investigations in a variety of settings and domains (Amabile, 1996; Conti, Coon, & Amabile, 1996; Ruscio, Whitney, & Amabile, 1998). Inherent in the model is the belief that there is a continuum that runs from the minimum levels of creativity observed in everyday life to historically significant advances in science, literature, and the arts; that there are degrees of greater or lesser creativity within any individual's work; and that the process of creative thinking in any domain involves the influence of task motivation, domain-relevant skills, and creativity-relevant skills.

I have adapted this model in order to relate it specifically to musical creativity involved in music composition. Figure 1 illustrates this adapted model with Amabile's terms in bold, while the terms in parentheses (and not in bold) are specific to the music-composition process and have been added by me. The top half of the model outlines the creative-thinking process, which is influenced by task motivation, domain-relevant skills, and creativity-relevant processes shown in the bottom half of the model. At any point, the cycle may be interrupted or affected by any of these three components.

Task Identification. The process begins with identifying the task, which is either self-imposed or imposed by others. The task is affected by motivation for the task (which includes intrinsic or extrinsic motivation, type of reward, and task parameters). Task motivation is heavily affected by social components, such as support from family, peers, or teachers, as well as the success or failure of previous tasks. There is little music-composition literature on how parent involvement or home environment factor into creative musical thinking. We might, however, learn about the social and environmental influences that affect children's creative composition skills by replicating the techniques used in studies that examined environmental factors affecting children's musical performance skills (e.g., Davidson, Howe, & Sloboda, 1997; Davidson, Sloboda, & Howe, 1996; McPherson & McCormick, 1999). Amabile (1996) believes that the social environment has a primary influence on creativity because it affects task motivation. Since task motivation contains several complex elements, I will discuss these in more detail later in the chapter.

Preparation. At the preparation stage, individuals either build or recall information. In music, this is the time for exploring sounds and practicing musical ideas, much like the problem-finding activities described earlier. The preparation stage is naturally affected by domain-relevant skills such as music aptitude, achievement, and experience. Amabile (1996) cites research supporting the idea that while a great deal of learning takes place in the preparation stage, children with greater domain knowledge need less time than others in this stage, as they only need to recall already-stored information about the task. The domain knowledge in music would have to relate specifically to music composition in order to positively influence this stage. In music classrooms, because there is so little composition instruction, students need this time to prepare and begin to cultivate ideas for the stages that follow. Often this preparation stage is compromised because of time constraints and the overemphasis on product. Research on creative thinking in music has consistently shown that, when confronted with creative tasks, most creative children feel comfortable exploring many options of sounds before making a choice (DeLorenzo, 1989; Hickey, 1995b; Levi, 1991; Moorhead & Pond, 1941). Opportunities for sound exploration and manipulation—playing around with sounds—in the composition process should be made available in order to help students begin to store ideas for creative music composition. Activities that involve brainstorming solutions to musical problems and that do not require one single right answer (such as creating several endings for the beginning of a musical phrase) should be the norm rather than the exception.

Figure 1. An adaptation of Amabile's componential model of creativity

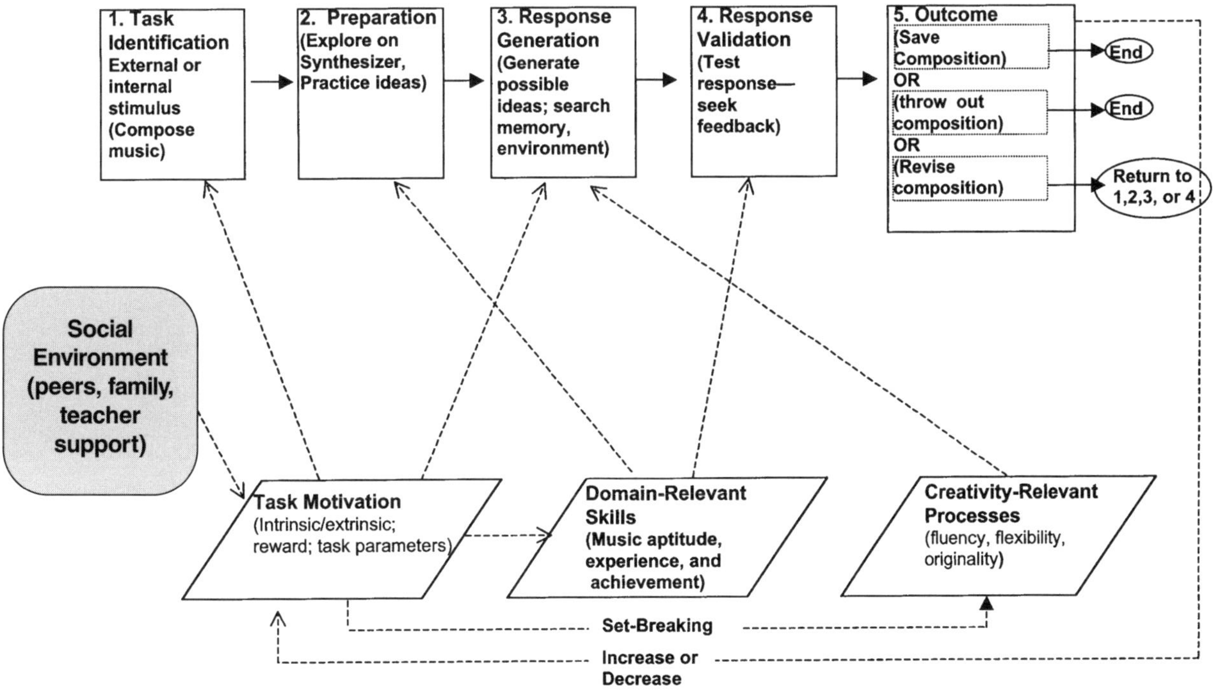

Note. From *Creativity in context: Update to the social psychology of creativity* (p. 113) by T. M. Amabile, 1996: Boulder, CO: Westview Press. Copyright 1996 by Westview Press, a member of the Perseus Books Group. Adapted with permission.

Response Generation. The response-generation stage is the point when the creator begins to generate possible ideas for the product by experimenting with new ideas, as well as remembering ideas heard or tried in the past. This stage is influenced by domain-relevant skills and creativity-relevant processes, such as playfulness, risk taking, fluency, and flexibility. These components of creative thinking influence the possibility of greater or lesser creative musical outcomes. Time is needed in this stage as there is some evidence suggesting that original outcomes are more likely to be produced later rather than earlier in the creative process (Johns, Morse, & Morse, 2001), and time is shown to have a linear influence on fluency and flexibility scores on creativity tests (Borland, 1988; Morse, Morse, & Johns, 2001). Music-composition tasks should be open-ended enough to permit considerable flexibility and creativity at this stage.

Response Validation. Naturally, students seek validation for their work in the creative process. The response-validation stage may include self-validation or responses from a peer or teacher. While the response-generation stage is the point where the process will be most influenced by creativity-relevant skills, the response-validation stage, which determines the extent to which the product will be pleasing, requires domain-relevant skills. Domain-relevant skills in the case of music composition, however, can have adverse effects on creativity. For example, I have discovered that experience can sometimes act as a detriment to creative outcomes, as in the case of young student composers who have had several years of piano lessons. Their C-major tonal focus and strong

scalar/arpeggio approach to the piano becomes prominent in their compositions, and little chromatic or nontonal experimentation takes place (Hickey, 1995a, 1995b). Webster (1990) and Hickey (1995b) also found no relationship between traditional music experience and musical-creativity scores. The influence of music aptitude, achievement, and experience on the creative quality of children's music compositions requires much further research.

Not only will musical achievement, aptitude, and experience affect the success or failure of the final composition, but they also will have an effect on students' confidence and ability for validation. Students are often quite enthusiastic to share their musical ideas as they approach the finishing stages of a musical composition; however, teachers must be careful to provide feedback that is honest yet positive without hurting the confidence of the creator.[1] Teachers often feel the least prepared to coach children at this stage because of their own lack of experience in music composition. We should encourage and strive for independence in children at this stage of the musical-composition process.

Outcome. The final stage is the creative outcome—in this case, the musical composition. If successful, the composition may be saved. If there is complete failure, it will be discarded. Some progress toward a successful composition may call for revision, in which case the individual goes back to Step 1, 2, 3, or 4 (task identification, preparation, response generation, and response validation). If task motivation remains sufficiently high, it is more likely a child will want to compose again or continue revising a composition. Students will gain domain-relevant music-composition skills as a result of getting to the outcome stage, regardless of success or failure.

Because the field of research into the creativity of children's musical products is relatively new, the outcome stage is the least informed. Though there are now several studies about children's musical composition (i.e., Barrett, 1997; Carlin, 1997; Emmons, 1998; Erkunt, 1998; Folkestad, Lindström, & Hargreaves, 1997; Gromko, 1996; Landányi, 1995; Robinson, 1995; Seals, 1990; Tsisserev, 1997; vanErnst, 1993; Wilson & Wales, 1995), there is little evidence to show what creative quality of compositions is typical at different developmental stages or what the revision process is like for the most creative students compared to the least.

Another aspect of the outcome stage that is intriguing, yet in need of much further examination, is revision. Evidence from Stauffer (1998) suggests that beginning child composers rarely revise or show any interest in revision until they gain experience with composing. My own anecdotal experiences support this notion. There is need for further research to understand more about the revision choices and processes of children as they compose music and how this affects the creative quality of their compositions.[2]

Task Motivation. An area of the Componential Model of Creativity that I will now examine more closely is the component of task motivation. Social and intrinsic motivation factors play a crucial role in the process of creative thinking, and research suggests that, for optimum creativity, assignment parameters, reward, and

task motivation must be carefully balanced—often in ways not necessarily characteristic of standard music teaching. All too often teachers present musical-composition assignments with strict rules and parameters and then assess based on the outcome and adherence to the parameters. Music teaching with a focus on the performance product, which is typical of many American music classrooms, requires very careful control and management from the teacher. It is inherently a teacher-directed activity in which students are managed and rehearsed to produce the best musical product. This approach is incongruous with the creative process and is possibly detrimental to creative output.

Reward. A consistent finding to emerge from research is that giving a reward for a creative product (such as a grade or points in a counting system) is often detrimental to the intrinsic motivation toward the task as well as the creative quality of the product (Amabile, 1996; Hennessey, 2000; Hennessey & Amabile, 1988; Kohn, 1993). Though teachers cannot let all musical work of children go without attention, music composition should not always be approached as an assignment to be completed and graded, but more as an ongoing activity in which students are given opportunities to experiment with musical sound. Students should be encouraged to compose, edit, revise, and doodle with their musical ideas as often as possible and to keep their sketches and final compositions in their own personal portfolios (much like visual artists who keep sketches and paintings). Portfolio assessment allows students to choose works for teachers to judge and keep works not to be judged. Assessment, critiquing, and evaluation of children's musical compositions need not be negative or squelching, but rather a process in which dialogue and learning take place between student and teacher in an ongoing reflective way that promotes students' ability to be their own best judges. Teacher sensitivity about the possible detriment of evaluation will make this atmosphere possible.

Assignment Parameters. Motivation toward a task is influenced by the types of parameters set up for the task. There is a tendency in first composition assignments to structure very strict assignment parameters in order to control the outcome. When one sets up a careful manuscript template with rules for the durations and notes to use, the number of measures, the time signature, and the beginning and ending notes, the chance for success at sounding tonal (which is often erroneously confused with good) is high. These "closed" assignments offer little room for exploration and imagination, much less error. While the intent is admirable, I suggest that teachers try just the opposite in their first (as well as subsequent) composition assignments. Offering few parameters and more open assignments, in order to give students the chance to explore and create something within their own boundaries, will stimulate creative thinking.

Figure 2 presents four possible compositional outcomes based on the interaction of the types of parameters given and the amount of craftsmanship rules followed. A closed musical assignment that has several parameters, yet is bound by no traditional craftsmanship guidelines, will most likely result in an exercise that is neither musical nor creative. I have witnessed this in music-

composition exercises where children follow strict guidelines regarding duration and range as they notate notes on a staff but have no aural sense of what they are doing. (They realize their compositions on a bell set or piano after they have dutifully written in notes.) At the other extreme, an open musical assignment with no parameters given ("compose anything you want") and devoid of any guidance or understanding of craftsmanship techniques may likely result in music that is plainly unorganized noise.

Yet another extreme is what I would describe as the *rules-bound,* unexceptional composition that results when the assignment is bound by too many parameters (e.g., key signature, time signature, length, style, and notes) and strictly follows prescribed part-writing rules. Music-writing exercises that require students to follow the rules of common practice might work well in theory class or in order to teach about these rules, but they will not likely result in very creative musical compositions.

The most successfully creative compositions are novel and follow some of our culturally bound music rules. The most successful composers are able to compose in this way. Ideally, children are taught and given many opportunities in music classrooms to experience music composition at this most musically creative level. Providing room for variety and uniqueness, while teaching techniques for good composition practice, will encourage the production of truly musically creative compositions.

Parameters and Reward. The issue of open versus closed assignments is inextricably linked to assessment. If the purpose of a composition assignment is specific (to teach how to write in rondo form) or is to teach a concept (such as 6/8 time), the assessment can and should be very specific. If a composition assignment is open, however, then simple feedback would be more appropriate than an evaluative assessment. Feedback on a composition that results from an open assignment is more critical—and fair—than giving a grade. Imagine the anxiety students would experience if asked to simply compose a piece of music that will be graded and are given no other guidelines except that it be something they like. This is not only unfair to the students but very difficult to do! On the other hand, if the assignment is to write an eight-measure melody in 6/8 time, it would be very easy and fair to evaluate students' understanding of, and their ability to write in, 6/8 time.

Researchers have found an interesting interaction between assignment parameters and assessment and the effects on creativity and intrinsic motivation. Folger, Rosenfield, and Hays (1976) discovered an inconsistency in literature related to effects of extrinsic motivation on creativity—specifically, the overjustification hypothesis, which states that external reward has a detrimental effect upon intrinsic motivation. They found that the variable of choice in a given task mediates motivation: a positive relationship exists between pay (external reward) and productivity (intrinsic motivation) under conditions where little choice is given in the task, while an inverse relationship exists between pay (external reward) and productivity (intrinsic motivation) under high-choice conditions. The overjustification hypothesis, then, must be qualified by the amount of choice students are given in a task.

Amabile (1979) also discovered that

Figure 2. Possible music composition outcomes

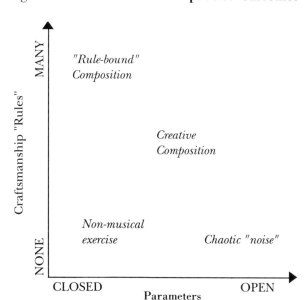

when subjects are given rewards for completing certain creative tasks, they indeed show more creativity. This contradicted her theory that nonrewarded tasks produce more creative products. The purpose of her 1979 study was to reconcile these contradictory findings by identifying instructional sets under which extrinsic rewards might undermine creativity and those in which these rewards might enhance creativity. The results showed that the evaluated (high external reward) groups scored significantly lower on creativity of their visual-art products than the nonevaluated (low external reward) groups, *except* where explicit instructions (closed task) were given. Though this group (closed task and evaluation) scored highest of all on creativity, they scored lowest in interest toward the required task. The group whose task was open and without evaluation (open task, low external reward) exhibited a high level of intrinsic interest and a high level of creativity. This finding was in agreement with Folger et al. (1976) in that the conditions

of the task will mediate the effect of external reward on intrinsic motivation and creative output. This interaction between instructional sets and types of reward and its effect upon motivation and creativity is illustrated in Figure 3.

The ideal condition, then, for supporting high intrinsic motivation and high creative output is one in which the individuals perceive that surveillance and external rewards are low and the tasks involved are relatively open (i.e., the upper right-hand box in Figure 3). Of course, the panacea for such complex issues as intrinsic motivation and creativity does not lie in the simple table presented in Figure 3. Children come to class with a multitude of personality and social traits that may inhibit or contribute to their creativity and motivation toward learning. Some students will have an easier time with strict parameters, while others will prefer the freedom of few parameters. Offering variety will give all students a chance for success. The optimal setting for creative thinking to thrive is one where there are

Figure 3. The interaction between instructional set and levels of external reward and its effect upon creative output and intrinsic motivation

	Instructional Set	
Reward	Closed (informed) Task	Open Task
Low External Reward	low creativity high intrinsic motivation	high creativity high intrinsic motivation
High External Reward	high creativity low intrinsic motivation	low creativity low intrinsic motivation

few parameters and no reward riding on the outcome. In reality, we know that different students have varying thresholds for such ambiguity and that closed assignments are necessary for achieving specific teaching goals. Too much of either extreme is not conducive to learning, much less creative thinking.

The best way to create a supportive and nurturing creative environment is to mix up all possible conditions when teaching music composition. Assignments for musical compositions should range from the specific, with strict parameters, to the loosely defined. And not all creative work should be evaluated—or even heard—by the teacher. Most importantly, the environment for music composition should be challenging and fun and invite the curiosity of the learner. Individual differences will demand an environment that is adaptable enough to entice even the most finicky learners to produce their creative best.

Summary. Amabile's (1996) Componential Model of Creativity provides music educators with a holistic framework in which to examine and nurture the musical creativity of children. New research, as well as creative musical-teaching methods, should consider the interaction and effects of all components of the model. In teaching music composition, there is often a tendency to hone in on only the domain-specific knowledge that we understand, when perhaps more benefit may come from cultivating the social, motivational, and creative interactions that are conducive to creative musical thought.

Creativity Development

Research on the development of cre-
ative thinking has direct implications for music education. Though research on the development of creativity in any of the art disciplines is sparse, it is interesting to note that both visual-art aesthetic development and general creativity development demonstrate similar and characteristic U-shaped growth. However, although there have been several studies about the development of musical skills (e.g., McDonald & Simons, 1989), there has been virtually no systematic effort to track the creative musical development of children.

Research on development in general creativity reveals a U-shaped curve that begins with a period of high creativity in early childhood (marked by play and freedom from conformity), is followed by a slump in the middle years, and then re-emerges in a more sophisticated form of creativity, for some, in adulthood (Albert, 1996; Keegan, 1996; Runco & Charles, 1997). There seems to be no consensus as to the exact age at which the slump occurs; however, it seems to be prominent either at the time children begin formal schooling or a little later, between the ages of 9 and 12. A similar developmental curve has been shown in aesthetic creative development in visual art (Gardner, 1982; Gardner & Winner, 1982). Gardner (1982) refers to the slump in the U as the literal stage, a time when children enter school—"and possibly, in part, as a result of this entry" (p. 100)—and become more aware of cultural standards and rules and feel less comfortable breaking these in creative ways.

While there is no model of creative development in music per se, Swanwick and Tillman (1986) propose a model of music development that could be used to examine creative growth in music. This model is based on assessments of 745 various composition and improvisation tasks by 48 children, ages 3 to 11 years. There were several different tasks, some in which children worked individually and others in which they worked in small groups. Unlike the U-shaped curve, Swanwick and Tillman's model suggests an invariant and progressive sequence of development.

Research by Kratus (1989) might also aid our understanding of creative music development. Kratus studied the amount of time that 60 subjects—ages 7, 9, and 11 years—spent in the activities of musical exploration (music that sounds unlike any music played earlier), development (music that sounds similar, but not identical, to music played earlier), repetition (music that sounds the same as music played earlier), and silence while creating a melody on an electronic keyboard. He then compared the time spent in each of these process stages by those subjects who successfully composed and repeated a song and those subjects who did not. Results indicated that significant differences existed across the age levels in the use of exploration, development, and silence. Older children used the compositional strategies of development and repetition more than exploration and silence. Younger children seemed unable to develop complete musical ideas and centered their time more on exploration and process-oriented—versus product-oriented—thinking. Kratus (1994) also infers that while early-elementary children are less able to generate and develop complete musical ideas than upper-elementary children, upper-elementary children do

this in ways similar to adult composers.

It is of interest to note that research by Swanwick and Tillman (1986) and Kratus (1989, 1994) suggests a linear progression in music composition development, while a U-shaped pattern is proposed in general creativity and in visual-art development. The difference may be that those who suggest a U-shaped development are examining aesthetic and creative ability while Swanwick and Tillman and Kratus follow children's progression toward more technical mastery of musical composition.

Some studies of children's music composition suggest alternatives to the sequence proposed by Swanwick and Tillman (1986). In studies of the development of 3- to 13-year-old children's intuitive music making, Davies (1986, 1992, 1994) compares her findings to those of Swanwick and Tillman and to the U-shaped curve proposed by Gardner (1982). Davies (1986) speculates that although progress occurs in children's spontaneous song making as they grow older, it is mainly portrayed as an increase of technical skills and greater confidence in handling musical material. Davies (1998) suggests that young children have the capacity for very early creative and imaginative facility in song making, hence an early output similar to that of the U-shaped curve. Marsh (1995) also found that very young children were capable of demonstrating abilities outlined in the highest levels of the Swanwick and Tillman model. More research is needed to observe children's creative musical development in a variety of settings and over substantial periods of time in order to inform the teaching of music composition and creative thinking.

Figure 4. Conceptual scheme for musical composition curriculum

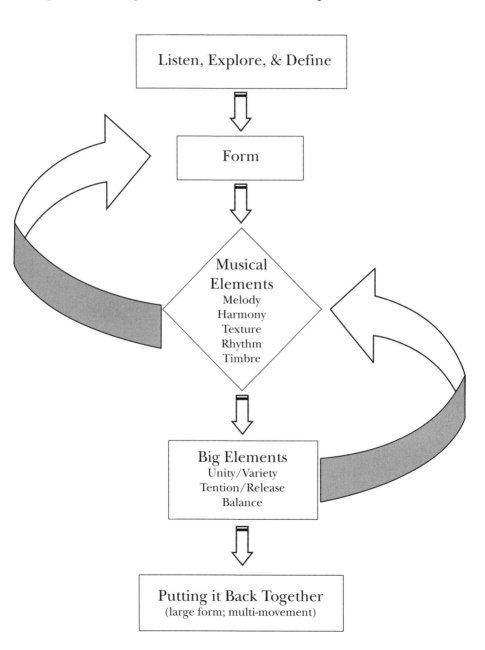

A Sequence for Teaching Music Composition

I conclude this chapter by suggesting a sequence for teaching music composition. It was developed based on concepts from the research literature on creative thinking, as well as through practice and experience teaching music composition to children. This sequence is diagrammed in Figure 4. The progression through this cycle could take one semester or four years, depending upon the amount and depth of time devoted to music composition in the classroom. This cycle is spiral: upon completion of the entire sequence at one skill level, one begins again and moves through the sequence at a deeper level, and so on.

The sequence begins with exploration of musical sounds—environmental as well as musical—as well as with listening to a variety of musics. This first stage also requires that students and teachers discuss and settle upon definitions of music and music composition. At this beginning stage, students can find immediate success and stimulate exploration and creative musical thinking by creating soundscape compositions (compositions that combine sounds to create an "effect") and compositions using found sounds.

The second step involves focusing on the organizing factors of music composition found in form. At the most basic level of form, we can build awareness of what musical factors help to create effective beginnings, interesting middle sections, and satisfying endings. Basic musical forms, such as rondo, can be successfully utilized while still using more sound-exploration approaches toward composition in this stage. Other forms such as song form,

theme and variations, and sonata-allegro form can be addressed as children advance progressively through the cycle.

As we move toward the middle of the sequence, we move toward more specific and limited assignments in order to focus on the domain-specific skills used in Western/tonal music. For very young children, it may be as simple as introducing melody and accompaniment or timbre and texture and having them compose simple exercises with these elements as the focus. As they progress in skill level, we can begin to teach children how to compose good melodies and to harmonize melodies using basic chord progressions.

Once students learn some basic domain-relevant skills through understanding and creating with specific musical elements, the sequence then moves out toward larger concepts in composition: unity and variety, tension and release, and balance. Here we stretch children's musical thinking by having them strive for these larger concepts in their compositions, drawing once again upon creative-thinking skills. A final goal of the sequence is the creation of a large musical composition, be it a multimovement work or a significant musical composition that reflects creative skills, musical skills, and music-composition skills.

The sequence for music composition provides one way of integrating not only musical skills but also creative and compositional skills. It is only an outline intended to guide teachers who are looking for a sensible sequence that allows for depth and breadth in the exploration of musical composition in the classroom.

Conclusion

By combining the field of music

composition with general creative thinking, we have greater chances to learn more about both. As we begin to look more closely at the literature in general creative thinking, it is clear that there are many questions to be examined in the field of music composition: What are the social and environmental factors that nurture or negate creative musical thinking in children? How does the success or failure of previous musical compositions affect motivation toward the next task? What types of motivation (intrinsic/extrinsic) seem to keep children most interested in creative music composition? What are the important domain-relevant skills for creative musical thinking? Can these skills be tested in a performance or with aptitude tests? Based on the answers to these and other questions, we need to provide classroom teachers with manageable pedagogical strategies for music composition.

There are many benefits to music composition in a classroom, musical as well as social. Students should learn the craft of, and appreciation for, writing a good melody above a simple chord progression and also learn to work in teams toward a goal of creating original music. While creative thinking in music can also be one of the benefits of music composition, we know that it requires certain dispositions, conditions, and environment in order to be nurtured. The more we learn about all of the components, the more we can assure success in creative musical growth of children.

Notes

1. Betty Anne Younker and Sam Reese offer chapters in this book that provide excellent ideas for providing constructive feedback to children's musical compositions.

2. In his chapter in this book, Peter Webster offers an in-depth discussion of the topic of revision.

References

Albert, R. S. (1996). Some reasons why childhood creativity often fails to make it past puberty into the real world. In M. A. Runco (Ed.), *Creativity from childhood through adulthood: The developmental issues* (pp. 43–56). San Francisco: Jossey-Bass.

Amabile, T. M. (1979). Effects of external evaluation on artistic creativity. *Journal of Personality and Social Psychology, 37*, 221–33.

Amabile, T. M. (1983). *The social psychology of creativity*. New York: Springer-Verlag.

Amabile, T. M. (1996). *Creativity in context: Update to the social psychology of creativity*. Boulder, CO: Westview Press.

Barrett, M. (1997). Invented notations: A view of young children's musical thinking. *Research Studies in Music Education, 8*, 2–14.

Borland, J. H. (1988). Cognitive controls, cognitive styles, and divergent production in gifted preadolescents. *Journal for the Education of the Gifted, 11*, 57–82.

Brinkman, D. J. (1999). Problem finding, creativity style and musical compositions of high school students. *Journal of Creative Behavior, 33*(1), 62–68.

Brown, R. T. (1989). Creativity. What are we to measure? In J. A. Glover, R. R. Ronning, & C. R. Reynolds (Eds.), *Handbook of creativity* (pp. 3–32). New York: Plenum Press.

Carlin, J. (1997). Music preferences for compositions by selected students aged 9–15 yrs. *Bulletin of the Council for Research in Music Education, 133*, 9–13.

Chand, I., & Runco, M. (1993). Problem finding skills as components in the creative process. *Personality and Individual Differences 14*(1), 155–62.

Conti, R., Coon, H., & Amabile, T. M. (1996). Evidence to support the componential model of creativity: Secondary analyses of three studies. *Creativity Research Journal, 9(4)*, 385–9.

Csikszentmihalyi, M. (1988). Society, culture, and person: A systems view of creativity. In R. J. Sternberg (Ed.), *The nature of creativity: Contemporary psychological perspectives* (pp. 325–39). Cambridge, England: Cambridge University Press.

Csikszentmihalyi, M. (1999). Implications of a systems perspective for the study of creativity. In R. J. Sternberg (Ed.), *Handbook of creativity* (pp. 313–35). Cambridge, England: Cambridge University Press.

Davidson, J. W., Howe, M. J. A., & Sloboda, J. A. (1997). Environmental factors in the development of musical performance skill over the life span. In D. J. Hargreaves & A. C. North (Eds.), *The social psychology of music* (pp. 188–206). London: Oxford University Press.

Davidson, J. W., Sloboda, J. A., & Howe, M. J. A. (1996). The role of parents and teachers in the success and failure of instrumental learners. *Bulletin of the Council for Research in Music Education, 127*, 40–44.

Davies, C. D. (1986). Say it till a song comes: Reflections on songs invented by children 3–13. *British Journal of Research in Music Education, 3*(3), 279–93.

Davies, C. D. (1992). Listen to my song: A study of songs invented by children aged 5 to 7 years. *British Journal of Music Education, 9*, 19–48.

Davies, C. D. (1994). The listening teacher: An approach to the collection and study of invented songs of children aged 5 to 7. In H. Lees (Ed.), *Musical connections: Tradition and change. Proceedings of the 21st world conference of the International Society of Music Education* (pp. 120–28). Tampa, FL: ISME.

Davis, G. A. (1998). *Creativity is forever* (4th ed.). Dubuque, IA: Kendall/Hunt.

DeLorenzo, L. C. (1989). A field study of sixth-grade students' creative music problem-solving processes. *Journal of Research in Music*

Education, 37(3), 188–200.

Dillon, J. T. (1982). Problem finding and solving. *Journal of Creative Behavior, 16*(2), 97–111.

Emmons, S. E. (1998). *Analysis of musical creativity in middle school students through composition using computer-assisted-instruction: A multiple case study.* Unpublished doctoral dissertation, University of Rochester, Rochester, NY.

Erkunt, H. (1998). *Computers as cognitive tools in music composition.* Unpublished doctoral dissertation, Boston University, Boston, MA.

Feist, G. J. (1999). The influence of personality on artistic and scientific creativity. In R. J. Sternberg (Ed.), *Handbook of creativity* (pp. 273–96). Cambridge, England: Cambridge University Press.

Feldman, D. H., Csikszentmihalyi, M., & Gardner, H. (1994). *Changing the world. A framework for the study of creativity.* Westport, CT: Praeger.

Folger, R., Rosenfield, D., & Hays, R. P. (1976). Equity and intrinsic motivation: The role of choice. *Journal of Personality and Social Psychology, 36*(5), 557–64.

Folkestad, G., Lindström, B., & Hargreaves, D. J. (1997). Young people's music in the digital age. *Research Studies in Music Education, 9*, 1–12.

Gardner, H. (1982). *Art, mind, and brain. A cognitive approach to creativity.* New York: Basic Books.

Gardner, H. (1993). *Creating minds: An anatomy of creativity seen through the lives of Freud, Einstein, Picasso, Stravinsky, Eliot, Graham, and Gandhi.* New York: Basic Books.

Gardner, H., & Winner, E. (1982). First intimations of artistry. In S. Strauss with R. Stavy (Eds.), *U-shaped behavioral growth* (pp. 147–68). New York: Academic Press.

Getzels, J. W. (1964). Creative thinking, problem solving, and instruction. In E. R. Hilgard (Ed.), *Theories of learning and instruction,* (pp. 240–76). Chicago: National Society for the Study of Education.

Getzels, J. W. (1975). Problem finding and the inventiveness of solution. *Journal of Creative Behavior, 9*, 12–18.

Getzels, J. W. (1982). The problem of the problem. In R. M. Hogarth (Ed.), *Question framing and response consistency* (pp. 37–49). San Francisco: Jossey-Bass.

Getzels, J. W., & Csikszentmihalyi, M. (1976). *The creative vision: A longitudinal study of problem finding in art.* New York: John Wiley.

Gromko, J. E. (1996). In a child's voice: An interpretive interaction with young composers. *Bulletin of the Council of Research in Music Education, 128*, 37–51.

Gruber, H. E., & Wallace, D. B. (1999). The case study method and evolving systems approach for understanding unique creative people at work. In R. J. Sternberg (Ed.), *Handbook of creativity* (pp. 93–115). Cambridge, England: Cambridge University Press.

Guilford, J. P. (1950). Creativity. *American Psychologist, 5*, 444–54.

Hennessey, B. A. (2000). Rewards and creativity. In C. Sansone and J. M. Harackiewicz (Eds.), *Intrinsic and extrinsic motivation: The search for optimal motivation and performance* (pp. 55–78). San Diego, CA: Academic Press.

Hennessey, B. A., & Amabile, T. M. (1988). Story-telling: A method for assessing children's creativity. *Journal of Creative Behavior, 22*, 235–46.

Hickey, M. (1995a, February). *Creativity, composition, and computers: Connections for the new century.* Presentation at the National Symposium on Research in General Music, Tucson, AZ.

Hickey, M. (1995b). *Qualitative and quantitative relationships between children's creative musical thinking processes and products.* Unpublished doctoral dissertation, Northwestern University, Evanston, IL.

Hocevar, D., & Bachelor, P. (1989). A taxonomy and critique of measurements used in the study of creativity. In J. A. Glover, R. R. Ronning, & C. R. Reynolds (Eds.), *Handbook of creativity* (pp. 53–76). New York: Plenum Press.

Johns, G. A., Morse, L. W., & Morse, D. T. (2001). An analysis of early vs. later responses on a divergent production task across three time press conditions. *Journal of Creative Behavior, 35*(1), 65–72.

Keegan, R. T. (1996). Creativity from childhood to adulthood: A difference of degree and not of kind. In M. A. Runco (Ed.), *Creativity from childhood through adulthood: The developmental issues* (pp. 57–66). San Francisco: Jossey-Bass.

Kohn, A. (1993). *Punished by rewards: The trouble with gold stars, incentive plans, A's, praise, and other bribes.* New York: Houghton Mifflin.

Kratus, J. (1989). A time analysis of the compositional processes used by children ages 7 to 11. *Journal of Research in Music Education, 37*(1), 5–20.

Kratus, J. (1994). The way children compose. In H. Lees (Ed.), *Musical connections: Tradition and change. Proceedings of the 21st world conference of the International Society of Music Education* (pp. 128–40). Tampa, FL: ISME.

Landányi, K. S. (1995). *Processes of musical composition facilitated by digital music equipment.* Unpublished doctoral dissertation: University of Illinois at Urbana–Champaign.

Levi, R. (1991). Investigating the creativity process: The role of regular music composition experiences for the elementary child. *Journal of Creative Behavior, 25*(2), 123–36.

Marsh, K. (1995). Children's singing games: Composition in the playground? *Research Studies in Music Education, 4*, 2–11.

Mayer, R. E. (1999). Fifty years of creativity research. In Sternberg, R. J. (Ed.), *Handbook of creativity* (pp. 449–60). Cambridge, England: Cambridge University Press.

McDonald, D. T., & Simons, G. M. (1989). *Musical growth and development: Birth through six.* New York: Schirmer Books.

McPherson, G. E., & McCormick, J. (1999). Motivational and self-regulated learning components of musical practice. *Bulletin of the Council for Research in Music Education, 141*, 98–102.

Michael, W. B., & Wright, C. R. (1989). Psychometric issues in the assessment of creativity. In J. A. Glover, R. R. Ronning, & C. R. Reynolds (Eds.), *Handbook of creativity* (pp. 33–52). New York: Plenum Press.

Moorhead, G., & Pond, D. (1941). *Music of young children.* Santa Barbara, CA: Pillsbury Foundation for Advancement of Music Education.

Morse, D. T., Morse, L. W., & Johns, G. A. (2001). Do time press, stimulus, and creative prompt influence the divergent production of undergraduate students? Yes, Yes, and No, Not very much. *Journal of Creative Behavior, 35*(2), 102–14.

Perkins, D. N. (1981). *The mind's best work.* Cambridge, MA: Harvard University Press.

Plucker, J. A., & Renzulli, J. S. (1999). Psychometric approaches to the study of human creativity. In R. J. Sternberg (Ed.), *Handbook of creativity* (pp. 35–61). Cambridge, England: Cambridge University Press.

Robinson, N. G. (1995). *An examination of the influence of visual feedback and reflection time on the pitch and duration characteristics of 9-year-olds' musical compositions.* Unpublished doctoral dissertation, Teachers College, Columbia University, New York, NY.

Runco, M. A. (Ed.). (1994). *Problem finding, problem solving, and creativity.* Norwood, NJ: Ablex.

Runco, M. A., & Charles, R. E. (1997). Developmental trends in creative performance. In M. A. Runco (Ed.), *The creativity research handbook* (Vol. 1, pp. 115–52). Cresskill, NJ: Hampton Press.

Ruscio, J., Whitney, D. M., & Amabile, T. M. (1998). Looking inside the fishbowl of creativity: Verbal and behavioral predictors of creative performance. *Creativity Research Journal, 11*(3), 243–63.

Sapp, D. P. (1997). Problem parameters and problem finding in art education. *Journal of Creative Behavior, 31*(4), 282–98.

Seals, K. A. (1990) A cross-sectional investigation of the melodic composition abilities of elementary and junior high school students (Doctoral dissertation, University of Kansas, 1989). *Dissertation Abstracts International, 50,* 3510.

Simonton, D. K. (1987). Musical aesthetic and creativity in Beethoven: A computer analysis of 105 compositions. *Empirical Studies of the Arts, 5,* 87–104.

Simonton, D. K. (1991). Emergence and realization of genius: The lives and works of 120 classical composers. *Journal of Personality and Social Psychology, 61,* 829–40.

Simonton, D. K. (1997). Creative productivity: A predictive and explanatory model of career trajectories and landmarks. *Psychological Review, 104,* 66–89.

Simonton, D. K. (1999). Creativity from a historiometric perspective. In R. J. Sternberg (Ed.), *Handbook of creativity* (pp. 116–33). Cambridge, England: Cambridge University Press.

Stauffer, S. L. (1998, April). *Connections between the musical and life experiences of young composers and the compositions they create.* Poster presentation at the biennial conference of the Music Educators National Conference, Phoenix, AZ.

Sternberg, R. J., Kaufman, J. C., & Pretz, J. E. (2001). The propulsion model of creative contributions applied to the arts and letters. *Journal of Creative Behavior, 35*(2), 75–101.

Swanwick, K., & Tillman, J. (1986). The sequence of musical development: A study of children's composition. *British Journal of Music Education, 3*(3), 305–39.

Torrance, E. P. (1963). *Education and the creative potential.* Minneapolis: University of Minnesota Press.

Torrance, E. P. (1974). *The Torrance tests of creative thinking: Technical-norms manual.* Bensenville, IL: Scholastic Testing Service.

Torrance, E. P. (1981). *Thinking creatively in action and movement: Administration, scoring, testing manual.* Bensenville, IL: Scholastic Testing Service.

Tsisserev, A. (1997). *An ethnography of secondary school student composition in music: A study of personal involvement within the compositional process.* Unpublished doctoral dissertation, The University of British Columbia, Canada.

vanErnst, B. (1993). A study of the learning and teaching processes of non-naive music students engaged in composition. *Research Studies in Music Education, 1,* 22–39.

Wakefield, J. F. (1985). Towards creativity: Problem finding in a divergent-thinking exercise. *Children Study Journal, 15,* 265–70.

Wakefield, J. F. (1991). The outlook for creativity tests. *Journal of Creative Behavior, 25*(3), 184–93.

Wakefield, J. F. (1994). Problem finding and empathy in art. In M. A. Runco (Ed.), *Problem finding, problem solving, and creativity* (pp. 99–115). Norwood, NJ: Ablex.

Wallace, D. B., & Gruber, H. E. (Eds.). (1989). *Creative people at work: Twelve cognitive case studies.* New York: Oxford University Press.

Wallas, G. (1926). *The art of thought.* New York: Harcourt, Brace and World.

Webster, P. (1990, March). *Study of internal reliability for the Measure of Creative Thinking in Music (MCTM).* Paper presented at the general poster session of the MENC National Conference, Washington, DC.

Webster, P. (1994). *Measure of Creative Thinking in Music-II (MCTM-II). Administrative guidelines.* Unpublished manuscript, Northwestern University, Evanston, IL.

Wilson, S. J., & Wales, R. J. (1995). An exploration of children's musical compositions. *Journal of*

Research in Music Education, 43(2), 94–111.

Maud Hickey is assistant professor of music education and technology at Northwestern University School of Music in Evanston, IL. Her teaching responsibilities include instrumental music methods, research, curriculum, and technology courses. Her research interests and publications have focused on creativity and composition in schools and the use of technology to facilitate these. A recent publication is a chapter on creativity research in music, visual arts, theater, and dance in *The New Handbook of Research on Music Teaching and Learning*, a project of MENC published by Oxford University Press in 2002.

3

What Do You Mean, "Make My Music Different"? Encouraging Revision and Extension in Children's Music Composition

Peter R. Webster

The scene is in a middle school general music classroom. Miss Williams is a music teacher working with a sixth-grade class on a composition assignment. Students are working in small groups with the help of computer-based music workstations. Miss Williams has asked the students to create some opening music for an act in a school play, and she hopes to have the groups present their pieces for class discussion. She has given her students some general parameters for length and form but has left much of the decision making up to the groups. This class has composed music many times before, so Miss Williams and her students are comfortable with this freedom. The music must be 2 minutes long and have a recurring timbre designed to organize the music. It also must start softly and build to the end. Megan, a leader in a group in the far corner of the room, has been working with her group for the last 10 minutes or so, but now the group looks bored and off-task. Miss Williams decides to investigate:

Miss W: Megan, how is the piece coming?
Megan: We're done.
Miss W: Done? Really? Could I hear it?
Megan: I guess.

Miss Williams dons the headphones and clicks play on the music-sequencing software. The music plays. It has a short ascending melody line played by the flute timbre that ends in a loud cymbal crash. The music is followed by a series of many more cymbal crashes, and then a brass timbre enters in the very low register with a growling sound. In less than 30 seconds, the music is over, falling far short of the intended parameters. Actually, much of the music of Megan's group in the last several projects has had the same instrument timbres, melodic patterns, and rhythms.

Miss W: Well, this seems like a nice start, Megan, but it is a bit short and seems a good deal like the last piece you created.

Can you make your music different by—
Megan looks confused and a little hurt
and quickly interrupts.
Megan: What do you mean, "Make my
music different"?

This chapter is about the wisdom of
using carefully crafted suggestions to actively encourage young composers to revise
and extend their work. By *revision*, I have in
mind the "return to exploration in which
composers test ideas that they previously accepted against new ideas while refining
their finished product" (Kaschub, 1997, p.
24). By *extension*, I mean a more specialized
revision that either adds new musical ideas
to an existing work or expands an existing
musical idea or set of ideas vertically or
horizontally (Folkestad, 1996).

In the vast and still emerging literature
on children's composition, it has been
demonstrated over and over again that
music teachers have good initial success
when they ask children to compose. Reports from the field have shown that children love to compose and that they enjoy
listening to their music and the music of
others (Glover, 2000; Moorhead & Pond,
1978; Upitis, 1992). What is far less clear is
just what music teachers do with all this
creative energy, besides celebrating its
presence in the minds and actions of those
they teach.

Initial music gestures, or what I have
come to call *primitive gesturals* (PGs), are
very easy for children to create, especially
with technological support (Greshiw-Nardi,
1994). Children can easily string together a
series of PGs, creating a wide variety of tim-
bral effects, spatial distance, and textural
diversity. I have personally seen and heard
hundreds of these pieces created rather
effortlessly by children, with or without
computer-based technology. The question
that these important examples of initial
creative thinking naturally raise in teachers'
minds is "What do I do next in my teaching
strategy?" Once these primitive gesturals
are formed, how can we guide children to a
more complete and extensive compositional experience? Or, indeed, should we?

Arguments against Revision and Extension

One obvious approach to the issue of
revision and extension is not to mention it
at all or to only encourage such activity
without ever insisting upon it. Teachers
who take this perspective believe that revision and extension suggested by an outside
force is not in the best interest of the child.
Three arguments are often advanced.

The first argument relates to the rights
of the child. This argument states that to
do anything more than suggest a process of
revision or extension is to impose the
teacher's thinking upon the creative
process of the individual child. To insist
that children revise and extend their work
is a violation of their rights as composers.
Revision and extension will probably happen naturally as the child gets more experience, anyway. Research on the composition
process as it naturally occurs suggests that
children are indeed happy with their initial
ideas and do not see the need for revision
(Kratus, 1989). Other work has documented
that children naturally do some revision
without being told to do so (Carlin, 1998).
If a teacher suggests a musical procedure
or a change in a given melody, harmony,
rhythm, timbre, dynamic, or other musical

element, the teacher is going well beyond the bounds of creative integrity. The child is not making aesthetic decisions but is being told what to do, thus increasing dependence on the teacher. Besides, if the child says the piece is done, then it is done.

A second argument centers on teacher competency. Because music teachers may not have studied composition personally, asking children to revise and extend is not based on any substantial personal experience with doing it. Teachers may wonder, "How can I do much more than give my kids a chance to compose? I can't really teach composition." Part of this attitude comes from our years of traditional music theory, which includes the study of tonal part-writing and the analysis of large masterworks. We have come to think of musical understanding in terms of highly technical knowledge that seems necessary to apply to a child's composition when we imagine ourselves as leaders of change.

A third argument is much more subtle and may not be spoken out loud. It has to do with the messiness and unpleasant reaction that naturally follows a request for revision and expansion. In the scene above, Miss Williams understands that she may be in for some hard work with Megan. Revision and possible expansion of a first set of ideas is not always easy. The initial gesture is often easy for students to find, but the working out and expansion of the idea requires real effort. This effort taxes the convergent and divergent thinking (Webster, 1990) of the child and the teacher. For some, this ruins the fun of introducing composition in the first place and adds still more time to the activity in a busy classroom, studio, or rehearsal hall.

These arguments, and ones related to them, are reasonable and worth careful study. A teacher should not dominate the thinking process to a point that discourages a creative child. Just as the overbearing band, chorus, or orchestra director robs children of a sense of creativity in performance settings, so too might composition teachers inhibit creativity by adopting a dictatorial posture. But is there a balance between dictating creative content and guiding creative discovery? If Miss Williams asks Megan to consider three other ways to use the crash cymbal sound, is she crossing the line of individual freedom?

Music teachers without composition experience may not initially be able to do what an experienced composer can do for a young composer. A teacher's feedback to a young composer might lack the expertise of feedback in the music teacher's more comfortable performance venue, but is that as important as we make it out to be? We all have instincts about sound designed to be expressive; we all can react with levels of craftsmanship and aesthetic sensitivity (Webster, 1990) and help a young composer think in sound by providing a new perspective. Cannot Miss Williams sense a rhythm or textural pattern in Megan's work that can be highlighted and built upon? Is not Miss Williams skilled enough to form directions that will lead Megan to discover this quality herself and perhaps expand it in a new way that might teach her something totally unexpected about music's power to express the ineffable?

Finally, creativeness is a messy business. Time taken to insist on revision and extension is time taken away from other valuable music experiences. But what students learn about music is absolutely worth the trouble. Children clearly do not like to revise, in part because they feel that if they are asked to revise then what they have initially done is seen as substandard. But do revision and expansion need to always be seen this way? Is it possible to design revision activities early and often enough to make this kind of activity a natural part of musical thinking? Group activity has been demonstrated to be conducive to the revision process (Kaschub, 1997), so might some council from Miss Williams reenergize Megan's group?

Why Revise and Extend?

I believe there are four convincing reasons why we should ask children to revise and extend. In describing these reasons, I hope to convince teachers to encourage children to routinely work beyond their first ideas and to think more deeply about sound formed to express feeling.

The Core of What Music Is as Art

First, and perhaps most important, is the notion that revision is part of how music is made. In the second edition of his classic text on music education philosophy, Reimer (1989) argues that

> the artist works on the material, the material immediately *works on the artist* [italics added], and the artist, with her sensitivity and imagination and craftsmanship, responds and decides and carries the act forward ... The art work grows and develops through the guidance of the artist's sensitivity to the feelings she recognizes, and imagination of their further potentials, and craftsmanly shaping of the material in which the expressive

encounter is being embodied. (p. 62)

Of importance here is Reimer's point that, at the core of creative work, the interaction of material initially created by the artist and the artist's continued work on this material becomes critical for the creative process. Revision is not only desirable but also necessary for creative expression.

In presenting a perspective on creative thinking, Elliott (1995) reflects on the need for creators to consider their material:

> Creative achievement requires that one be continuously on the look out for promising musical ideas and plans. This positive, inquiring mindset is another aspect of supervisory musical knowledge. It develops when students are guided and encouraged to reflect in, on, and about the originality, significance, and creative promise of the musical ideas they are generating and selecting. (p. 226)

Supervisory musical knowledge, in Elliott's thinking, is part of musicianship. It relates to the metacognitive aspect of musical thinking where musicians "monitor, adjust, balance manage, oversee, and otherwise regulate one's musical thinking" (Elliott, 1995, p. 66). It seems clear that the thoughtful review of musical ideas is necessary if real musical thinking is to occur.

Many other theorists implicitly or explicitly identified revision as part of creative thinking. For example, in his famous process model, Wallas (1926) speaks of a verification phase where creative ideas are "worked out." His model is based on anecdotal evidence from many artists describing their processes, and it has been verified since by many professionals speaking about their creative processes.

A more modern treatment of this notion can be found in the work done at Harvard's Project Zero (Gardner, 1989). The model of perception, production, and reflection forms the theoretical heart of this important project. Reflection, carried forth not only in music but in other arts as well, plays an important role in the thinking process.

In my own work, I have included revision as a key part in a model of creative thinking in music. Figure 1 displays the most recent version of this model. In the core, between divergent and convergent thinking, I have included the "working through" aspects in context with other steps in the creative process. Key here are the notions of revising, editing, and extending. Other researchers have included similar endorsements of revision and extension in models that have flowed closely from actual observation of composition processes (Carlin, 1998).

Naturally Present in Children's Actions

The second reason to consider revision and extension a required step in teaching children to compose is that it naturally happens to some extent during free periods of composition. Several empirical studies have focused on the compositional process, and most have reported periods of "exploration" or "reflection." The well-known work by Kratus (1989) on time use by children reliably demonstrates the presence of exploration and development. The more qualitative studies of Younker (1997) and Younker and Smith (1996)

show how both inexperienced and experienced composers work with musical ideas by naturally using revision and extension techniques. Folkestad (1996) reports similar behaviors in his subjects when working with technology.

The point of these studies was not to examine the effect of revision or even to study its presence directly. *In fact, a review of the music literature on creative thinking in music reveals not a single study that isolated revision or extension as a focus of study.* What these studies do tell us is that children spend at least some time working through musical material without being explicitly asked to do so. If a teacher can devise clever ways to build on this behavior without being too dominant, children may well feel that this is a natural part of learning how to compose.

Educational Value

A third reason for encouraging revision is what the child can learn about music. As Megan and her group begin to experiment with that rising flute line by extending it into the body of the composition, creating a contrasting line in a new timbre that moves downward, interrupting the movement with something unexpected, adding the low brass sounds earlier in the work, or trying any of a thousand similar extensions or revisions, they learn about music. They are not just gaining a surface understanding of how melodies, textures, or timbres work; they are learning about the power they have as composers to manipulate the materials of music to create a sense of meaning that is otherwise unavailable. Miss Williams understands that when she encourages group members to look beyond

59

Figure 1. A model of creative thinking in music

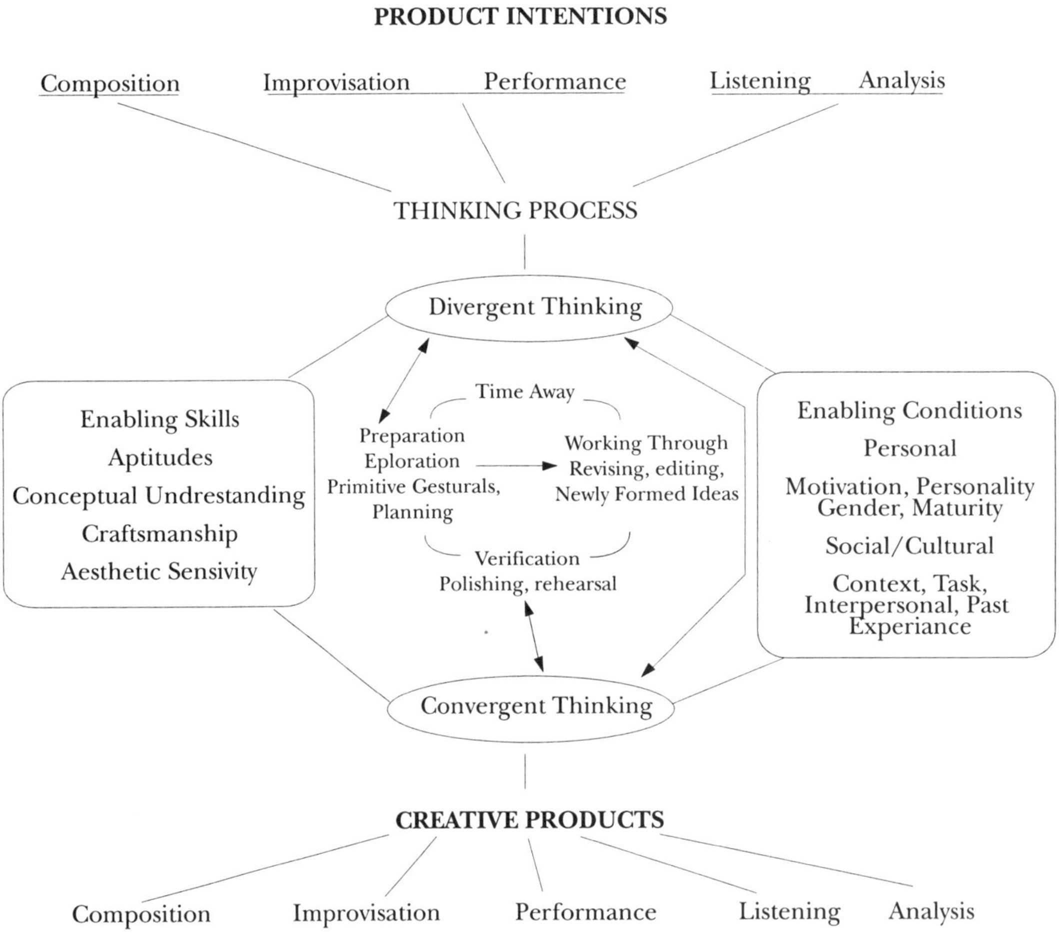

PRODUCT INTENTIONS

Composition   Improvisation   Performance   Listening   Analysis

THINKING PROCESS

Divergent Thinking

Time Away

Enabling Skills
Aptitudes
Conceptual Undrestanding
Craftsmanship
Aesthetic Sensivity

Preparation
Exploration
Primitive Gesturals,
Planning

Working Through
Revising, editing,
Newly Formed Ideas

Verification
Polishing, rehearsal

Enabling Conditions

Personal

Motivation, Personality
Gender, Maturity

Social/Cultural

Context, Task,
Interpersonal, Past
Experiance

Convergent Thinking

CREATIVE PRODUCTS

Composition   Improvisation   Performance   Listening   Analysis what they are comfortable doing, learning happens. Once children understand that such a request is not a result of something being "wrong" with the music in the first place, but rather that it is about taking the initial ideas further for the sake of a deeper musical experience, the whole idea of revision and extension will seem logical and important.

One example of this is in a study reported by Kaschub (1997). This research profiles the processes of two composition projects, one with six sections of sixth-grade general music students and one with a high school choir. In each project, a composer worked with the groups to create works cooperatively. The article is rich with examples of how the children gained a stronger understanding of music by participating in the composition project and learning revision and extension strategies. This is one example from the high school project:

> Once the high school students began to gain confidence in their ability to generate melodic material, the guide [composer] challenged them to think in layers. He began by suggesting that the students sing the opening melody and then to try it as a canon. As students experimented with different compositional techniques they began to offer ideas that were developed beyond just the melodic frame. Students began to sing in duets and trios … and presented multiple ideas until idea generation had to be put on hold so that the ideas already offered could be explored. Several students mentioned that their confidence in their ability to generate musical material grew rapidly. (Kaschub, 1997, p. 21)

In the conclusion section of this study, Kaschub points to the great benefits that come from engagement in composition in learning music. Studies by Christensen (1992) and Auker (1991) have empirically confirmed these benefits.

On a practical level, the books by Paynter (1992) and Schafer (1979) provide music teachers with hundreds of strategies for helping individual and group projects that surround revision and extension. These books are based entirely on the idea of helping the music teacher, regardless of composition background, to encourage children to experiment with sounds as a way to express and understand music better.

Basis for Assessment

This last reason is a compelling one as we strive to assess compositional thinking. Since the spotlight was placed on compositional thinking as part of the National Standards for Music (Consortium of National Arts Education Associations, 1994), music educators have struggled with how to assess composition product and process.

Hickey (1999) and Brophy (2000) offer good starting points in thinking about the design of rubrics, checklists, and rating scales for assessing the revision and extension process. By creating such instruments and sharing them with those who are being assessed, teachers are emphasizing process over product. Overall product assessment, of course, is possible and may be important at key points in a teacher's work with children; however, by recognizing the importance of the manipulation of musical materials, the teacher is placing value on the creative-thinking process.

How might this work for Megan's

group? Miss Williams might have set up the assignment to reflect the need for more than just a product at the end. In addition to the project parameters dealing with length and overall form, the children might be provided with an evaluation rubric to complete at the end of the time period. The children would be responsible for showing evidence of melodic extension, rhythmic variety, development of form, and many other possibilities. Another possibility would be for students to write reflections about the compositional process and how the group arrived at final solutions. Such reflections can be very strong evidence of who is engaged in the musical thinking and how it has transpired.

The point here is that the insistence on "working through" the potential of a musical idea and the documentation of this process benefits both the teacher and the children involved. The focus for quality includes not just the final product but also the journey to get there—this journey is often where the real learning occurs.

Making Revision and Extension Happen Practically

Very little is known about how best to teach compositional thinking. Even the literature on adult pedagogy for composition is very limited. One way to think of how to interact effectively with young composers is to consider stages based on where the composer is developmentally. A first stage might be a formative period during which a child is discovering how to engage and work with initial musical ideas. A second stage could be more related to craftsmanship; individuals in this stage are looking for help in how to accomplish a task. The

third stage might be a more expert stage in which a person can metacognitively understand the measured process of composition and experiment with more holistic techniques related to thinking and feeling in order to find a personal voice.

Stage One: Formative

This stage requires care on the part of the teacher in offering structure versus freedom. In her excellent article on teacher control and creativity, Wiggins (1999) warns about the delicate balance in teacher feedback between being too directed and offering too little structure for improvement and growth. She raises legitimate concerns about children producing music that is the teacher's idea of good music rather than the product of the children's own decision process. She writes:

> When teachers use expressions like, "I want you to do _____ with your piece," students can be overheard saying, "He doesn't want it like that. He wants us to do _____." They are more concerned about what will please the teacher than what will serve their own purposes. Teachers also need to think about how they respond when students make their work public by sharing their finished products or works in progress … Criticizing and altering students' work can give students the impression that they are composing for the teacher and not for themselves. They tend to lose ownership of the work, which is a critical part of engaging in the composition process in the first place. (1999, p. 35)

Wiggins (1999) suggests that if the

teacher senses that the pieces being composed lack, say, dynamic contrast, an acceptable approach might be to do class activities that focus on this concept before continuing with another set of composition assignments. She encourages the teacher to praise the last set of pieces in general terms but also to point out that they were all at one dynamic level and that the class will now study music that has marked contrasts so that students might include these contrasts in their next compositions.

Although this approach has clear merit in preserving the sense of the whole that comes from children's "final" compositions while attempting to broaden their musical vocabulary by example, I worry about the missing of a "teachable moment" when reacting to student work this way. When children have the materials close at hand and "in their heads," teachers need not completely avoid insisting that young composers try out revised and extended patterns in the music. This is especially true if there is no evidence that a child or a group of children has actually thought in these terms.

Comments like "I want you to add some contrast in dynamics here in measure 5 so that it sounds better" are clearly inappropriate and dictatorial; the following is a more meaningful approach:

> **Megan:** What do you mean, "Make my music different"?
> **Miss W:** Well, are you completely happy with your music?
> **Megan:** It's ok, I guess.
> **Miss W:** What do you like least about your music?
> **Megan:** I guess it's kind of boring to me.

> **Miss W:** What can you do to make it more interesting?
> **Megan:** I can make it longer, I guess, by adding a bunch more notes.
> **Miss W:** Yes, you could do that—like we talked about the other day when we changed that melody in class, remember? Or you could add another voice if you wanted to, or you could play around with the dynamics.

This kind of interchange can lead to further experimentation without dictating content. Of course, Megan and her group may still not revise and extend this particular music enough to make it more interesting to all parties concerned, but at least a way of dealing with music materials is established.

Stage Two: Craftsmanship

As children become more experienced with working past initial musical ideas and moving on to revision and extension, the teacher's role might change. Instead of working as a watchdog to be sure revision and extension happen and striking a balance between dictator and facilitator, the teacher becomes more of a coach or a consultant. In this stage, the child is comfortable with revision and extension but needs practical help in solving sticky problems with the music.

For example, a high school student is participating in an on-line distance-learning project focused on composing. The student submits a MIDI-based composition for review on-line, and a teacher/critic comments on the piece. Perhaps the young composer has indicated a section in the music that is of major concern and hopes someone can offer a solution. In this case, the teacher/critic can use a different kind of approach to revision and extension, focusing on a specific musical problem. Here the intent for improvement and growth is the same as in Stage One, except that the level of musical understanding is different, and there is less concern that the teacher is dominating.

Stage Three: The Expert

Here, the teacher becomes a mentor and an engineer for helping students discover their complete potential as composers. Students in the expert phase actively seek alternate approaches to composing music. For example, students may choose to enter a composition program at a college or university and study with a composition teacher. The teacher's role is similar to those in Stage One and Two, but in this stage more subtle relationships between approaches emerge.

In an article from the adult literature on the pedagogy of composition, Carbon (1986) proposes four approaches as possible entry points into compositional work: thinking, sensation, feeling, and intuition. He explores how each of these approaches to pedagogy can be tried with different students, depending on what is needed at the time. The *thinking* approach involves experiments in serial writing or other systems for creating initial ideas and revising them. *Sensation* is approached by using improvisation as a major way to generate content, demonstrating that improvisation and composition have a close relationship—one that has intrigued many music educators (Burnard, 2000). Improvisation also plays a role in the *feeling* approach in which Carbon suggests creat-

ing short improvisatory sequences based on emotions, such as rage or fear. *Intuition* is approached by having students create works that are more "stream of consciousness" pieces (Carbon, p. 119). It is interesting to speculate about whether this particular system of helping expert students fully explore their potential as composers might also take some form in Stages One and Two.

Concluding Thoughts

The issues surrounding revision and extension are fundamental to how we teach music composition, and perhaps all music. In preparing this chapter, I became very much aware of one stunning fact: we desperately need more evidence from practice and research on the roles revision and extension play in developing musicianship. The Megans of our world require nothing less.

References

Auker, P. (1991). Pupil talk, musical learning and creativity. *British Journal of Music Education, 8,* 161–66.

Brophy, T. (2000). *Assessing the developing child musician: A guide for general music teachers.* Chicago: GIA.

Burnard, P. (2000). Examining experiential differences between improvisation and composition in children's music-making. *British Journal of Music Education, 17*(3), 227–45.

Carbon, J. (1986). Toward a pedagogy of composition: Exploring creative potential. *College Music Society, 26,* 112–21.

Carlin, J. (1998). Can you think a little louder? A classroom-based ethnography of eight- and nine-year olds composing with music and language (eight year olds). *Dissertation Abstracts*

International, 59(5), 1503.

Christensen, C. (1992). *Music composition, invented notation and reflection: Tools for music learning and assessment.* Unpublished doctoral dissertation, Rutgers, The State University of New Jersey, Camden, NJ.

Consortium of National Arts Education Associations. (1994). *National standards for arts education.* Reston, VA: MENC.

Elliott, D. (1995). *Music matters.* New York: Oxford University Press.

Folkestad, G. (1996). *Computer based creative music making.* Göteborg, Sweden: Acta Universitatis Gothoburgensis.

Gardner, H. (1989). Project Zero: An introduction to "Arts Propel." *Journal of Art and Design Education, 8*(2), 167–82.

Glover, J. (2000). *Children composing, 4–14.* London: Routledge.

Greshiw-Nardi, T. (1994). Creativity with instant feedback. *Teaching Music, 2*(3), 36–37, 55.

Hickey, M. (1999). Assessment rubrics for music composition. *Music Educators Journal, 85*(4), 26–33, 52.

Kaschub, M. (1997). A comparison of two composer-guided large group composition projects. *Research Studies in Music Education, 8,* 15–28.

Kratus, J. (1989). A time analysis of the compositional processes used by children ages 7 to 11. *Journal of Research in Music Education, 37*(1), 5–20.

Moorhead, G., & Pond, D. (1978). *Music of young children.* Santa Barbara, CA: Pillsbury Foundation for the Advancement of Music Education.

Paynter, J. (1992). *Sound and structure.* London: Cambridge University Press.

Reimer, B. (1989). *A philosophy of music education* (2nd ed.). Englewood Cliffs, NJ: Prentice Hall.

Schafer, R. (1979). *Creative music education.* New York: Schirmer.

Upitis, R. (1992). *Can I play you my song?* Portsmouth, NH: Heinemann.

Wallas, G. (1926). *The art of thought.* New York: Harcourt, Brace.

Webster, P. (1990). Creativity as creative thinking. *Music Educators Journal, 76*(9), 22–28.

Wiggins, J. (1999). Teacher control and creativity. *Music Educators Journal, 85*(5), 30–35, 44.

Younker, B. A. (1997). *Thought processes and strategies of eight, eleven, and fourteen year old students while engaged in music composition.* Unpublished doctoral dissertation, Northwestern University, Evanston, Illinois.

Younker, B., & Smith, W. (1996). Comparing and modeling musical thought processes of expert and novice composers. *Bulletin of the Council of Research for Music Education, 128,* 25–36.

Peter Webster is John Beattie Professor of music education and music technology in the School of Music at Northwestern University in Evanston, Illinois, where he also serves as the academic dean. Webster advises doctoral students and runs the doctoral center at Northwestern.

The Developing Composer

4
Children Composing: Inviting the Artful Narrative

Joyce Eastlund Gromko

Two values of MENC: The National Association for Music Education support my interest in studying the developing composer: embracing diversity and including composition in children's music education curricula. In this chapter, I will argue that music educators' responses to the call for embracing diversity should be based on a value for the individual differences that are expressed when children draw on their own cultures as they create original compositions. Further, I will argue that the inclusion of composition in our curricula should be based on a view of musical composing as *artful narrative*—defined as a temporal sequence of musical events with a beginning, a middle, and an end that is communicated through musical sound and recorded within the symbol system of music. Further, I will illustrate with examples from children as young as 3 years old that children's musical compositions reflect their past musical and extramusical experiences. We can learn something about children from their musical compositions. I will illustrate with examples from elementary-age students that children's metanarratives—their stories about how they composed—are "spontaneous autobiographies,"

analogous to the autobiographies described by Jerome Bruner in *Acts of Meaning* (1990). In the autobiographical narrative that Bruner describes, the storyteller constructs "a longitudinal version of Self" (p. 120). In their metanarratives, children construct a version of themselves as artists and composers.

We Value Diversity

The documents that followed from the Tanglewood Symposium in 1967 emphasized the value of the cultural diversity of American society. In 1969, MENC's Goals and Objectives (GO) project called on music educators to "lead in efforts to develop programs of music instruction challenging to all students, and directed toward the needs of citizens in a pluralistic society" (Mark, 1986, p. 58). Unfortunately for those children who were disenfranchised by the school systems in 1969, the nature of music education did not change radically. Music education's response to the official call from MENC was, by and large, to teach more ethnic music (Barresi & Olson, 1992; Mark, 1986). Often, however, ethnic music (e.g., the music of Africa or Indonesia) was taught using "colonial models" and "standards foreign to the culture" of the ethnic music being taught (Goetze, 2000). Although reading music from a notated score may be the most efficient and effective approach to learning European music, reading music from a notated score misrepresents the way songs and dances are often learned in non-Western lands. Protecting the integrity of ethnic music, however, requires an understanding of the culture from which the music emanates and the culture's traditions for transmission of its music. Mukuna (1997) explains:

> Colonial models continue to provide moulds in which traditional musical materials are organized and students' progress is measured according to standards foreign to the culture. These models are rigid; their implementation leaves little room for interpretation. Often they have an established mould in which all musical materials must fit, or they are considered inferior. The fear of establishing these standards outside their respective cultural context often leads to the denial of the existence of the diversity of cultural teaching processes. (p. 49)

To ignore the cultural context from which music emanates is to misrepresent the music, particularly where music is aurally transmitted or inextricably bound to spiritual rituals or social traditions. Likewise, if teachers ignore or deny the cultural and social context of their students and the need for their students to connect what they are learning to their lives, then students are disenfranchised from the school community. As Herb Kohl (1991) reminds us, disenfranchised students learn how *not*

to learn from us. They do not perform well by the standards imposed upon them, they drop out of the officially sanctioned school music ensembles, they may not want to come to school, and they seek other ways to protect their identity and to express what they have to say:

> Not-learning tends to take place when someone has to deal with unavoidable challenges to her or his personal and family loyalties, integrity, and identity. In such situations there are forced choices and no apparent middle ground. To agree to learn from a stranger who does not respect your integrity causes a major loss of self. The only alternative is to not-learn and reject the stranger's world. (Kohl, 1991, pp. 15–16)

In 1974, the call to embrace diversity came directly to me from my school principal when I was hired to teach in four California elementary schools, three of which served children in low-income neighborhoods. Music teachers were hired to teach music in these schools so the elementary classroom teachers could have preparation time. My teaching experience up to that time had been in predominantly white, middle-class neighborhoods. The principal had worked in his racially diverse community school for 20 years when I was hired to be his school's first music teacher. He asked to meet with me before he would permit me to enter his classrooms, and at that meeting, he laid out his program for embracing diversity at his school:

■ The children were to *make* music.
■ No conventional system of reading or

writing music was to be imposed on the students. If the students and I wanted to make up a system for writing down our music, we could.

■ The children were to teach me *their* music and guide me in selecting the music we would learn together.

I agreed to the principal's terms. I explained, however, that if I were to effectively facilitate the children's learning by doing, then I would need instruments (e.g., guitars, Autoharps, a string bass, hand drums, bongo drums, and conga drums), a record and tape player, and a budget to buy music that the children selected. The principal agreed. Over the next 4 years, my principal's plan proved effective for embracing the school's musical diversity. Students programmed and choreographed concerts that they performed in a gymnasium packed with relatives and friends. I learned from this teaching experience that the urge to create is strong in all children. When they have the opportunity to sing and play music that is meaningful to them, they want to join together to express themselves through music.

The following principles for practice align with my principal's plan: When children make music, they are engaged in personalized encounters with music. When children invent their own systems for documenting their music making, they are reflecting on what they believe is salient about their musical experience. In other words, they are creating symbols that represent what is meaningful to them. In this way, their music is directly associated with their actions, feelings, and thoughts. Finally, when the children's experiences are the

starting point for music making, children's expressions are honest, idiosyncratic, and connected to important events in their lives.

We Value Composing

In 1957, the Contemporary Music Project for Creativity (CMP) was inspired and ultimately funded by the Ford Foundation with the express purpose of increasing the creative aspect of music in the public schools (Mark, 1986, p. 35). From 1959 until 1968, the CMP's Young Composers Project funded residencies for adult composers within public schools, where adults composed works for school ensembles.

Although the CMP project is laudable for its infusion of contemporary music into the public schools, its approach defined the adult composer as the expert. In such a view, the adult composer stands in juxtaposition to the child, and development becomes a linear path by which a child aspires to be like an adult composer. In the "adult-as-standard" model, achievement is measured according to a set of benchmarks, and the worth of children's compositions as art is often devalued. Although children's compositions can be subject to evaluations of goodness, as all objects of art can, I argue against judging goodness in relation to an adult, or expert, standard. Rather, goodness in children's compositions can be determined by describing their compositional process: the integration of the multiple ways of musical knowing, the expression of the children's artistic voice (what they want to say and the ways they say it musically), the usefulness of the children's invented systems for notating what they are saying (Gromko, 1994), and the relation of their musical art to their social and cultural context.

Therefore, I suggest that a theory of development with composing like an adult as the desired end is too narrow and too uniform. Instead, I propose that the rationale for including composition in our curricula be grounded in a philosophy of culture and in cultural psychology. When creating compositions, children draw on their past experiences in order to express themselves to others. Drawing on my observations of children composing, I shall describe individual differences in young children's compositions, or artful narratives, and compare what children say about their compositions to the autobiographical narratives described by Bruner in *Acts of Meaning* (1990). Finally, I will suggest implications for music education.

Philosophical Foundations for Developing Composers

For my philosophical grounding, I turn first to the philosophy of culture espoused by philosophical anthropologists Mikhail Bakhtin (1975/1981) and Valentin Voloshinov (1929/1973), both members of the Bakhtin Circle, and Ernst Cassirer (1925/1946), a German philosopher and historian. From 1918 until Bakhtin's death in 1975, the Bakhtin circle addressed in philosophical terms the social and cultural issues posed by the Russian Revolution of 1917. Dialogism—the belief that culture both responds to and solicits responses from the individuals in the culture—is the hallmark of Bakhtin's thought (Audi, 1999). Audi asserts that Bakhtinian philosophy "signals the birth of a new philosophy of responsibility that challenges and trans-

gresses the Anglo-American tradition of 'rights talk.' Epistomologically, it lends our welcoming ears to the credence that the other may be right" (1999, p. 71).

In Henderich's (1995) words, "From this emerges a conception of personhood where we dialogue with others and subject to the reinterpretations they give us" (p. 76). Bakhtin, in particular, seemed intent on deflating the pretensions of an official language and ideology and instituting a popular-collective learning process (Brandist, 2000), in which students define problems around themes and topics relevant to them. Music educators will recognize these ideas as the roots of reforms in education that invite more voices to be heard in an increasingly pluralistic society.

For Voloshinov (1929/1973) and Cassirer (1923/1953), the symbolic function—the ability to use symbols (e.g., words, numbers, or images) to convey meaning—is common to all areas of knowledge and takes a specific form in each area of knowledge. Because each form is equally valid, a plurality of symbolic forms results. Cassirer (1925/1946) explained that "any symbolic form, of language, arts or myth" is a "particular way of seeing, and carries within itself its particular and proper source of light" (p. 11). Music educators may recognize in these ideas the antecedents of arguments against a general intelligence and toward a theory of multiple intelligences based on the plurality of symbol systems.

Howard Gardner (1983) has argued for a view of intelligence that grants music equal status as a specific form of intelligence among several other symbolic forms. The developing composer is learning to express ideas within the particular symbol system of music, even while calling upon extramusical symbol systems. Thus, music is one symbolic form among a plurality of equally valid symbolic forms.

While members of the Bakhtin circle were addressing the social and cultural issues posed by the Russian Revolution in philosophical terms, Lev Vygotsky, Russian psychologist and philosopher, was concerned with the formative role of culture on children's development. Vygotsky (1934/1986) stressed the close connection between the acquisition of language and the development of thinking. Butterworth and Harris (1994) explain Vygotsky's context:

> Like many educated Russians, he was able to read French and so was acquainted with Binet's ideas about intelligence and Piaget's writings on language and thought in the child. In some respects, then, Vygotsky's intellectual heritage was similar to Piaget's. However, Vygotsky was formulating his ideas during the revolutionary period in Russia, when great emphasis was placed on the way in which the social organisation channels human potential. (p. 21)

Vygotsky's ideas influenced Jerome Bruner, who introduced Vygotsky's ideas to scholars outside Russia. In his writings, Bruner argued that children learn language in the context of social exchanges with their parents and caregivers. Thus, language fluency derives from children's experience of language in their daily life and from their cognitive and linguistic abilities (Butterworth & Harris, 1994, p. 126).

In summary, the philosophical under-

pinnings for a theory of development in support of children's composing can be found in the writings of philosophical anthropologists who posit that there is a plurality of symbolic forms and who emphasize the importance of the social and cultural context in which children develop and express symbolic function. Children's musical compositions are symbolic forms, artful narratives that "meaningfully structure committed time" (Bruner, 1996, p. 133) and that embody children's particular understandings that have evolved through their musical experiences and social interactions within their culture. From this perspective, all children are potentially artists with something to say that is inextricably connected to the social and cultural context of their world. Children's compositions embody their understandings in deciding what to say and how to say it. Furthermore, the comprehension of a composition involves multiple participants who bring their own understandings. Therefore, the comprehension of the narrative has no "single, unique construal" (Bruner, 1996, p. 137). The performance of the work, if not performed by the composer, is subject to the performers' understandings as they interpret and re-create the work. The audience also brings a set of understandings when listening to the composition. Therefore, the interpretations of the composition are multiple and open for negotiation.

In this view, a child's musical composition embodies an intersection of musical, social, and cultural meanings. The composition's worth cannot be judged according to objective standards imposed upon it by a critic who stands at a distance. Rather, the role of the critic (e.g., the teacher or the audience) is to unfold the composition's layers of meaning in consultation with the child. Therefore, assessing the composition's goodness requires an investigation into the various layers of understanding that have contributed to the composition's creation, its performance, and its comprehension. In this way, the critic, with the help of the child, may understand the musical composition's meaning and evaluate its goodness.

Psychological Foundations for Developing Composers

Influenced by Darwin's naturalist approach to observation, Piaget observed children's development within their environments and posited a theory of symbol formation (Kaye, 1982). Piaget's model of development is a self-regulating one between the child and the child's environment. According to Piaget, inner development progresses through qualitatively different stages as the child gradually acquires the conventional symbols used to communicate with others (Piaget, 1945/1951; Piaget & Inhelder, 1966/1969). In contrast, Vygotsky (1988) emphasized the importance of social interactions for children's development. Bruner (1990), in turn, believed that a theory of children's psychological development must be organized around meaning-making and meaning-using processes that connect people to their culture (p. 12).

Acknowledging the importance of both intrinsic (Piagetian) and extrinsic (Vygotskian and Brunerian) influences on a child's development of the symbolic function, Kaye (1982) proposed that the development of the symbolic function begins at

birth with the social interactions between infant and parent. Kaye organized his thinking about children's development of the symbolic function along two dimensions: conventionality and intentionality. Conventional signs or symbols are socially defined and have meaning within a particular cultural context. Intentional signs or symbols are intended by their producers to transmit meaning. Symbols that are conventional and intentional possess the highest degree of shared meaning. The infant's earliest representations are neither conventional nor intentional. They are literal memories for objects, actions, or events (Butterworth & Harris, 1994, p. 116). They are like footprints left by the infant who is engaged in playful exploration. Intermediate signs or symbols vary on one of two dimensions: conventionality and intentionality. A child who is developing within a particular community gradually internalizes the conventions of that community's culture and invents signs or symbols that are intended to transmit a message. Kaye, like Vygotsky (1988), conceived of symbolic development as a social process in which giver and receiver share meanings through increasingly context-specific signs. Furthermore, the meanings are culturally situated in ways "that assure their negotiability and, ultimately, their communicability" (Bruner, 1996, p. 3).

In summary, if we say we value diversity in music education, then we will need to work and play within a context that is meaningful to our students, teaching them the tools and the skills that they will need to compose and improvise. If we say we value composition in music education, then we will need to provide opportunities for our students to compose sound structures (e.g., artful narratives) using the tools and skills they have learned in our classrooms, to hear their compositions performed by capable peers, and to reflect on what they have learned (i.e., to construct a metanarrative).

In the next section, I will describe how children as young as 3 years old approached composing while in individual sessions in my studio. The purpose of these sessions was to observe children as they engaged in creative musical play that might prompt original musical compositions and invented notations of their compositions.

Composing Children: At Play

Learning to compose involves, at the very youngest of ages, making decisions about what sounds to use and how to organize them. During the fall of 1995 and throughout the winter of 1996, I interacted with very young children in weekly individualized 45-minute sessions in my studio. Depending on the age and the inclination of the child, our sessions included exploring various instruments (e.g., unpitched and pitched percussion instruments, piano, and recorders), learning new songs, singing familiar songs, playing familiar songs on instruments, creating original compositions, working on the computer, and inventing notations for familiar folk songs and original compositions. The children generally directed the activities, and I followed their lead.

Available in my studio were a variety of pitched and unpitched percussion instruments, wooden blocks, marker pens, tactile materials, a large drawing pad for every composer, a CD and tape player, CDs, tapes, a metal cookie sheet, magnets,

magnetic letters, magnetic numbers, dolls, African and Native American drums, rattles, bells, cabasa, a computer, notational software, and interactive CD-ROMs about music. All the children chose to use familiar sounds while composing. Their organization was idiosyncratic and based on their previous musical and nonmusical experiences at home, at play, and with media. In the following paragraphs, I will describe five young children's earliest compositions. I engaged all children in exploration of sound sources and asked them to "make a song." When they had made a song and sung or played it for me, I would ask them to "draw (show me) the way the song goes." I provided a variety of materials, including paper, pencils, pens, colored markers, colored shapes, fabric, wooden blocks, pipe cleaners, magnets, plastic letters and numbers, clip-art pictures, plain colored round stickers, glitter glue, buttons, and pictures of hands clapping or feet stomping. I did not direct the children to use a particular material; they chose the material and developed their own approach for organizing their drawing.

Maggie

At her first session when Maggie was 2 years old, she sang "Itsy bitsy spider went up the wah, water pah-do-rah, water pah-do-rah, and go up the wall again!" As I sang "Itsy Bitsy Spider," she placed a plastic egg shaker in a baby doll's arms and began to sing and sway the doll in response to the rhythm of the song. As I sang, Maggie shook her plastic egg shaker while I shook mine. In response to the taped version of "Itsy Bitsy Spider," she shook an egg shaker and danced her doll. When nearly 3 years old,

Maggie made her first sound composition. She had often played with the brightly colored egg shakers when we listened to recorded music and sang songs together. With a set of multicolored egg shakers, her large white drawing tablet, and a bag of multicolored magic markers by her side, Maggie made short lines on her white tablet; she then matched the color of the egg to a line she had drawn of the same color, "cracking" the blue egg on the blue line, the pink on the pink, and so forth, hitting the eggs against the lines. Starting in no particular spot and following in no particular order, Maggie replayed her "Egg Song" in subsequent weeks, first choosing an egg and then hitting it against the tablet on the line of its corresponding color.

Max

When Max was 3 years old, he announced, "Let's make a song! Let's play on this instrument!" He selected hard rubber mallets and played on the xylophone, and he handed me the felt mallets, directing me to play on the glockenspiel. After playing on the xylophone, Max began to make several green *H*s on his drawing pad. He placed the triangle on the drawing pad and traced around the triangle, announcing, "I writed it! Now we have to draw a line around that" (referring to the striker). He placed the striker for the triangle below the triangle shape and drew a line around it (see Figure 1). In performance, I pointed at the green *H*s, and Max played on his xylophone. When I pointed at the triangle outline, Max played the castanet. For Max, a composition was a series of musical sounds.

Thea

At age 4, Thea built a crescent shape out of wooden blocks, explaining that it was a dinosaur that moved on the ground, ate people, lived in Mean Land, but was trying to get to the Magic Land where its mother lived. She went on to explain, "The mouth is the beginning, the middle is the tummy, and that's the tail [she added four more blocks]. The whip and the triangle are for the mouth. The egg shakers take us to the tummy. The ankle bells are in the tummy because he ate a lot of people! You shake those while I crack this. You keep playing these sticks while I play this [the agogo bell] for the tail." She wrote in green coils on her tablet, explaining that she was writing the song in French (see Figure 2).

Ben

Ben, age 5, used wooden blocks to build a maze with walls, bounded on the front end by a "gate." He pointed at the yellow door, walked his Z-bot plastic toy through the form, and described the middle as "orange" and "rectangle." Explaining how his wooden-block maze could serve as a frame for his sound composition, he said, "The beginning is different from the middle, but it is similar to the end. This makes it different [pointing to the green rectangle at the end]. The song begins at the yellow door because that's a squeaky door." He chose the triangle and hit the triangle continuously from the time my Z-bot toy left the door and until it got to the middle of the maze. He then picked up the whip. I matched my Z-bot's movement to Benjamin's whip sounds. He chose the jingle bell and jingled as I walked the Z-bot to the green rectangle. I turned the Z-bot around

Figure 1. Max's song

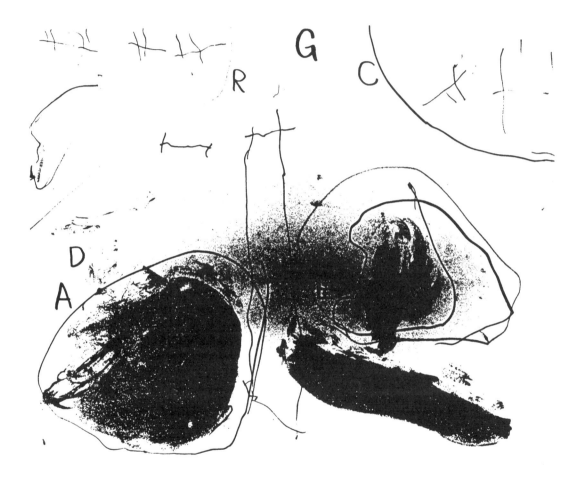

The drawing records Max's exploration of the xylophone, triangle, colored markers, and glitter glue.

Figure 2. Thea's "Dinosaur Song."

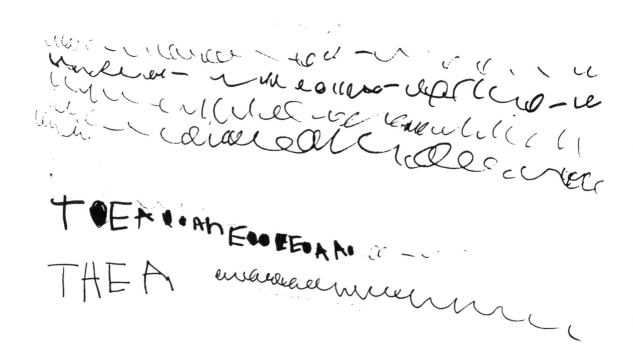

The writing is Thea's song written in French.

Figure 3. Benjamin's "Maze Song" for the plastic toy

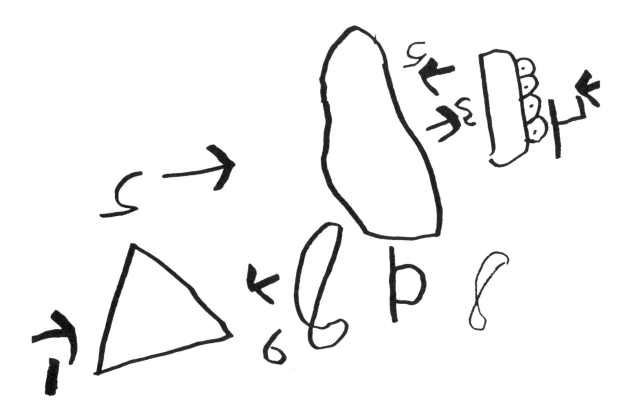

His numbers signify numbers of sounds; the shapes signify
sound sources; his arrows show temporal direction.

and began to walk it back toward the middle. Benjamin picked up the whip again as the toy approached the middle. "When he hops up there [the yellow door] that's the ending," he announced. His invented notation of the sound composition (Figure 3) consisted of outlines of each of his instruments, with numbers to indicate how many times the instrument should be played and arrows to indicate temporal direction in the playing.

Nathan

Nathan, age 6, built a "B-2 bomber" from colored wooden blocks. He built the midsection first, stacking rectangular blocks into a rectangular shape. Next, he built diagonal and symmetrical wings that sloped downward from the top of the midsection to the floor on both sides of the midsection. The wing span measured approximately 2 feet across, and the midsection was approximately 8 inches high. He explained, "These are the things that are hooking on because of gravity. That's a blocker for some things it will be ramming into. That's just where the electricity goes into this and this uses the electricity. The human beings sit down in the London Bridge part, about 25 of them. The pilot sits right here. This is a gun and he steers. The other people are there for emergencies, if the pilot goes down."

"If you had to divide this into three parts, where would they be?" I asked.

"The parts that are going to be stuck together? I would keep this part together and take this part [the wing] off and this part [the other wing] off," he explained.

"Which of the three parts are a lot alike? Assign some letters to the parts," I said.

"ABA," he replied, pointing at the wing, the body, and the other wing.

He said that the little triangle made a different sound, so it should be in the B section. He picked up the finger cymbals and compared their sound to another pair. They sounded the same, so he put one pair beneath each wing. He picked up the ankle strap bell, shook it, compared it to the other ankle strap bells, placed the two that sounded alike (one with a beige strap and one with a red) near the A sections and the one with the black strap near the B section of his sculpture. The jingle bells sounded the same, so he placed one near each A section. He performed the A section of his sound composition with triangle, claves, egg shaker, jingle bell, ankle bell, and finger cymbal; the B Section consisted of an agogo bell and the ankle bell with the black strap, and then he repeated the A section.

"There's something weird about this," Nathan told me. "See these two [the ankle strap bells]? They look different, but they sound the same. The difference, see, compared to these: these are lower, so they went in the A section. So what I did was I put the matching ones to the A sections. I put the unmatching ones in the B section. I matched the sounds. I divided them each with some things that sound the same. In their color, they look different, but they hear the same."

Children's Decisions

The children's decisions about what sounds to use were influenced by what sounds were accessible and familiar, as well as whether the sounds heightened the drama of the story they were imagining. The youngest children's decisions about their sound compositions revealed connections to personal experiences. Maggie had watched eggs being cracked at home and was imitating the experience. She used color to indicate which sound source she had explored. Max used outlines of the instruments to indicate the sound sources he had explored. The older children's organization of their sound compositions was based on stories they imagined. Thea's dinosaur was going to meet its mother, Ben's Z-bot was working its way through a maze, and Nathan's bomber was equipped for a mission. Telling stories "is the most natural and the earliest way in which we organize our experience and our knowledge" (Bruner, 1996, p. 121). For children, a spoken narrative can provide the framework for their arrangement of musical sounds. The music children compose embodies their experiences and imagination and tells us something about them. According to Bruner,

> Education is not simply a technical business of well-managed information processing, nor even simply a matter of applying "learning theories" to the classroom or using the results of subject-centered "achievement testing." It is a complex pursuit of fitting a culture to the needs of its members and their ways of knowing to the needs of the culture. (p. 43)

In summary, even the youngest children arranged sounds in a temporal sequence, drawing on previous musical and extramusical experiences. The metanarratives of the older children in this group revealed their tendency to organize their temporal sequence of musical sound according to stories they imagined. As the figures show, the children's invented notations are unconventional and idiosyncratic.

In the next section, I will describe how fourth-, fifth-, and sixth-grade children approached composing within their elementary-school music class. The purpose of the semester-long project was to prepare children to compose through the study of eight masterworks that they would perform and 28 compositions that they would listen to outside class. The fourth-, fifth-, and sixth-grade children were at more advanced levels of musical development than the children in the previous section and were working within a school setting rather than in individual sessions with me in my office.

Composing Children: At School

In preparation for composition within a school setting, I formed a percussion ensemble as a preliminary activity to recruiting a composers' club 4 months later. I thought it was important that the children learn to perform masterworks that were based on sheerly musical ideas (versus extramusical ideas) so that the children could experience and understand how the musical ideas were developed within Western (e.g., American, African-American, Central American, Belgian, and German) musical structure. I chose eight masterworks written for children; the pieces had different forms and used different combinations of percussion instruments and were written in different musical styles. I taught all the music by rote, explaining how the musical ideas were developed so that the children would understand the structure of the music and the way their individual parts contributed to the musical whole. After we learned each piece, we consulted the musical score in order to locate the individual parts and to see how the composer notated the music using traditional notation. I wanted the children to have played a variety of pitched and unpitched percussion instruments so that they would be familiar with a number of sound sources. Eighteen children, ranging in age from 8 to 12 years, joined the percussion ensemble. Together, they learned to perform two 4-part canons, one jazz piece with vocal improvisation, a hand-drum duet, a Calypso piece that featured recorder and pitched and unpitched percussion instruments, and three pieces scored for a variety of pitched and unpitched percussion instruments featuring particular timbre collections.

The children and I met for 24 group sessions from January until April. At the end of April, we performed in concert for parents and friends. During May, 12 of the 18 children elected to form the composers' club. To build the children's listening repertoire, I selected 28 listening maps from a collection of 80 listening maps provided in the examination copies of teachers' editions for Silver Burdett Ginn's *The Music Connection* (1995). I compiled the maps into a booklet and created a master tape of the selections from the CDs. The children individually listened to the music and followed the maps as part of their regular classroom activities over a period of 4 weeks. I chose maps that I thought were easy to follow, accurate in representation of the music's rhythm and melodic contour, and helpful in showing how musical patterns can be arranged to create whole musical structures. I chose to structure their composition experiences in ways that

prompted social and musical interactions among the children.

Assignment One

For their first composition assignment (Figure 4), I asked the children to form small groups. Each group was to find a rhythmic spoken text and to use the text, along with fragments of the text that served as ostinati, as the basis for an unpitched rhythmic composition. The children chose their spoken texts from books in the school library. They chose a speech segment to serve as an ostinato, and then they transformed the speech into body percussion, transferring the body sounds to unpitched

Figure 4. Sounds with words

Word Rhythms

1. Choose a poem that is rhythmic.

2. Read it out loud. Does it have a beat?

3. Choose a short phrase from the poem as an accompaniment ostinato.

4. Read the poem again while one of your friends performs the accompaniment ostinato.

Word Rhythms into Sound Structures

1. Substitute vocal sounds or body sounds in place of the word rhythms.

2. Substitute percussion sounds in place of the word rhythms.

instruments. In the small-group sessions, I observed that social goals seemed to predominate during the composing processes, such that musical goals either coexisted with the social goals or were entirely lost to the social goals as children negotiated their way to a group composition and performance.

In her analysis of children's English-language compositions, Anne Haas Dyson (1995) constructed a category system to describe children's social goals when composing. Among these goals were affiliation, solicitation, allowance, control, compliance or resistance, and negotiation. As I observed the children composing musical compositions, I found affiliation (i.e., emphasizing one's similarity to others) to be operative when the children formed their small groups. Once in a group, the self-appointed leaders chose to control, solicit, and resist, while the followers chose to allow or comply. In groups where the members perceived themselves to be similar in status and somewhat advanced in musical ability, there was evidence of negotiation (i.e., mutual accommodation, with each participant seeking some control) and a free exchange of ideas. In groups where the members perceived themselves to be similar in status but not musically advanced, the members consulted or recruited more knowledgeable members from other groups to help them. In one child's case, no affiliations were formed, so the child opted to use a tape recorder to record family members performing the speech-fragment ostinati, over which he performed his speech segment.

Assignment Two

For the second composition assignment (Figure 5), I asked children to complete the assignment by themselves at home and bring their notation to school for a performance. During music class, each child composer chose three or four performers to interpret the notation and perform the composition while the composer conducted from the notation. If the composer was satisfied with the performance, we would videotape. If the composer was not satisfied, he or she would

Figure 5.
Colors of sound: Aleatoric music

1. Choose one sound color (e.g., beads, metallic, skin, or wood). Choose three "hues" of your sound color by selecting three instruments that produce that color (e.g., the plastic egg shaker, the wooden shaker, and the cabasa; or the glockenspiel, the metallophone, and the finger cymbal).

2. Create a score of your sound-color composition. Using a white background and moving left to right, lay out each of the three "hue" parts in blocks of color on horizontal lines. Lengths of blocks signify duration. Color signifies sound. Space between blocks signifies silence. By varying the lengths of the blocks, you can create patterns.

3. Choose three friends to perform your sound-color composition. Assign each friend one of the horizontal lines on your score and one of the instruments you have selected (in Step 1 above). Moving left to right with a wand, conduct your composition. You determine the tempo.

change instruments or make suggestions to the performers (e.g., "I want you to play more than one note at a time," "I want you to keep playing until I get to the white," or "I want you to play softer so I can hear the softer instruments"). If the other composers, who made up the audience, had suggestions, they could offer them to the composer, who was obliged to acknowledge the comment and encouraged to try out the idea. Again, social goals were operative. Affiliation showed itself in the composer's choice of performers. Negotiation was practiced between the composer and the performers and between the composer and the audience critics. In his metanarrative about his composing process, Sam, a 9-year-old, explained:

> I got up Tuesday morning and did it. [It was sort of] Random. I tried to make it so it weaved, so that there was always a sound going on. Sometimes they mixed; sometimes they didn't. There's always a main sound. Sounds come in at certain parts. There's a main sound, but the main sound changes. The metallophone is my favorite. The bass makes a big deep sound. I forget the name of the last one. I needed it just to come in at certain places, a light sound. The high one was the metallophone. I didn't want a heavy sound for that part. I wanted it really light; I wanted something that could be heard when the metallophone rings and the basses boom. The xylophone is one that did that. First, I chose my instruments, then I just wove those in and out at random. I just sort of had my performers just play it. I think it sounded better just doing that. I didn't know what

notes; they just had to play it. I liked how the metallophone had just random notes. I didn't mean for the piece to have any certain beat or tempo. It was supposed to be random notes. I just sort of made it [into] shapes. I looked at the shapes, not the sounds and how long they were going to play. I just sort of went through that. I wanted them all to get a chance to play—sometimes others, sometimes not. I wanted them to end together because I thought it made an interesting sound to have them all ending together. The beginning was just the start of pattern. I think it vibrates quite a lot. Sometimes the xylophone gets sorta lost, then it gets found again. You listen to how it sounds, then you change that sound till it sounds just the way you want it. It makes it sound better to know what you want the instruments to play. If I compose something in my mind, I can never play it the same way twice. [I try] Writing it down sometimes. I know sometimes it doesn't get the same effect when you play it back as when you've written it down, but if it's an interesting effect, I sit down and just keep playing it until it sounds right.

In her metanarrative about her composing process for this assignment, Rachel, an 11-year-old, explained:

> These shapes were supposed to be footsteps, the soprano xylophone. I actually had a different idea of what it would sound like, but I think it turned out okay. I started with the footsteps, then I added different patterns. I wanted this to be a quick instrument that you could shake. I

wanted instruments that had high and low, chords and stuff. First, I had these [the soprano xylophone footsteps], then I added these [the bass], then I decided that in the middle, everything would stop except the maraca, then they [the pitched instruments] would go alone. I wanted them to end on a note that sounded right. And have it be loud at the end. The beginning [sounds] just like you're walking along and you hear some sounds. I thought of the title ["A Day in the Park"] first, then I came up with all this stuff to go with it. It didn't come out the way I thought it would. I liked the first time we played it better. I liked how the musicians played it. I sort of in my mind had notes, a low one and a high one, but the assignment was called "Aleatoric Music." It was totally chance what your players would think about playing it. I kind of like it how it is. It is like chance, so it's however it turns out.

Assignment Three

For their third composition assignment (Figure 6), I asked children to complete an ostinati composition by themselves at home and bring their notation of this to school for a rehearsal and performance. The composers chose three or four performers to perform their precisely notated ostinati and one performer to improvise over the ostinati. The composer rehearsed the parts and conducted the performance. When the composer was satisfied, we videotaped. By this stage in our process, groups had solidified. Because so much of the performance was controlled by the composers, given the precision of the notation and the clear idea they seemed to have of what they wanted,

musical goals seemed to predominate in group interactions. In her metanarrative about her composing process, Emily, a 10-year-old, explained:

> [My idea came] from "Body Rondo" [a piece in ABACA form performed with sounds created on and with the body], but this sounded better, and it was harder too. When I actually had the full

Figure 6. Sound patterns

1. Choose two or three interesting sound sources that are unpitched.

2. For each sound source, create a rhythmic pattern in different lengths or meters (for instance, 3 unit pulses in a group, 4 unit pulses, or 5 unit pulses).

3. Notate each pattern horizontally on your orange paper. Use stickers to represent a language. All unit pulses should line up vertically.

4. Choose a friend to perform each of your patterns. Conduct each unit pulse. Make sure the unit pulses sound together.

5. Ask one friend to "improvise" using a pitched instrument (for instance, xylophone, recorder, or singing voice). Your friends' patterns will repeat, but the pitched improvised part will vary.

6. Figure out how you will signal (with the conductor's baton) when your sound structure should end.

7. Make a title for your sound structure and write it on your orange paper.

thing, I had learned from other people that it was a little too hard, so I had to change it a little bit. When I was thinking of the times, I wanted to be sure they fit together. I adjusted it so it would sort of contrast, but not really. I don't know exactly how I thought of it. It was like all complicated in its own way, but the easiest overall was making [the clave] part and thinking of a bass. I like the sound of it. I like the agogo sound; Rachel went back and forth with it and I liked that; and the claves, they're a bass. And the tambourine, it's a nice little extra. I like how they all fit together, even though they sound a little different, they all fit together in some way. [The xylophone part is] improv, so you can't decide what she plays. I didn't even limit her from any notes; she could just play what she wanted.

In talking about her plans to continue composing, Emily went on to say:

We got these listening tapes. I really liked Shostakovich. My mom really likes him too. I like his Polka. That's the one I really like out of the whole entire tape of 90 minutes. I like the different ways he puts it together. I liked the xylophone. It stood out, I think. He used all these other instruments, while the other ones were mostly violin, flute, and oboe. I think this one used the trumpet. The xylophone and different ones that the other ones didn't use. It stood out a lot. He goes to the trumpet and goes to the xylophone. And so it contrasts. [The sections] aren't blended together. I can hear that's "B."

Lessons Learned

It is tempting for us as music educators to assume that learning has taken place when we see tangible products of our assignments. However, we need to ask the children about what they learned. The metanarrative is one way children can construct a longitudinal view of their artist selves, by reflecting in the company of others (their teachers and their capable peers) and by entering into a dialogue with others. Bruner (1990) suggests that we capture the autobiography of children, that is, "an account of what one thinks one did in what settings in what ways for what felt reasons" (p. 119). Furthermore, Bruner adds, "It does not matter whether the account conforms to what others might say who were witnesses, nor are we in pursuit of such ontologically obscure issues as whether the account is 'self-deceptive' or 'true'" (p. 119). I am interested in extending an invitation for children to think and talk about what they were doing, why they thought they were doing it, and what they think they learned from doing it. In the data I collected, the school-aged children created artful narratives that embodied their experiences. In their metanarratives, they talked about why they made the choices they did and what kinds of problems they encountered along the way. Asking the children to create compositions is fundamental to children's development as musical artists. In this way, children contribute to, and don't just absorb, a cultural heritage.

Clifford Geertz (2000), cultural anthropologist, asserts that "culture is socially and historically constructed … narrative is primary … [and] we assemble the selves we live in out of materials lying about in the society around us" (p. 196). As is evident in the ways the children organized their compositions, they drew on the culture around them even as they were creating culturally embedded symbolic forms—musical, linguistic, visual-spatial, and social. The young children framed their compositions on the basis of their personal experiences and stories they imagined. The older children organized their compositions on the basis of past musical experiences and in the midst of social interactions, creating autobiographical and artful narratives. Bruner (1990) states that "in the end, even the strongest causal explanations of the human condition cannot make plausible sense without being interpreted in the light of the symbolic world that constitutes human culture" (p. 138). In their creation of symbolic forms, children weave themselves into the culture they are making. In summary, the strongest rationale for developing composers derives from the call to embrace diversity and to offer all students the chance to create symbolic representations that embody their experiences, their culture, and their imaginations. At the same time, others are invited to join them in the process.

Implications for Practice

Composing as artful narrative implies that the musical composition is symbolic of children's lived experience. Given the decisions that children make about sound and its organization while composing, a rich and varied experiential background in music will be invaluable. At the stage in their development when children begin to engage in symbolic play, they enjoy making up songs; drawing pictures that represent their experiences; using costumes, puppets, and props to act out stories they have heard or made up; and using gestures and movement in response to musical sound. When children are just beginning to talk, their songs, like their words, are a series of expressive sounds. As children's memories, their concepts of space and time, and their vocabularies grow and as they gain experience with stories, musical songs, and motor activities, their compositions begin to reflect their growing inner library of sounds and lived experiences. By the time children are in elementary school, they are able to draw on considerable life experience, to borrow from symbol systems outside music, and to use the tools and skills they have been taught in music classes to compose organized sound structures. Furthermore, children welcome the chance to talk about what they have made, why they made it the way they did, and what they learned in the process.

Students' Roles as Performers, Listeners, and Composers

As we observed, all the children used sounds and sound sources from their inner library, based on the youngest children's sheer explorations and on the older children's performance and listening repertoire. The youngest children's compositions were characterized by personal statement, spontaneity, and playfulness. The older children used the structure of the assignments as starting points for their compositions, choosing their sound sources and interpretations from ideas stored in their inner library of sounds.

The group compositional process revealed children's social styles. Each composer in the group process played multiple roles—composer, performer, and audience critic. Based on what the children revealed in their metanarratives, the children learned about composing through collaborating in the solving of compositional problems exposed when the works were first performed. The more experience each child accumulated as composer, performer, and listener, the more likely the participants in group projects were to practice negotiation, rather than control and submission. The older children enjoyed watching their tapes and making adjustments to their compositions. Rachel noted:

> It didn't come out the way I thought it would. I liked the first time I played it better. I liked how the musicians played it. I sort of in my mind had notes, a low one and a high one.

Emily added:

> I didn't know exactly what I wanted, which is why we had to tape three times. First time, I was going to have them play anything, so I said they could play two notes. I had absolutely no idea what notes they would play.

Playing it again and again added to their experience of possibilities and prompted their ideas for their next compositions. Rachel shared:

> I like improvising, because it's like composing, except it's never the same. Since you didn't actually have to put certain notes, it didn't take that much. You could have things in mind—it was easier. [While I was improvising,] I was thinking

about all the different pieces I played.

About her next composition, Emily said:

> Actually, I started a song. It's cool. I have the whole part *A* of it. I started this before composer's club, but I'm still working on it. It's called, "Sunshine Song." I'll probably keep on working on that. It's for bass xylophone, soprano metallophone, the conga, and the soprano glockenspiel. I think that's all. I like the xylophones a lot. From "Painted Bunting" [a masterwork by Jim Solomon that Emily had performed], there was a pattern that I liked. I did that same thing, but I changed it a little bit. It was a dotted quarter note and I just changed that around a little bit. Rachel, because she can get harder pieces easier than other people can [and] she gets them quicker, … I'd probably give the harder parts to her. Justin can keep a steady beat on the bass, so I'd give the bass to him. Maybe Jimmy would play the conga thing. Lauren could play pretty much anything … At school I know what the instruments sound like. Listening at school, I know what they sound like. I'll probably finish it by fall.

Children's musical compositions are richly varied narratives that draw from the whole of children's experiences. Among these few children, we observe connections to poetry, stories, books, media, number, language, color, and shapes.

The Teacher's Role as Musician, Facilitator, and Critic

Before I close, I want to describe my

role as music specialist. In my individual sessions with the very young children, I taught songs and provided a variety of instruments for exploration that little hands could play. I was an earnest listener and imaginative responder, intent on learning from and through my experience with the very young children. I was a playmate and a musical companion who shared my experience and my expertise in musical conversations. In my sessions with school-aged children, I remained attentive to the musical and social needs of the children, lending knowledge when appropriate, encouraging through questioning, providing resources and materials, and facilitating the children's development of independence as musicians. I observed that, as the children accumulated experiences with both composing and social interactions while composing, the dynamics within the group changed from one of leaders and followers to one of peers in negotiation.

Even as I am promoting a student-centered orientation, I want to stress the profoundly important role played by a professional musician who is also a gifted teacher. Orienting education to the children's individual needs and interests requires the teacher not to do as much overt teaching in the traditional sense, but to be more keenly aware, socially astute, and musically flexible in response to the children's direction and ideas. As the children's narratives revealed, the composers called upon ideas they had learned in their previous musical experiences, which is to say composition cannot replace, but will most certainly extend, traditional musical activities. If music experiences are to generate musical ideas, then performance and listening repertoires need to demonstrate ways of organizing and combining sounds and illustrate the myriad effects possible through such organizations and combinations.

In conclusion, I have argued that composing with children is one way to embrace diversity by allowing children's voices to contribute to our cultural heritage. I believe that children, when given access to sound sources and performing and listening opportunities, will build their repertoire of musical ideas and thus enrich and improve their compositions. Children need guidance and support in creating effective compositions. The teacher's primary role is to invite the artful narrative in such ways that children can trust they will be heard and understood, that is, to let children know they have something worthwhile to say and to help them find a way to say it.

References

Audi, R. (Ed.). (1999). *The Cambridge dictionary of philosophy* (2nd ed.). Cambridge, England: Cambridge University Press.

Bakhtin, M. (1981). *The dialogic imagination: Four essays* (C. Emerson & M. Holquist, Trans.). Austin, TX: University of Texas Press. (Original work published 1975)

Barresi, A., & Olson, G. (1992). The nature of policy and music education. In R. Colwell (Ed.), *Handbook of research on music teaching and learning* (pp. 760–72). New York: Schirmer Books.

Brandist, C. (2000). The Bakhtin circle. In J. Fieser (Ed.), *The Internet Encyclopedia of Philosophy*. Retrieved June 29, 2000, from http://www.utm.edu/research/iep/b/bakhtin.htm

Bruner, J. (1990). *Acts of meaning*. Cambridge, MA: Harvard University Press.

Bruner, J. (1996). *The culture of education.* Cambridge, MA: Harvard University Press.

Butterworth, G., & Harris, M. (1994). *Principles of developmental psychology.* Hove, England: Erlbaum.

Cassirer, E. (1946). *Language and myth* (S. Langer, Trans.). New York: Dover. (Original work published 1925)

Cassirer, E. (1953). *Philosophy of symbolic forms* (R. Manheim, Trans.). New Haven, CT: Yale University Press. (Original work published 1923)

Dyson, A. (1995). Writing children: Reinventing the development of childhood literacy. *Written Communication, 12*(1), 4–46.

Gardner, H. (1983). *Frames of mind: The theory of multiple intelligences.* New York: Basic Books.

Geertz, C. (2000). *Available light: Anthropological reflections on philosophical topics.* Princeton, NJ: Princeton University Press.

Goetze, M. (2000). Challenges of performing diverse cultural music. *Music Educators Journal, 87*(1), 23–25, 48.

Gromko, J. (1994). Children's invented notations as measures of musical understanding. *Psychology of Music, 22,* 136–47.

Henderich, T. (Ed.). (1995). *The Oxford companion to philosophy.* Oxford, England: Oxford University Press.

Kaye, K. (1982). *The mental and social life of babies: How parents create persons.* Chicago: University of Chicago Press.

Kohl, H. (1991). *I won't learn from you: The role of assent in learning.* Minneapolis, MN: Milkweed Editions.

Mark, M. (1986). *Contemporary music education* (2nd ed.). New York: Schirmer Books.

Mukuna, K. (1997). The universal language of all times? *International Journal of Music Education, 29,* 47–51.

The Music Connection. (1995). Morristown, NJ: Silver Burdett Ginn.

Piaget, J. (1951). *Play, dreams and imitation in childhood* (C. Gattegno & F. M. Hodgson, Trans.). London: Heinemann. (Original work published 1945)

Piaget, J., & Inhelder, B. (1969). *The psychology of the child* (H. Weaver, Trans.). New York: Basic Books. (Original work published 1966)

Voloshinov, V. (1973). *Marxism and the philosophy of language* (L. Matejka & I. R. Titunick, Trans.). New York: Seminar. (Original work published 1929)

Vygotsky, L. (1986). *Thought and language* (A. Kozulin, Rev. & Trans.). Cambridge, MA: MIT Press. (Original work published 1934)

Vygotsky, L. S. (1988). The genesis of higher mental functions (J. V. Wertsch, Trans.). In K. Richardson & S. Sheldon (Eds.), *Cognitive development to adolescence: A reader* (pp.61–79). Hove, England: Erlbaum. (Reprinted from *The concept of activity in Soviet psychology,* pp. 145–88, by J. V. Wertsch, Ed., 1981, Armonk, NY: M. E. Sharpe.)

Joyce Eastlund Gromko is professor of music education at Bowling Green State University in Bowling Green, Ohio. Since 1970, she has taught preschool through college-aged students. Since 1992, she has developed field sites in general music at private and public schools near her university. Her undergraduate work was done at Luther College in Decorah, Iowa, where she sang with the Nordic Choir under the direction of Weston Noble. Her doctorate in music education is from the School of Music at Indiana University in Bloomington.

5

Identity and Voice in Young Composers

Sandra Stauffer

"The study of the creative process is an extremely delicate one," composer Igor Stravinsky wrote. "In truth, it is impossible to observe the inner workings of this process from the outside" (1970, p. 49). Indeed, those who study creativity in music can examine only the external manifestations of a process that unfolds in the minds of those who create. Even to watch a composer or improviser at work is to observe the creative workings of the musical mind after the fact, though the time lapse may be measured only in milliseconds.

Still, what composers and improvisers create is recognizable by performers and informed listeners as uniquely *theirs*—as something of, from, or by particular individuals. We may not be able to observe the inner workings of Stravinsky's creative process, but we do recognize Stravinsky's music as Stravinsky's music. Put another way, just as a rose is a rose is a rose, Stravinsky is Stravinsky, and Miles Davis is Miles Davis. Furthermore, connoisseurs of the compositions of the former or the improvisations of the latter can discern subtle variations in the music of either master and identify their works as early or late

examples of their genius.

Turn on the radio. Go to a concert. Listen to a recording. The music starts; we perceive the sounds and identify them, or with them, in some way. Our complex cognitive capacity for processing what we hear enables a broad spectrum of responses and reactions. When musical sounds and gestures are sufficiently familiar, we know that the music is from a certain culture, in a particular style, or even performed or created by specific individuals for specific purposes. In Western cultures, where musical works of all kinds are attributed to the individuals who created them, we say the composer has identity or voice.

What is identity or voice? In music, the composer's *identity* is made up of the unique qualities of musical sound that allow the informed listener to associate a work with its composer. Furthermore, the qualities that are particular to a composer's identity persist, allowing the listener to recognize a certain sameness in different examples of the individual's collective works over time. In other words, regardless of transformations in style or character, the essential qualities of an individual's creative works in music remain consistent, recognizable, and unique. Stravinsky sounds like Stravinksy, whether one is listening to the *Rite of Spring* (1913) or *The Rake's Progress* (1951).

The term *voice* is also used to describe the uniqueness of a single composer's works. Voice is associated with identity, but the two are not synonymous. Identity has to do with qualities that make up the particular sound of the individual composer. The composer's works are also, however, singularly meaningful and uniquely expressive. Identity is a matter of the materials of music—gestures, structures, and their combination; voice is a matter of expression and meaning.

In the literature of psychology and sociology, the term *identity* is linked to the concept of self, or "who we are in relation to ourselves, to others, and to social systems" (Johnson, 1995, p. 249). In the pages that follow, I use *identity* to mean the unique qualities of a composer's works. I propose that both identity (characteristic gesture and structure) and voice (expression and meaning) are indeed linked to social systems, even among young composers, and, further, that compositional identity is linked to seeing oneself as a composer.

In this chapter, then, our task is to consider identity and voice in young composers—children and adolescents. What is the nature of identity and voice in young composers? When and how do identity and voice emerge? How are identity and voice linked to the process of composing? What are the implications for pedagogy? To answer these questions, we begin with an examination of traditions in the study of identity and voice, and we then turn to examples of identity and voice in the works of several young composers and to thoughts about our own practices for including composition in music classrooms and ensembles.

Studying Identity and Voice

In traditional academic circles, the composer's identity is studied in music history and theory classes, where works are analyzed, salient features are described, and pieces are placed in both biographical and broader historical—and sometimes social—contexts. Voice has become the province of philosophers, historians, and theorists. Both identity and voice are typically examined in reference to mature composers who have a collection of works available for analysis and reflection. In this context, the only child composers worthy of study are those who were prodigies in their youth and masters in adulthood.

Examination of the composer's voice and identity is further linked to long and powerful traditions in Western art music of studying canonized works, otherwise known as *masterworks,* and composers whose compositional and life histories and sociohistorical contexts have been documented. For the most part, scholars look back in time, analyzing composed works, poring over sketch books and manuscripts, examining letters and diaries written while a work was in progress, interviewing composers about their works, describing one work in the context of other works by that composer or works by that composer's contemporaries or predecessors, and viewing compositions through the lens of the composer's personal beliefs and history as well as the *zeitgeist.* Such research culminates in composer biographies; scholarly papers in history, theory, and philosophy; and even program notes. Young composers, particularly children, hardly qualify for study, as they have neither extensive life histories nor, in most cases, significant bodies of work available for examination.

The tradition of scholarship described above is also tied to performance practices of Western art music, where the composer's voice is venerated. In *The Composer's Voice*, a book whose title makes the point, Cone (1974) notes that "it is the duty of the performer or performers to make clear" the intentions of the composer and, further, that "the performer ... is a living personification ... of the mind whose experience the music is" (p. 5). In *The Composer's Advocate*, Leinsdorf (1981) asserts that "great composers knew what they wanted" and suggests that performers, particularly conductors, "can enter into the mental processes of a composer" by examining "representational music," by studying "the ways in which he learned from earlier composers," and by "explor[ing] in depth works that he has revised" (pp. 23–37). This point of view leaves little room for consideration of identity and voice in young composers.

For the most part, researchers in music education and the psychology of music who are natives of Western cultures have been raised in intellectual and artistic traditions similar to those of historians, theorists, and performers of Western art music. We should not be surprised, therefore, to find similarities among them in the study of composers and composition. Sloboda (1985), for example, suggests four possible means of studying the creative process: (a) examination of

sketches, notebooks, and manuscripts; (b) examination of what composers themselves say about their works and processes; (c) observation of composers at work; and (d) observation of improvisers at work. The examples Sloboda provides to illustrate these methods of inquiry are studies of mature composers and improvisers—individuals who have developed some kind of recognized expertise. Most references to young composers or improvisers are from the point of view of adults reflecting on their childhood experiences, and, while valuable, they do not reflect the thinking of children as composers in the act of creating.

Apart from ties to the practices of Western art music and its scholarly traditions, matters of voice and identity among young composers have been on the side burner of the music education research agenda for another reason. With the exceptions of historical and philosophical inquiry, the tradition of scholarship within the music education research community is firmly rooted in the study of perception, cognition, and learning. The primary questions that drive research in music education have centered on how children and adolescents perceive music and how we can best shape our practices so that teaching enables learning. From the extensive and valuable body of literature, we know a great deal about students' attitudes, aptitudes, preferences, skills, and knowledge. More specifically, we have systematically studied children in the act of creating music to discover how age, experience, prior musical training, stages of development, aptitude, and other characteristics affect composing. We have rarely, however, examined children as composers with intentions, meanings, gestures, and structures that are their own, separate and distinct from adult expectations. Questions of identity and voice have remained largely unexamined.

The momentum of music education scholarship has shifted, however, in the past few decades, and a different branch of inquiry has emerged in the research community as the writings of Bruno Nettl, John Blacking, and Christopher Small, among others, have gained currency in music education circles. In the opening chapter of *Songs in Their Heads,* Campbell (1998) provides an excellent summary of how the interests of researchers in anthropology and ethnomusicology have intersected with those of music educators. The result has been a growing body of literature in which the culture of children's music and of children as musicians is at the forefront of thinking and inquiry. The underlying premise of these investigations is that children are already music makers and creators in their own right and that their music is worth studying as a representation of the culture of children and as a subset of the larger cultural context.

Campbell (1998) notes that "educators have just begun to apply aspects of the ethnomusicological (and ethnographic) method to children's songs and musical play, in an attempt to discern the complexity of both children's performance practice and the contemporary musical environment in which they are enculturated" (p. 6). Because ethnographic researchers observe children in natural environments where they are engaged in playful interactions with each other, it is not surprising that a majority of studies in this literature focus on singing games, playground songs,

and children as song makers. Indeed, some of the children described in Campbell's book and other studies invent new songs and reinvent familiar ones based on music they already know. But it is not only their voices that children lift up in acts of musical creating. They compose with whatever means are at their disposal, from objects to computers to instruments of all sorts. Still, the question remains: Do these young composers have identity and voice?

Do Young Composers Have Identity and Voice?

Whether children are creating songs or making some other kind of music, the answer to the above question depends, at some level, on one's view of children as creative beings. If one does not think children are creative, then matters of voice and identity are of little consequence. Notwithstanding various studies and models of creativity in music and other domains, Runco and Charles (1997) document "a surprising debate in this area of research ... concerning the possibility that children's creativity is not actually creative" (p. 140). The debate derives from views of creativity as purposeful and goal-directed and children's creations as accidental or serendipitous, from the tendency to apply adult models and norms of creativity to children, and from problems in studying a human experience (i.e., creativity) that is inherently subjective. Runco and Charles argue the point:

> Surely it is reasonable to view a child's subjective creative acts as creative, but at the same time view accomplishments during adulthood, be they personal,

workaday, or eminent, as creative. The difference is merely frame of reference. For the child, the comparative standard is the child him- or herself. Many creative acts are original and useful, if only for that individual child. Adult acts are creative in the same sense of being original and useful, although the standard may differ (perhaps being the individual's oeuvre, or even a movement or genre) ... What we are suggesting may sound like a sliding scale, but that should not surprise anyone, given that relative norms are already used in creativity research. ... The creativity of children may only qualify as such if we acknowledge that originality and appropriateness must be defined relative to individual children rather than relative to larger, objective norms. (p. 127)

To accept the premise that children are creative beings and that they can and do create in original and meaningful ways is to align one's thinking with the philosophical position that children can and do have "signified and signifying world[s]" (Greene, 1995, p. 55) that they manifest on their own for themselves in ways particular to their individual contexts and development. Indeed, the creative acts of children are no less renderings of their own construction and meaning than the private worlds rendered public in the works of adults who have earned the sociocultural label of *artist* or *composer.* Whether adults or children, individuals create what is meaningful to them on their own terms. From this perspective, young composers *do* have identity and voice—the identities and voices of children acting from their perspective,

place, and time.

If we accept the premise that young composers do have identity and voice, how do they emerge and of what are they comprised? Neither adults nor children function apart from cultural frames of reference. In other words, both the individual and the context matter in acts of creating music. Scholarship in cognitive psychology, anthropology, and sociology has led to understandings of how knowledge and action are culturally grounded and sociologically situated. We know what we know and do what we do because of who we are and because of the sociocultural contexts in which we live, and, by our actions, we continue to construct our contexts. In Geertz's words, "Without men, no culture, certainly; but equally, and more significantly, without culture, no men" (1973, p. 49). Geertz's oft-quoted passage furthers the discussion:

> The concept of culture I espouse ... is essentially a semiotic one. Believing, with Max Weber, that man is an animal suspended in webs of significance he himself has spun, I take culture to be those webs, and the analysis of it to be therefore not an experimental science in search of law but an interpretive one in search of meaning. (1973, p. 5)

We might make use of the Geertz-Weber metaphor of "webs of significance" to consider young composers' contexts for creating and how voice and identity emerge and are manifested in their music.

Composing occurs within a multidimensional web comprised of cultural and experiential strands wound around and supporting each other in complex ways. Put another way, because young composers have knowledge that is embedded in culture and experience, they create music grounded in their own lives. Children who play musical games together day after day are likely to create—individually or collectively—according to the musical forms and norms of their social-musical group (Harwood, 1993), just as music connected with popular media and art forms is part of the collective culture of children and emerges in their creative musical expressions (Stauffer, 1998b, 1999b). The music that children know constitutes part of the web in which they exist. Similarly, a child's individual musical experiences shape the web. Children who play an instrument, for example, have knowledge derived from the physical act of making music, the mental work of playing, their own feelings about their music and music making, the responses of others to what they do, and so on.

Music education researchers have investigated various strands in the web, including young composers' age, experience, and developmental level (Hedden, 1992; Hoffman, Hedden, & Mims, 1990; Kratus, 1989, 1994; Swanwick & Tillman, 1986; Wilson & Wales, 1995), musical training (Stauffer, 1998b; Wilson & Wales, 1995), musical ability/audiation (Kratus, 1994), ability to conceive musical wholes (Wiggins, 1995), and learning style (Moore, 1990). Still, while the musical and individual considerations described above are no doubt important, they remain a rather one-dimensional and limited view of the "web of significance" from which the young composer operates.

Elsewhere I suggest that young composers begin creating from a place that has to do with the whole of who they are at that moment—the circumstances of their lives, the nature of their interests and motivations, and their basic "states," which include the state of their ideas and their global affective state (Stauffer, 1999a). Who individuals are and how they feel on any particular day matters as much as their contextual frames. In a discussion grounded in neurobiology, Demasio (1994, 1999) describes the nature and functioning of certain core states of feeling and consciousness in individuals. Background feeling, one such state, is part of the persistent and continuous condition of our core sense of self. Demasio (1994) elaborates:

> A background feeling is not what we feel when we jump out of our skin for sheer joy, or when we are despondent over lost love; both of these actions correspond to emotional body states. A background feeling corresponds instead to the body state prevailing *between* emotions. ... The background feeling is our image of the body landscape when it is not shaken by emotion. (pp. 150–51, italics in original)

Similarly, core consciousness, one's basic sense of self, is the fundamental state of consciousness, which functions not verbally but at the level of images. Demasio (1999) describes it as providing us with "*the very evidence, the unvarnished sense of our individual organism in the act of knowing*" (p. 125, italics in original) as we interact "with particular objects within [ourselves] or in [our] surroundings" (p. 89). According to Demasio (1999), our basic states of core self and consciousness underlie autobiographical self, autobiographical memory, the "feeling of what happens," reasoning, extended consciousness, and even conscience. The state of the individual matters in the shaping of voice and identity in general and specifically in composing.

We are, in effect, the *sum* of who we are—biological and experiential, individual and collective, educated and encultured, with core states of consciousness and higher levels of reasoning and abstraction—and what we create arises from all of this. In other words, in the "web of significance" within which the young composer operates, everything counts to some degree. The web includes musical and all other culture, life as experienced in sociocultural frames, characteristics and states of the individual, and the individual's interactions with everyone and everything. The web is both comprehensive and specific, and it is out of this condition that voice and identity in composers of all ages is possible.

One more idea merits attention. Both the individual composers and their "webs of significance" constantly evolve. Neither is static. Both may change suddenly and radically or evolve slowly and imperceptibly in a process of constant remodeling engendered by experience. In fact, the very act of composing precipitates changes in the composer and web. "The practice of composition itself moves on in an inexorable process of change," Leinsdorf notes (1981, p. 59), and although he refers to masterworks and mature composers, the same idea applies to young composers. The past compositions and the experience of composing them exist in the web. The individual carries forward to the next composing experience all that was gained or learned, consciously or unconsciously, in previous episodes of composing. The next starting place cannot be the same. Something is changed or gained in the act of creating. We may be hard-pressed to state exactly the nature of the gain, the direction or degree of change, or the import of either, but that change has occurred is certain. No experience is irrelevant.

Examples of Identity and Voice in Young Composers

The argument put forward to this point is largely theoretical. What evidence is there of identity and voice in young composers? The following examples are drawn from a longitudinal study (1994–2001) of children and adolescents participating in an after-school program in which they composed in a lab using computers and various software packages. The young composers ranged from 5 to 11 years old when they began participating in the composition lab, and their tenure in the project ranged from a few weeks to 7 years. In presenting the cases of these individuals and their works as evidence for the ideas set forth in the previous pages, I recognize the limitations of looking through the lens of a single project and a single medium for creating, as well as the limitations tied to the idiosyncrasies of both researcher and participants.

Three short notes about the project are necessary. First, the participants composed using the computer and software only, without the use of auxiliary hardware such as synthesizers or piano-type keyboards. Over 7 years, when a keyboard synthesizer was available, all except 2 of the nearly 40 participants rejected its use, preferring instead point-and-click or click-and-drag methods of entering their music. Second, the protocol of the study was noninterventionist and noninstructional; the participants composed, and the researchers observed. Adults were available to answer questions about software and hardware, but they did not instruct, direct, or otherwise guide the composition process. I purposefully chose this protocol in order to observe what and how the participants created without adult intervention and thereby gain insights into the participants' thinking. Third, in this discussion and in other reports from this study, only the works that the participants called compositions are presented. If the participant did not consider a work to be a composition, then a well-meaning adult could not call it a composition. With these caveats in mind, we turn first to a piece entitled "Trombone Fun" (Figure 1).

Hilary

Hilary, a sixth-grade girl who started playing the trombone in fifth grade as part of an elementary school instrumental music program, composed "Trombone Fun." At the time, she was a member of the middle school band and a second-year participant in the composition study. In her description of her piece, Hilary indicated that the trombones (bass clef) play the "interesting" parts while all the other instruments (treble clef) "play the same thing over and over again plus all the slow notes." At first glance, "Trombone Fun" is Hilary's response to the "boring" parts she felt were usually assigned to her and her fellow trombonists in the middle school band, and I have written elsewhere that the piece is an example of how students' instrumental experiences, including their experiences in ensembles, influence their compo-

sitions (Stauffer, 1998b). But there is more to the story.

Hilary's music tells us something about her perceived ability as a musician and her role in the ensemble. By writing sixteenth notes into her part, she is saying, in effect, that she is at least as competent a player as her fellow sixth-grade band members. She is signaling not only that she is given boring parts to play but also that *she* is bored— she is not having fun. She is, however, interested and engaged enough to know that other instrumentalists are playing more interesting parts and that they play in clefs that are different from the one she reads. By writing this piece, she offers her commentary about the incongruencies she perceives between her ability, motivation, and interest and the challenges provided to her in the sixth-grade band repertoire, and she proposes a solution.

There is meaning, or voice, in her work, but is there identity? Would we recognize "Trombone Fun" or another piece by Hilary as Hilary's? What is it about her music that makes it hers? For that, we must place "Trombone Fun" in the context of other pieces Hilary has written.

"Trombone Fun" is the only one of the 14 compositions written during her sixth-grade year in which Hilary specifically designated a trombone part. However, she composed nearly all of her pieces on a two-staff treble and bass clef system, even when she was aware that she had other options. The bass clef parts usually appeared to be characteristic of beginner-level music for her chosen instrument but with twists of rhythm or melody that made them more interesting than "the same thing over and over again plus all the slow notes." As she continued

Figure 1. "Trombone Fun"

Hilary Roge

playing through middle school and into high school, Hilary joined the jazz band and began to compose for small ensembles of wind and percussion instruments, but not keyboards, found in jazz groups. In these pieces, one instrument typically carries the melody, while others accompany. Melodic patterns outlining triads appear in some instrument parts and repetitive rhythms in others, while the harmonic rhythm is typically slow and chord structures basic. The final

composition in her sixth year in the composition study was a rather effective arrangement of "Happy Birthday" for her high school jazz ensemble.

Given that information, one might recognize a piece written for a small ensemble of wind instruments usually associated with jazz groups with hints of jazz idioms and with "interesting" parts for the bass clef instruments as Hilary's work. In fact, none of the other participants in the composi-

Figure 2. "Vietnam"

tion study wrote pieces like this, although some had very similar musical experiences. Hilary indeed has identity as a composer, based on these works alone. But Hilary also saved several short compositions with relatively limited ranges and single instrument designations that are nothing like her other works. She wrote these "songs" for presentations given by young children in a local Montessori school where she spent time as an aid. Recognizing that "the kids probably can't sing that," she enlisted one of her siblings and a few friends to play the melodies to support the children's presentations. For Hilary, composing was tied to the ensemble, people, and music of the moment. The same could not be said of Lee, one of Hilary's peers.

Lee

"Vietnam" (excerpts in Figure 2), a work Lee composed during his fourth year

measures 25-33

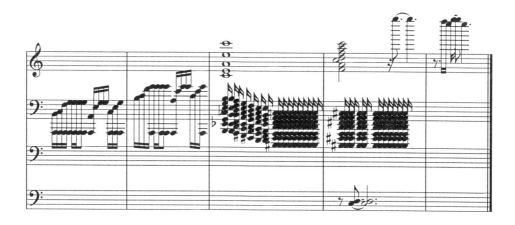

in the composition lab, has none of the characteristics of Hilary's compositions. It does not include the instrument (euphonium) he played as a seventh-grade student, and it is not composed for any particular ensemble. Instead, Lee chose MIDI timbres (celeste, cello, "sound tracks," and slap bass) to suit his purposes, and, unlike most other students in the study, he composed the piece primarily by exploring gestures on a keyboard and then transforming them in various ways. Not only was Lee uninterested in composing for particular instruments, people, or ensembles, but he also was unconcerned about making his music look like the notation he was capable of reading. That he could hear his music on a computer, record it on a CD, and take it home and listen to it was sufficient. "Vietnam" may look unreadable and unplayable, but that was of no consequence to Lee, who was interested in the sound, the mood, and the gestures. In that respect, he succeeded. Hearing "Vietnam" leaves one with the impression of drama, urgency, despair, and even irony when the opening gesture, a gentle celeste melody, returns and fades in the last two measures of the piece—a deliberate choice by Lee and one of which he was quite proud.

What can be learned from "Vietnam" about Lee's voice and identity as a composer? How are this and other works he composed related to his "webs of significance"? Like Hilary's compositions, Lee's works include surface connections and deeper meanings. Lee revealed that one of his parents, now a successful professional, was a Vietnam veteran, but he mentioned this bit of family history only once during the 6 years of his participation in the study. More

evident throughout his lab sessions and his music was his interest in themes of conflict, conspiracy, and justice related to the content of his social studies classes, current events, and plot lines of certain television programs. Lee was also interested in movies and epic stories, and he frequently referred to his compositions as sound tracks for movies he would like to make, often including story cues in his scores. Justice usually prevailed in his music works, and, in fact, Lee stopped coming to the composition lab when he became a student lawyer in a school-based court system for solving campus problems.

Attention to details of timbre and dramatic gesture was characteristic of Lee's working style, and if the timbres and gestures he initially selected did not produce the effect he intended, he reworked the composition section by section until he achieved a sound that satisfied him—a sound recognizable as his compositional identity. The repeated musical motives and gestures, as well as the rhythmic drive and intensity, found in "Vietnam" are characteristic of Lee's works. These are also qualities of his twin brother Luke's compositions, but not in exactly the same way.

Luke

The title of Luke's "Rhythm and Pogroms" (Figure 3) tells the story of his composition; the music is about drive and drama. The distinguishing quality of Luke's music, in contrast to Lee's, is that the rhythmic motion is constant, with specific motives and gestures shifting between parts instead of being relegated to one timbre or line only. In this piece and others, Luke achieved rhythmic intensity and structural

Figure 3. "Rhythm and Pogroms"

by Luke S.

unity by copying, repeating, transforming, and transposing gestures he liked. Like Lee, he was relatively unconcerned about whether his works were playable ("Rhythm and Pogroms" is written for piano, and Luke thought "a really good player" could perform it), except when writing for his own instrument, the oboe. Unlike Lee, Luke was interested in correct notation, and his skill improved considerably over the 7 years of his participation in the study.

Although the brothers' compositional identities are similar, they are also clearly different. Luke wrote a greater variety of works than Lee, including short pieces limited to the piano timbre and works for solo oboe or oboe with one or two other instruments. He performed one of the latter compositions at a school recital of solo and small-ensemble pieces and another at a memorial service for a relative. While both boys' music was typically driving and dramatic, Luke's oboe works could also be lyrical and delicate.

Likewise, their working styles were similar, but different: Luke concentrated on transforming small motives or composed in longer sections that he would either retain or scrap entirely, while Lee composed in phrase-length chunks that he manipulated in various ways.

The brothers' identities and voices were shaped by their shared musical-cultural web, which included instrumental music performance experiences and various kinds of music from popular media. Luke often expressed his preferences for certain artists, composers, and pieces. He insisted, for example, that I see the film *Gladiator* because he believed the score would be nominated for an Academy Award. When I

hadn't seen it some time later, he brought a disc of the movie to the lab, and as we watched he explained why the music was particularly effective in certain episodes. When the score was indeed nominated for an Academy Award, Luke commented that it probably wouldn't win because it was "too subtle … they won't get it." The award went to another score.

Although both brothers wrote "epic" pieces with programmatic titles and cues in the music, Luke's compositions typically reflected his concern about individual matters of fairness rather than Lee's large-scale social themes. Luke's collected works include a piece commenting on a school incident in which he perceived a classmate was treated unfairly, music for a projected movie about a homeless boy, and parts of a projected opera in which the two main characters are two women—one a body without a soul and the other a soul without a body.

Luke was aware of the origin and development of his own musical ideas. He could explain how he conceived of pieces and how they evolved as he worked on them. He talked about composing in his head by whistling (which his friends confirmed), by playing the oboe, or by exploring at the piano (though he said he knew nothing about "the fingers or the notes" and had no interest in learning how to play it). He sometimes brought to the lab bits of music scribbled on the back of various school papers, and one of his parents described watching him walk through the backyard with his head bobbing as though he was listening to music, though he wasn't wearing headphones. Luke also composed at home, particularly during the summer months when the lab was closed, using either a computer or the oboe and staff paper and pencil.

As a seventh-year participant in the composition lab, Luke sometimes composed for 2 hours or more without interruption. At other times, he seemed distracted or lost, sometimes stating that he "[didn't] have any ideas." *State of idea* clearly affected his work. For example, when a new program became available for him to try, he waved it away, saying, "Not now. I haven't been here for a couple of weeks and my head is full." On another day, he emerged from his work space after a short period of composing and scrapping bits of music and said, "I'm done. I don't have any ideas. Nothing is coming. I'm going home." During one "no idea" session, I broke with the research protocol and suggested that he attempt a piece that contrasted with a dark and dramatic work he had recently finished. He resisted, saying that "adults always want kids to do happy stuff" and that was not how his music went.

Luke referred to himself as a composer, and he was critical of his work and aware of his progress. Although "Rhythm and Pogroms" was one of his favorite pieces during the year he composed it, he later rejected it as being written in "last year's style." Periods of "style" development could also be observed in the work of other students, including Meg.

Meg

Meg, a third-grade composer whose work is described elsewhere (Stauffer, 2001), composed in two style periods over 7 months using a non-notation-based composition program. Styles became evident as she composed using the same musical gestures in new pieces during each session rather than revising works composed in previous sessions. Meg's identity as a composer was obvious, for her pieces were similar from week to week. When she did change styles, the specific musical gestures changed, but larger structures and her working strategies remained consistent. Consequently, "Hills" (Figure 4), from Meg's first style period, is both similar to and different from "Marching Ants" (Figure 5), from her second style period. Both were created by adding chunks of music to the composition, changing timbre

Figure 4. "Hills"

with each chunk, and then listening. Both are thin in texture, one of Meg's stated preferences for her music. But the melodic material is different.

Like the work of other composers, Meg's musical works reflect the sociocultural and individual strands of her web. Raised in a family of writers and teachers, Meg was playful with language and with musical sounds. As she continued in the lab for another 2 years past her initial 7 months and learned to use notation programs, instruments she played and personal events (e.g., an adjustment of her braces, the death of a schoolmate following an illness) prompted compositions.

Cautions and Caveats

Based on the work of these individuals and others, I am increasingly convinced that young composers do indeed have voice and identity, that voice and identity emerge early in their works, that their works are based in their own webs and reflect their individual lives and states of being, and that their works are significant and signifying to them. But I offer these examples and my convictions with caution.

We may perceive all kinds of connections between the creations of young composers, their webs of significance, and their various individual states, but forging ahead without taking time to understand the children and to listen to what the young composers have to say about their own works may lead to wrong inferences, misguided conclusions, and inappropriate assumptions.

I sat one afternoon with Carrie, a fifth-grade composer who had recently and enthusiastically taken up Scottish highland dancing. We listened to a piece on which she was working, a short work made up mostly of alternating long and short notes on a single pitch. The resulting music had a triple-meter feel. "I'm going to call this 'Song of Star,'" she said. "Can you guess why?" To her amusement, I guessed that it was modeled on a highland dance piece, a Scottish song, a bagpipe piece. "No," she giggled, "it goes like this," and she chanted the rhythm, "Daaah-dah, daaah-dah, daaah-dah …" After a few more of my inept guesses, she gave up and sang, "Star of wonder, star of light," the first phrase of a carol Carrie and her family knew from their church. "Get it?" she asked.

Figure 5. "Marching Ants"

Toward a Pedagogy of Composition

Greene (1995) tells us that "to enable children to have a signified and signifying world is among the crucial concerns of a human and critical pedagogy" (p. 55). If we accept the premise that children are creative beings, that they can and do create music on their own, and that their musical creations are expressions and extensions of themselves, then what are the implications for a pedagogy of composition? Do our practices support the developing identities and voices of young composers, or do we hinder them, particularly in school settings? Three qualities of composing experiences in school contexts require our attention: opportunities for composing, the nature of group and individual composing activities, and the use of models for composing.

Opportunities for Composing

Whatever the young composers described above have learned about music and composing, they have learned because of repeated opportunities to compose over time. I argue elsewhere that time, tools, and technique interact in the composition process (Stauffer, 2001). Young composers need time to gain facility with the media for composing and time to develop their working strategies. More important, they need time to form and evolve the gestures that will become part of their compositional identities and time to find their compositional voices. Time for composing implies not only sessions that are long enough for exploring and developing ideas, but also repeated opportunities to create in consecutive sessions so that young composers can become familiar with the process of composing. As Howard (1991) suggests, one acquires the fluency and mental agility to get better at doing something when one engages in that activity with frequency and some regularity—in short, with practice. Students get better at composing by composing, and composing takes time.

Time is a commodity in short supply in schools. When composing is included in the curriculum, sessions may be limited to a portion of a class meeting or ensemble rehearsal, and they may be included in class or ensemble activities only occasionally. These conditions seem to be the antithesis of what is required for students to develop identity and voice, let alone to develop complete musical works or a sense of self as composer.

But educators' perceptions of the constraints of time may be confounded by a narrow conception of children as composers. Neither schools nor music teachers hold proprietary claim on the creative ability or potential of children. Times and places for creating and composing can and do occur outside the educational environment, for, as Campbell (1998) notes, "music is already in the possession of children prior to school or specialized training" (p. 5), and it is certainly in their possession beyond the classroom or rehearsal hall. We should teach composition in order to extend abilities and open possibilities for more composition, most of which will occur *outside* of school. From this perspective, time might be invested not only in "whole composition" tasks but also in composition studies or "etudes" that focus on component skills, such as exploring sound potentials of the medium or discovering how sounds or gestures can be manipulated to achieve specific ends.

Nature of Group and Individual Composing Activities

If we allow the time for composition in school music classes and ensembles, then we must also consider the nature of group and individual composing activities and their impact on the development of identity and voice. The young composers described above worked as individuals, and each composer developed an idiosyncratic working style, as well as a distinctive compositional identity and a unique voice. Would the same individual qualities have emerged for these young composers if the majority of their composition time had been invested in group composition experiences that are typical of creative experiences in general music classes in the United States?

Group composition experiences are not without merit. An individual in a "no ideas" state as described by Luke may be motivated by the contributions of others in the group. Young composers may learn new gestures from one another and then accept, reject, or adapt these gestures for their own work both within and apart from the group. Similarly, students working in groups may learn strategies or processes that are profitable in later individual composition experiences. In the end, however, the group composition is about corporate voice and identity rather than the voice and identity of individual student composers.

Certain unspoken assumptions also underlie group composition experiences. Group composition assumes an overlap of the individual sociocultural and musical webs of the students in the group. At the very least, there is an expectation that students can negotiate a shared space in which they can work and find meaning together. While that may indeed be the case, it is equally likely that when webs overlap, certain ideas and meanings prevail over others. Further, group composition experiences are not typical of how adult composers function, at least in Western cultures.

Although researchers (DeLorenzo, 1989; Wiggins 1994, 1995, 1999/2000) and music educators have found group composition projects to be an effective means of including creative activities in the classroom, students should also have opportunities to compose individually. Each child occupies a different place on the contextual web in which composition occurs, and no two children are likely to have identical musical ideas or strategies for working on a composition. Individual composition projects, though more difficult to implement in the context of a classroom, may allow students to develop strategies and gestures that are covered or subsumed by others' ideas during group projects.

The Use of Models

Another point at the intersection of development of voice and identity and the teaching of composition has to do with the use of models as a pedagogical strategy. Composition activities may include tasks in which students imitate or compose within certain structural or stylistic models. One question we should ask is whether the implicit expectations and constraints that come with models are appropriate for the developmental level of children. Imitating the ideas of others may not allow the children's voices to emerge or may not be the appropriate means by which to allow children to discover their own voices and identities. To exercise voice within a model may be more limiting than to compose from one's own web, unless one already has developed gestures and strategies and can use them fluently within the specified context.

The question, then, may be one of timing. When can students use models to their own best effect without impeding the development of voice or identity? It is likely that we are overly concerned with having children conform to the model before they have had time to explore and develop identity and voice as composers. Subotnick (1995) suggests that when one has learned to play with the sounds and the sounds are one's own, then one has an identity as a composer and can look at the models to develop expertise. My own observations of children in the composition lab suggest that their cultural experiences provide them with musical models from which they intuitively explore and create. When students have a sense of themselves as composers, then models as pedagogical tools may be more useful than in earlier stages of development.

Finally, regarding the role of the teacher, Campbell (1998) suggests that "while children are musical without expert guidance, they become more musical as a result of it" (p. 196). Guiding composition while respecting the emerging identity and voice of young composers requires active attention to works in progress, the mental and musical agility to recognize the emergence of gestures, patience as students work and rework ideas, and the ability to ask questions or redirect actions in order to

motivate students while maintaining the integrity of their work.

Do young composers have identity and voice? Children are capable of significant and meaningful works of music. They are young, creative composers whose pieces are powerful and expressive and whose music is uniquely their own. Our task is to develop a pedagogy that both supports and respects the identity and voice of young composers.

References

Campbell, P. A. (1998). *Songs in their heads: Music and its meaning in children's lives*. New York: Oxford University Press.

Cone, E. T. (1974). *The composer's voice*. Berkeley, CA: University of California Press.

DeLorenzo, L. C. (1989). A field study of sixth-grade students' creative music problem-solving processes. *Journal of Research in Music Education, 37*, 188–200.

Demasio, A. R. (1994). *Descartes' error: Emotion, reason, and the human brain*. New York: G. P. Putnam's Sons.

Demasio, A. R. (1999). *The feeling of what happens: Body and emotion in the making of consciousness*. New York: Harcourt.

Geertz, C. (1973). *The interpretation of cultures*. New York: Basic Books.

Greene, M. (1995). *Releasing the imagination: Essays on education, the arts, and social change*. San Francisco: Jossey-Bass.

Harwood, E. (1993). Content and context in children's playground songs. *Update: Applications of Research in Music Education, 12*(1), 4–8.

Hedden, S. K. (1992, April). *Qualitative assessment of children's compositions*. Paper presented at the National Biennial In-Service Conference of the Music Educators National Conference, New Orleans, LA.

Hoffman, K., Hedden, S. K., & Mims, R. (1990). *Music composition processes in children aged seven through nine years.* Paper presented at the National Conference of the American Orff-Schulwerk Association, Denver, CO.

Howard, V. A. (1991). And practice drives me mad; Or, the drudgery of drill. *Harvard Educational Review, 61,* 80–87.

Johnson, A. G. (1995). Self. In *The Blackwell dictionary of sociology* (pp. 249–50). Malden, MA: Blackwell.

Kratus, J. (1989). A time analysis of the compositional processes used by children ages 7 to 11. *Journal of Research in Music Education, 37,* 5–20.

Kratus, J. (1994). Relationships among children's music audiation and their compositional processes and products. *Journal of Research in Music Education, 42,* 115–30.

Leinsdorf, E. (1981). *The composer's advocate: A radical orthodoxy for musicians.* New Haven, CT: Yale University Press.

Moore, B. R. (1990). The relationships between curriculum and learner: Music composition and learning style. *Journal of Research in Music Education, 38,* 24–38.

Runco, M. A., & Charles, R. E. (1997). Developmental trends in creative potential and creative performance. In M. A. Runco (Ed.), *The creativity research handbook* (Vol. 1., pp. 115–52). Cresskill, NJ: Hampton Press.

Sloboda, J. A. (1985). *The musical mind: The cognitive psychology of music.* Oxford, England: Oxford University Press.

Stauffer, S. L. (1998a, April). *Children as composers: Changes over time.* Paper presented at the biennial meeting of the Music Educators National Conference, Phoenix, AZ.

Stauffer, S. L. (1998b, April). *Connections between the musical and life experience of young composers and the music they create.* Poster session presented at the biennial meeting of the Music Educators National Conference, Phoenix, AZ.

Stauffer, S. L. (1999a, February). *Beginnings of the composition process among children and adolescents.* Paper presented at the Desert Skies Symposium on Research in Music Education, Tucson, AZ.

Stauffer, S. L. (1999b, February). Social and cultural cues in the compositions of children and adolescents. In M. S. Barrett, G. E. McPherson, & R. Smith (Eds.), *Children and music: Developmental perspectives: Proceedings of the Second International Music Education Research Symposium* (pp. 294–98). Launceston, Tasmania: University of Tasmania.

Stauffer, S. L. (2001). Composing with computers: Meg makes music. *Bulletin of the Council for Research in Music Education, 150,* 1–20.

Stravinsky, I. (1970). *The poetics of music.* Cambridge, MA: Harvard University Press.

Subotnick, M. (1995). The music and musicians of the future. In S. L. Stauffer (Ed.), *Toward tomorrow: New visions for general music* (pp. 31–42). Reston, VA: MENC.

Swanwick, K., & Tillman, J. (1986). The sequence of musical development: A study of children's composition. *British Journal of Music Education, 3,* 305–39.

Wiggins, J. H. (1994). Children's strategies for solving compositional problems with peers. *Journal of Research in Music Education, 42,* 232–52.

Wiggins, J. H. (1995). Building structural understanding: Sam's story. *The Quarterly Journal of Research in Music Education, 6,* 57–75.

Wiggins, J. H. (1999/2000). The nature of shared musical understanding and its role in empowering independent musical thinking. *Bulletin of the Council for Research in Music Education, 143,* 65–90.

Wilson, S. J., & Wales, R. J. (1995). An exploration of children's musical compositions. *Journal of Research in Music Education, 43,* 94–111.

Sandra Stauffer is professor of music education at the school of music at Arizona State University in Tempe where she teaches both undergraduate and graduate courses. She is active as a general music clinician throughout the United States and abroad, and she has written education materials for music textbooks, curriculum projects, and symphony orchestra programs. Her recent research and publication has focused on children and adolescents as composers.

6

Imagination in Education: Strategies and Models in the Teaching and Assessment of Composition

Jonathan Stephens

The journey of life takes us from familiar landscapes to unfamiliar territories, from the world of ideas and ambitions to a realization of our aspirations. Those who explore more than their immediate surroundings discover the rich variety that life can offer, and to the intrepid explorer, "life has more imagination that we carry in our dreams" (quotation at end of Scott, 1992).

Education is also a journey that, in its broadest sense, seeks to expand individual and collective horizons and to challenge ideas and assumptions. Formal education that emphasizes mechanistic, assessment-led approaches to teaching and learning may focus too much on acquiring knowledge and skills perceived to be relevant to the world of employment rather than on encouraging creative thinking and a broadly based understanding that will enable individuals to better adapt to an ever-changing world. Commenting in the mid-1980s on the trend toward greater precision in curricula in the areas of content, standards, and objectives, Elliott (1986) predicted that there would be a growing emphasis on goal-directed, functional approaches to

teaching, learning, and assessment. For many of us, that prediction is now a reality.

Training for a possible career undoubtedly has an important place in personal development, as well as in society. An imbalance occurs, however, when it becomes the primary focus of curricula. Highly structured, task-oriented approaches that emphasize conformity over diversity may not sufficiently value the place of imagination as a motivating force in personal development (Stephens, 1994). In many parts of the world, there has in recent years been an emphasis on competence-based teaching and learning (Dolloff, 2000). This trend indicates a shift from the flexible educational approaches prevalent during the 1970s in the United Kingdom and elsewhere to more defined models of education that are based on perceived employment needs. Moreover, the changing and often uncertain face of employment has itself had a notable impact on curriculum design and student choice (Favaro, 2000). In the present educational climate, it is important to reaffirm that a broad understanding, the acquisition of knowledge and skills, aesthetic development, and training for a career are all essential to a balanced curriculum and fulfilled life (Jorgensen, 1996; Swanwick, 1990).

Functional models of education are a consequence of an economically driven society, where survival depends on maintaining a competitive edge over one's peers. In our rapidly changing contemporary cultures, an emphasis on early specific training is surprising in view of the recognized need for flexibility and creativity in the workforce. Indeed, our survival at personal and collective levels is predicated on our ability to adopt imaginative solutions to problems (Stephens, 2000).

The benefits of the "creative leaps" in scientific and medical research that often transform reasoned calculation into an effective solution underline the importance of imaginative thinking. When it comes to formal teaching and learning, however, it is far easier to focus on those aspects of the educational process that are easily taught and assessed. In this regard, it would appear that many music teachers consider performing and listening to be an easier option than composing. It is, of course, neither necessary nor feasible for everything to be addressed in school curricula. The fact that none of our musical activities would be possible were it not for the act of composing, however, should lead us to question the serious imbalance where composition is relegated to a subsidiary position or excluded altogether. If our commitment as teachers is to enrich the lives of those in our care, then we should help individuals to better understand themselves and the nature of music through a wide range of listening, performing, and com-

posing activities.

A greater concentration on composition need not threaten the performance-oriented culture of much of American music education; rather, it should enhance music provision in schools. The following questions should help in our appraisal of current priorities in music curricula:

- To what extent does an emphasis on performance (particularly its technical aspects) address matters of musical understanding and sensitivity—a feeling for "the music beyond the notes"?
- What is the purpose of focusing on a factual knowledge of composers and their works rather than developing a more intimate understanding of musical expression by engaging in its creative processes?
- How far does the subculture of school music reflect the educational and musical needs of individuals and the world outside the classroom?

Many teachers who have not studied composition are understandably anxious about their ability to engage students in worthwhile compositional activities. There are substantial political and educational hurdles to be surmounted if composition is to attain a level of respectability in American music education. The fact that it has achieved such status in other parts of the world (such as the United Kingdom and Scandinavia) and in other educational programs (such as the International American Schools' music program and the International Baccalaureate) means that we are not chasing an impossible dream in seeking a central place for composition in all schools. The benefits of raising the profile of composition in music education are many: the process of composing develops creative thinking, encourages students to take personal responsibility for their learning, and brings together aspects of listening and performing. This union of composing, listening, and performing can help students make sense of musical activities both in and out of the classroom.

Many texts on teaching composition in schools have been published over the past 30 years (e.g., Harris & Hawksley, 1989; Howard, 1989; Paynter, 1982, 1992; Paynter & Aston, 1970; Schafer, 1979; Thackray, 1965; Tillman, 1976; Wiggins, 1990; Winters, 1986). It is not the purpose of this chapter to summarize these texts or provide lesson plans, but rather to focus on broader theoretical and practical issues related to teaching, learning, and assessment in composition. The following pages outline some of the problems and possible solutions with regard to including composition in music education. The intention is to provide teachers with a number of possibilities for extending current practice to encompass approaches that are considered more *creative* than *re-creative*. The encouragement of imaginative dimensions in our lives would not only enrich current thinking and practice in many schools but also transform much of what purports to be education to a higher level. It is hoped that this brief overview will provide a springboard for music composition to become a central aspect of music education in the United States.

Models and Approaches

If we accept the premise that composition should have an important role in music education, how might it be featured in those curricula where short-term goals,

attainment targets, and clearly defined learning outcomes receive high priority? The problem is twofold:

■ Such a curricular model does not support those aspects of learning where observable development often takes place over many months or years.
■ When composition is included, it may be forced into a mechanical, staged approach of clearly defined steps, similar to painting by numbers, where each stage is prescribed and imaginative response is discouraged.

A question to be considered at the outset, therefore, is whether composition, other than as a series of staged exercises measured by specific assessment tools, sits comfortably in formal education. Such a problem has faced music educators in the United Kingdom since 1988, when the national curricula in England and Wales (Department for Education, 1988/1992) and Northern Ireland (Department of Education for Northern Ireland, 1989/1996) and curriculum and assessment guidelines in Scotland (Scottish Office Education Department, 1988/1992) set out defined attainment targets and learning outcomes for all pupils.[1] This has affected the way some teachers approach compositional activities. For example, instead of encouraging a range of compositional activities, a teacher may focus on assessment requirements and adopt an approach that is more competence-based and atomistic (i.e., a fragmentary approach that emphasizes individual elements rather than holistic understanding). There are, of course, benefits in establishing common standards;

clarity and direction in teaching and assessment encourage effective learning. However, the nature of individual subjects, together with appropriate learning models and approaches, should be respected in curriculum design and implementation. Standardization may neglect this important aspect of teaching and learning.

Education should be challenging, and in this regard direct experience of the processes of composition should provide learners with valuable opportunities to develop problem-solving skills that impact both musical and nonmusical development. As individual and collective needs become apparent, appropriate strategies for addressing them can be devised. Once again, a wealth of published material deals with teaching and learning strategies in improvising and composing (e.g., Bennett, 1976; Bunting, 1987; Campbell & Scott-Kassner, 1995; Dennis, 1975; Ellis, 1987; Forster, 1983; Gamble, 1984; Hennessey, 1998; Paynter & Paynter, 1974; Salaman, 1988).

Learning from the Past

During the late 1960s and early 1970s, many British music educators reacted to the largely passive music curriculum prevalent at the time. Essentially, there were two basic components to music teaching in schools:

■ an emphasis for all students on knowledge about composers and their works (typically constructed around singing, music history, and listening to classical music)
■ technical and theory-based approaches (harmony, counterpoint, instrumental tuition, and ensemble activities) for the few who were considered to demonstrate potential to benefit from such specialized instruction.

In response to this situation, progressive educators adopted a new and largely experimental "music-for-all" approach that was influenced by the work of avant-garde composers, artists, and writers. Exploration of sounds made with voices, instruments, and everyday objects formed an important part of the teaching and learning process advocated by the reformers. Today, influences are more likely to come from tonal popular music, expressed through electronic keyboard and synthesized and computer-generated sounds, than from experimental art forms. Interestingly, the earlier emphasis was on high art, valuable for both illuminating the world of the contemporary composer and reflecting on the classical tradition. The contemporary use of tonal, popular, and media-influenced models reveals the more functional, purpose-based approaches that characterize much current thinking in education. Though it is possible to be inventive in any musical genre, it might be easier for many teachers to develop more imaginative approaches within an experimental, exploratory framework, using the highly developed language of classical music, rather than by focusing exclusively on the popular medium.

The more accessible, less challenging tonal language in much contemporary "classical" music contrasts with the inventive, groundbreaking work of those composers who, in the third quarter of the twentieth century, became the models for much creative work in the classroom. Paradoxically, as Richard Wolfson (2001) observes, rock music is now the avant-garde genre from which classical music might learn: "Perhaps it's time for the classical tradition to take note, and return the compliment paid to it 30 years ago, when pop musicians showed themselves willing to learn from another culture" (p.7). While experimentation is not a prerequisite of an imaginative approach, creative thinking and practice flourish where there is interaction, exchange, and even conflict between ideas and traditions.

A Matter of Relevance

Experiential approaches do not in themselves guarantee interesting and varied results. Those teachers who have used avant-garde models will have recognized the limitations and apparent sameness of much of the work produced by students. In the early stages (as with learning a language or an instrument), such uniformity is to be expected. The level of progress and development depends on the teacher's skill, guidance, and enthusiasm, as well as the student's ability. For the student, personal motivation derives from the perceived relevance of both the task and the musical language. This does not mean that only popular models should be employed; otherwise, education would revolve around limited common denominators. Effective teaching and learning should not merely reinforce the obvious but also explore the less obvious. An experienced teacher will devise suitable challenges and structures to address deficiencies in students' abilities and help them overcome limitations that prevent the realization of their compositional intentions. The teacher's task, therefore, is to widen perception of what is con-

sidered relevant, while encouraging a culture in which an individual's work is valued.

In our search for appropriate models to stimulate and support composing in schools, it is useful to consider the process of creative development outside the music classroom. In this regard, let us look at the world of the child, the visual artist, and the composer.

The Child. Some would consider the early expressions of a young child to be simply unstructured experimentation and exploration, but these dimensions are important in the life of all creative artists. Are composers, artists, and writers, in fact, more in tune with the world of the young child than those people for whom formal education might have dampened early imaginative and creative potential?

Exploratory approaches in education have tended to receive bad press in recent years, not least because of the absence of measurable stages of development within what some perceive as a "free for all," "anything goes" culture. During the past 20 years, certain British politicians have criticized the perceived educational excesses of the 1960s and 1970s and those teacher education courses that focused on open-ended programs of child-centered learning. Partly as a result, the national curriculum in the United Kingdom now emphasizes standardized approaches, attainment targets, and clearly defined learning outcomes.

Apart from the fact that we do disservice to early education by typifying it as unstructured (according to an adult-defined, time-economic process of progression), experimental and open-ended approaches can encourage vital learning and lead to highly developed levels of understanding and skill. This is evidenced, for example, in the way children learn language: informally, within a family setting, and away from the professional interference of teachers. Indeed, this natural approach could provide a useful model for learning other languages later in life.

In advocating more exploratory and less structured approaches in the teaching of composition, it is important still (through direct and indirect means) to encourage essential progress and development in knowledge, skills, and understanding. In creative activities, there is not always a sharp division between the stages of exploring and shaping ideas; the learning process for each individual is complex and integrated. In this, the model of child development provides a valuable resource for music educators. Our ability to create and make music is fundamental to humanity:

> It is the most natural thing in the world for human beings to make up music. Even now, as we look back on the twentieth century with its extraordinary record of scientific achievement, all over the world people continue to create songs and dance intuitively more or less as they have done for thousands of years. (Paynter, 2000, p. 6)

Campbell (1998) supports this view in *Songs in Their Heads,* a fascinating book that describes the creative world of young children and the ways they explore and value music. Children are far more capable than formal education might allow; there is a need for greater trust and respect for what they are able to accomplish with minimal input from teachers, as well as through the guidance and inspiration of good teaching. Research undertaken in recent years by many educators supports this view (e.g., Marsh, 1995; Scott-Kassner, 1992; Upitis, 1992). The issue is not that there is limited value in unstructured, informal, and exploratory activities, but that a conflict of interests may occur when such child-based approaches to learning are placed within the conformist setting of the school.

The Visual Artist. In support of the "music-for-all" ideal advocated in the 1960s and 1970s, contrasts were drawn at the time between a typical music lesson and a typical art lesson. It the art class, all students were encouraged to experience direct involvement with the medium of paint and materials through perceiving, making, and doing (Paynter, 1992, Paynter & Aston, 1970). During this time, the model for visual-art education was the creative artist rather than the art historian or appreciator. The underlying belief was that encouraging creative understanding as a *maker,* rather than as a *knower* or *reproducer,* heightens perception, appreciation, skill, and understanding.

My own education at the secondary school level was enriched by a skilled visual-art teacher who was also a practicing artist. He encouraged individual perception and understanding of the visual world and supported the development of technical ability in drawing and painting. The interest and confidence created by such teaching motivated me to engage in artistic pursuits outside of school and sparked a lifetime interest in the relationship between the natural environment and constructed world of the artist. This in turn has influenced my own compositional progress, both in terms of a transfer of skills and understanding from the visual to the aural dimension and in the use of structures and textures to prompt compositional ideas. While such interests were already part of my childhood world, they were enhanced through perceptive and creative teaching.

The work of British music educators such as Brian Dennis (1975), John Paynter (1982, 1992, 2000), George Self (1967, 1976), and many of those involved in the UK Schools Council Project ("music in the secondary schools curriculum") based at the University of York in the 1970s owed much to the world of visual-art education. The outcome of this project influenced a generation of teachers in the United Kingdom and elsewhere. In North America, Murray Schafer (1979) similarly demonstrated that starting points and structures for music composition activities could be found in the natural world and the visual arts.

The experimental era of the 1960s and 1970s saw many composers working across the traditional divisions between the arts and producing works where musical scores and performances revealed strong associations with the visual arts. During this inventive period, developments in music education followed closely the work of avant-garde composers, artists, and writers, demonstrating an essential integration of the creative process with the world of education.

The Composer. A third model for composition in music education can be derived from the compositional processes and works of professional composers. In this regard, the 1960s and 1970s provided sympathetic music educators with a multitude of possibilities as every musical and social tradition was open to challenge and redefinition. Exploratory approaches were

the order of the day, and recognition was more likely to arise from novelty or even notoriety than from widespread appreciation by the public. Traditional boundaries between areas of musical expression and practice, and even between music and the other arts, were broken down.

Unfortunately, much of the motivational and philosophical basis of these newer ways of working was misunderstood by some teachers or inadequately articulated by proponents, particularly with regard to matters of progression and development, skill acquisition, and quantifiable musical understanding. To some teachers in the United Kingdom during those early days of composition advocacy, it seemed that traditional views of musicality and assessment were being sidestepped and that important aspects of musical training were being ignored in favor of less quantifiable activities in improvisation and composition (Stephens, 2000).

An underlying problem during the 1970s and 1980s in the United Kingdom was the lack of composition courses in teacher education programs. The majority of teachers had not studied composition at the higher-education level and therefore lacked confidence in developing programs of study beyond the exercises presented at in-service courses. Fortunately, advocates of a composition-based curriculum continued to enthuse about their beliefs. The cause was assisted during the 1980s and 1990s by the publication of various texts on improvisation and composition in schools and a growing number of teacher education courses that included composition. By the mid-1980s, composition had become a requirement for secondary school examinations in the United Kingdom and later was included as a fundamental part of national curricula in England and Wales and Northern Ireland and curriculum and assessment guidelines in Scotland.

Institutional support for an area of the curriculum is important to its status, but it does not necessarily address operational difficulties in the classroom. A fundamental problem still exists for many teachers: namely how to encourage and identify student progress in composing. Educators such as Ross (1995) and Spencer (1993) have observed deficiencies in school practice that raise questions concerning the place of composition in formal music education programs. Paynter (2000) refers to these concerns and offers a way forward based on encouraging progress in students' composing.

Every country and culture will face particular difficulties and propose different solutions to its educational problems. It is likely, however, that the stages of introducing composition that have been experienced in the United Kingdom over the past 30 years will have their counterpart in the United States and elsewhere. In learning from each other's experience, it is important not to be discouraged at apparent setbacks in the establishment of composition programs in schools. As the old saying reminds us, "Nothing ventured, nothing gained!"

What can we draw from child development, art education, and the activities of composers to help us develop models and materials for teaching and learning in composition? Common to each of these worlds is the exploration of materials and making connections between similar and disparate

language development and acquisition. There are clear parallels with the stages of compositional development. In both areas, an individual moves from listening and observing, to experimenting with sounds and structures, to devising extended linguistic or musical statements. Progress in our ability to perceive, consider, and respond to differing perspectives typifies both the evolution of artistic and reasoning skills and an increased confidence in dealing with compositional processes. While styles of composing come and go, the human need to create remains constant; the purpose of seeking appropriate compositional models is to help us structure our musical ideas in effective and appropriate ways.

Changing Perspectives

During the 1960s and 1970s, many composers and music educators who advocated exploratory approaches were themselves products of a conventional music education. In their enthusiasm to provide students with a meaningful and interesting range of musical experiences, some appeared to disregard the benefits of their own educational background in allowing them to progress beyond the early stages of exploration and discovery. They had climbed the ladder that allowed them to see beyond the boundary wall, and they expected students to benefit from a similar perspective when the lower part of the ladder had been removed.

In seeking a place for composition in today's curriculum, it is beneficial to learn from earlier situations. Assigning composition a central position need not lead to the exclusion of other areas of musicianship. Even the thorny issues of music theory, harmony, and counterpoint are not automatically excluded; it is *how* such aspects are taught that is crucial. In discussing a recent research project on the place of composition in schools (Paterson, 2000), George Odam revealed that many students sought instruction in harmony and counterpoint in order to more fully realize their compositional ideas.[2] When students perceive a need, they are motivated to learn. Effective teaching consists of both encouraging and recognizing such need in students.

Musical understanding should develop hand in hand with skill, technique, and knowledge. As an individual progresses in one area, further possibilities open up in other areas. The heady days of the 1960s have been assigned to history. At the start of the 21st century, we have to contend with the earlier ideals of personal freedom and the more recent influences of postmodern thinking, with its advocacy of relative values and pluralism. Such influences inevitably affect curricular design, resulting in our questioning whether there are any universal ideals in music education. There is a risk of impotence in our politically correct, all-inclusive cultures. We hesitate to question or advocate a particular focus in music education lest we be accused of devaluing another area or of setting an elitist position against a "music-for-all" philosophy. In our desire to make school music culturally inclusive and representative, are we in danger of presenting conflicting messages? In the world outside the classroom, mass media and commercial interests have eroded many indigenous cultures, yet pop and world musics happily coexist in our culturally representative curricula. While such diversity of musical expression is to be wel-

comed, it sometimes appears that educational, cultural, and social factors have not properly been addressed. Where everything is of equal worth, how is value defined?

The polarization of exploratory approaches and structured curricula does not help us obtain an appropriate balance in music education. While clearly defined goals are essential to progress, creative thinking and experimentation allow us to challenge boundaries and so contribute productively to personal and social development. Improvisation and composition, therefore, should not be considered to be in conflict with a structured curriculum, although it is important not to limit the benefits of compositional activities by emphasizing a prescriptive approach to teaching, learning, and assessment. *Knowledge about* is always easier to teach than *experience of*, although the latter may have more lasting impact on an individual's development.

In the information that accompanies his stained glass work entitled *The America Windows*, the artist, Marc Chagall, refers to the importance of creativity in our lives, stating, "I prefer a life of surprises." As educators, concerned with enabling students to progress in their journey of discovery, to move from the known to the unknown, have we neglected the vitality of "a life of surprises"? The challenge is to balance the need for unity of purpose and design with the variety that is inherent in human communication—a challenge fundamental to the art of the composer. The task for the teacher is to encourage a diversity of expression and to foster divergent thinking in order to help the student develop a personal voice rather than to emphasize only convergent or conformist approaches.

Back to Basics

During my almost 30 years of teaching composition, I have been aware that many difficulties faced by students result from trying to deal with complex areas of melody, harmony, and counterpoint while having limited direct experience of the basic building blocks of music. The model in Figure 1, based on a house, focuses attention on essential areas of thinking and practice in this area.

It is my contention that compositional activities at the first-floor level would be far richer and more satisfying if there were more work in the initial stages of teaching and learning at the foundation and ground-floor levels. Musical communication consists of a combination of sounds and silences; exploration of these elements equips the student with an awareness of the technical and expressive possibilities of music. The six parameters at the ground-floor level underpin the first-floor activities. Investigation of pitch, for example, provides the student with a better understanding of melody, harmony, and counterpoint. Similarly, work in duration enriches one's understanding of rhythm, while consideration of timbre and articulation informs thinking about texture and orchestration. By exploring the ground-floor parameters individually and in various combinations, students gain valuable experience in developing musical statements and communicating ideas. This allows for better control of the more complex areas of musical expression found on the first floor. The model is applicable to music of all cultures, not only at the foundation and ground-floor levels but also—to varying degrees—at the first-floor level. In classical Indian music, for example, melody and rhythm will figure more prominently; in Chinese music, the concept of melody is highly regarded; while in much African music, rhythm and texture are dominant.

The purpose of this model is not to suggest that once students experience first-floor activities, the foundation and basic parameters of musical expression can be forgotten. When entering a house, we are reminded of the need for a secure foundation. Before we climb the stairs to the first floor, an appreciation of the surroundings on the ground floor provides a sense of location. There is no benefit in removing the stairs once we arrive on the first floor. Just as experienced composers continue to experiment as part of their creative work, students should return periodically to consider those foundation and ground-floor aspects that underpin more highly developed compositions. For the creative artist,

Figure 1. Model of a house

- **First Floor**
Melody Harmony Counterpoint
Rhythm Texture Orchestration

- **Ground Floor**

Pitch	Duration	Tempo
Dynamics	Articulation	Timbre

- **Foundation**
Sound and Silence

the additional years of focused activity provide a richer and more structured context for all aspects of the creative process, including that of experimentation. The above model encourages us to think of music in an integrated and holistic manner.

A Personal Note

Many years before I developed this model or understood much music theory, my early childhood experiences in improvisation and composition strongly motivated me to gain a more complete understanding of the nature of musical expression. The presence of a player piano in my home prompted hours of exploration, discovering how the paper rolls produced music and how the various parts of the machinery worked. When I punched random holes in sheets of rolled paper and then drew them over the sound-producing aperture, new and unusual patterns and combinations of fragmentary musical statements presented themselves to my young ears. I discovered that by pedaling lightly, I could further vary the performance by eliciting quieter sounds and faster renditions of my music. Conversely, when I increased the air supply through heavy pedaling, the paper was drawn tightly to the air holes, creating loud and sustained sounds and extending the length of the pieces. Alongside these activities, I used the pedals and tempo control to alter the musical parameters in my performances of commercially produced paper rolls, effectively "re-composing" the pieces by varying the composer's intentions. These experiences opened my ears to a fascinating world of sounds that was far beyond my performance capability and how I imagined sounds might be com-

bined. They extended my musical horizons, influencing my thinking as an aspiring composer and providing a basis for acceptance of irregular, atonal, and somewhat random sounds. This was an aural experience of my own making, all the more fascinating because it was unpredictable. Incidental understanding of the dimensions of sound and silence; the six parameters of pitch, duration, tempo, dynamics, articulation, and timbre; and the combination of sounds that produced these unusual melodic fragments and harmonic patterns provided a valuable basis for later musical development.

The randomly produced music of my unusual compositions inspired attempts to create similar-sounding patterns with my own limited piano technique. The fact that such music was neither tonal nor predictable (in direct contrast to the pieces I should have been practicing for my long-suffering piano teacher) added to the excitement and interest. Like Chagall, I reveled in "a life of surprises." Although the motivation for this activity was compositional (in terms of exploration and experimentation), the dimensions of listening and performing were very much in evidence in my decision-making process. This illustrates both the need to preserve the unity of composing, listening, and performing in music education and the benefit of a composition-based approach in providing a cohesive and holistic musical experience. Moreover, those hours of exploration gave me a heightened appreciation of natural and composed sounds and encouraged curiosity about how other composers dealt with compositional problems and structures. From such a simple beginning, aspects of my development as a musician and teacher were formed.

Approaches to Teaching and Learning

What musical understanding and skills are we trying to develop through teaching composition? If we are not clear concerning our objectives, we will have difficulty planning worthwhile experiences and defining progress, though we might encounter interesting activities and results. *Musical sensitivity* is a key dimension of a developing musicianship, and ways to support it should therefore be valued. A rich and varied musical diet, incorporating a range of approaches, is more likely to encourage musical sensitivity than a limited curricular focus. Variety of context and approach provides a basis for healthy growth in musical understanding.

Earlier in this chapter, reference was made to the areas of informal learning and the problems that arise when unstructured activities are brought into the formal environment of the classroom. Formulaic approaches to teaching and learning, like painting by numbers, might appeal to some for their apparent ease in achieving results. An undue emphasis on technique, however, apart from a natural engagement with a task, can reduce creative endeavors to mere exercises. Even the area of teaching and learning can succumb to an overemphasis on systems, thereby reducing teachers to technicians and discouraging spontaneity in the learning process. John Paynter (1992) writes:

> Indeed, this [i.e., suggestions for approaches to teaching musical composition] is one area where methods are to

be avoided, because they are the very antithesis of the creative mind. When you find you've developed a system for teaching composition, that is the moment to give up! (p. 30)

Such a view regarding the place of composition in formal education would appear to be at odds with current thinking on the necessity for systematic, structured methodologies in curricula. It also suggests that assessment-dominated education in schools is not the best context in which to encourage vital learning opportunities in composition. In a 2000 BBC 2 television documentary, American composer Aaron Copland echoes similar sentiments to Paynter with regard to providing guidance to composers:

> I don't like to generalize about what composers ought to do with their music or how they ought to do it, since I am so very much aware that composers are very different in their personalities and you have to give them lots of leeway to do the thing that comes natural to them, instead of setting up ideas in their minds as to what they ought to do. (Thompson)

Both Paynter and Copland question the validity of establishing clearly defined teaching methodologies or setting limits on the creative process of composing music. While such cautionary remarks should be heeded, they do not preclude the possibility of employing models and strategies to aid the compositional process or of devising appropriate assessment categories and criteria to evaluate teaching and learning in this area. Best (1985) cautions against implying that a subject cannot be properly assessed or that clearly defined learning goals cannot be described, as this effectively devalues its place in the curriculum. According to Best, there should be no significant incompatibility between "the importance of reason, and those important aspects of artistic experience on which the subjectivist rightly insists" (p. 15). He advocates devising appropriate objective measurements of knowledge, skill, and understanding in order to secure an important place for the arts in a curriculum where political and educational requirements value subjects on the basis of their perceived objective worth. The challenge for teachers, therefore, is how to balance political and societal expectations with good educational practice.

Copland's (Thompson, 2000) remarks on the need for sensitivity to the autonomy of the individual composer are at odds with our mass-produced culture and its influence on the educational process. A prescriptive curriculum achieves results and is considered attractive for its economic use of time and resources. A uniform approach to teaching composition is not desirable, however, because it tends to encourage conformity rather than the development of an individual voice, and it emphasizes technical skills over a broadly based musical sensitivity. Divergent thinking develops where there is variety rather than uniformity; even the problems experienced by students in acquiring listening and performing skills differ from one individual to another and therefore require distinctive teaching approaches. A composer's ability does not automatically improve over time; early works may be considered "better" than later examples. Yet educational systems pre-

suppose a staged development and require precise measurement. Once again, it is important to recognize different types of progression in individual development and to relate our thinking and practice in this area to the real world of the composer.

Idea, Technique, and Structure

The creative process in the arts consists of a relationship between materials, their manipulation, and their overall organization—or, more simply, between idea, technique, and structure. While a work of art is a skilled integration of these three elements, it is helpful to consider each separately within the educational process.

The Importance of Idea

The perceived value of a composition depends not only on the skill of a composer in organizing sounds but also on the quality of the musical ideas themselves. Although a skilled artist will be able to make much out of what might initially appear to be unpromising material, the nature of the initial material itself plays an important part in determining the musical quality and shaping the overall structure of a composition. Some ideas are more appropriate for one type of work than another: the content of a short story differs from that of a novel, a piano miniature from that of a symphony, a sketch from that of a complex landscape. Copland (Thompson, 2000) expressed concern over teacher intervention in the compositional process, of "setting up ideas in their minds as to what they ought to do." His reference to doing "the thing that comes natural to them" draws a helpful distinction between student intuition and teacher imposition. How can teachers foster an appropriate environment in which ideas flourish and intentions are realized? Effective teaching and learning in this area include discussion with students of the reasons for their choices as they select ideas and outline strategies for developing and concluding their compositions. Stimulation and motivation are therefore important for both the student and the teacher in evaluating and shaping ideas.

Attitudes and perceptions are influenced by earlier experiences; in composition, this includes the range of our musical and extramusical backgrounds. For highly gifted students, imagination and motivation often make up for any lack of prior experience, while intuition serves as both a useful instigator and commentator on all creative efforts. As students progress, a growing self-awareness and ability in self-evaluation further affect their conception and development of ideas. Our goal as teachers is to make ourselves redundant and to encourage greater independence on the part of our students. The relationship between teacher and student has much in common with that of parent and child, where there is a movement from total dependency to increased independence. While the intention is the same for each individual, the rate of development cannot be absolutely defined. In encouraging students to develop musical ideas, therefore, it is helpful to foster reflection on their own and others' material rather than to adopt a more prescriptive, teacher-based approach. This is not to deny the value of devising common starting points for student pieces or setting defined tasks or even compositional exercises. Copland's remarks, after all, are more pertinent to composers with some experience than to novices.

The Importance of Technique

Technical know-how is vital to learning. In the area of composition, it involves being aware of what can be accomplished and how goals might be achieved. In this regard, experimentation with the medium (instrumental, vocal, electronic) is essential. Finding out what can be done is necessary for individual development, as witnessed in the way a young child learns to walk or relate to its environment. Exploring and testing boundaries generate many creative possibilities. Stravinsky characterized this process in his observation, "Fingers are not to be despised: they are great inspirers, and, in contact with a musical instrument, often give birth to subconscious ideas which might otherwise never come to life" (as cited in White, 1966, p. 242).

At the heart of this approach is the important technique of variation; our ability to perceive, respond to, and change ideas is fundamental to the compositional process and enriches our experience of music as listeners, composers, and performers. The imaginative teacher will stimulate student thinking by providing a range of models of how composers, artists, and writers vary their ideas. Composing is both an art and a craft, where familiarity with skills and techniques enables individual ideas to be shaped according to both recognized and unusual patterns. Sensitive teaching consists of knowing when to intervene and guide learning in order to maximize time and resources and enrich the compositional experience.

The Importance of Structure

The human mind is designed to create, appreciate, and respond to structures and routines. Composers, artists, and writers have generated many ways of organizing their sounds, materials, and ideas. Essentially there are two main options available:

■ to work with imposed structures (such as the range of tonally-based musical forms)
■ to work with organic structures (where the overall form grows from an opening idea or musical cell).

In both scenarios, there are a host of possible approaches, and many choices have to be made in the organization of the individual elements of a work. The quality of the ideas and the way these are arranged in a final product distinguish the ordinary from the extraordinary, the banal from the inspired. An important part of the teaching process, therefore, is to present students with a range of models for their work, not in order to restrict their ideas, which Copland cautions against, but in order to liberate their thinking. Just as we develop our ability to speak by listening to others, so our development as composers is encouraged through listening to and considering a wide range of musical examples and observing how compositional problems are presented and solved.

Because the language of music is more abstract than spoken or written language, music often communicates at a deeper level than words. The question of *meaning* is therefore important to consider with students, not so much in terms of representation, but rather in relation to intention and response. The way sounds and silences are structured is particularly important in this regard; questioning the reasons for selecting individual sounds, patterns, and larger forms enables student and teacher to en-

gage in useful discussion concerning the quality and impact of musical ideas and structures.

In linguistics, the issues are more straightforward, as the following example illustrates:

> Spend to like I this not is my Tuesday the way.

Here we recognize and understand the words individually, although when the sentence is taken as a whole, its meaning is somewhat obscure. Parts of the sentence are more intelligible than others, but the individual sounds that make up the statement could be ordered more clearly. There are several ways we could proceed, and each reordering has a different meaning. The majority of English speakers would most likely select the following version as the most appropriate: "This is not the way I like to spend my Tuesday."

Appreciation of linguistic and musical structures is related to cultural context. The arrangement of subject, verb, and object in the above example resonates with the way native English speakers' brains have been programmed during the early years of our development, based on the aural environment in which we learned our native language. A German might be more comfortable if the verb was placed at the end of the sentence. In the following Japanese haiku by Buson (1985), the deferment of the subject has both cultural and poetic significance, transforming a simple statement (subject, verb, and object) into something far more beautiful:

> On the temple bell

Settles—and is sleeping—
A butterfly.

The sense of expectancy created by the delay in establishing what is "on the temple bell" has an aesthetic quality that informs our appreciation. Its effect is retained even on repeated readings.

Similarly, in music, we learn patterns of scales, frames of reference, and styles that enable us to respond intuitively to musical structures. To a Chinese or Greek ear, there are no missing notes in the pentatonic scale. This natural and learned appreciation of musical patterns and structures is demonstrated within the stages of child development, as Campbell (1998) observed in *Songs in Their Heads*. A consideration of musical meaning and the *optimum* order of sounds provides teacher and student with a valuable learning opportunity in composition, while the presentation of alternative models, including those from other cultures, allows for further exploration. In this regard, it is interesting to consider to what extent it is the *unusual* quality of a poetic, artistic, or musical statement that affects us. To an ear accustomed to hearing a subject placed at the start of a sentence, its displacement to the end is particularly attractive because of its unexpected nature. The relationship between expectation and surprise, unity and variety, is fundamental to the creative process.

Musical and Artistic Starting Points

In my own music education, writing in the style of other composers provided one way of developing musical and technical knowledge, understanding, and skill. This method not only provided an inside view of the elements of a composer's musical language and how ideas are developed, but also encouraged fluency in dealing with melodic, harmonic, and contrapuntal forms through understanding something of the nature of musical expression. Admittedly, there is a danger of superficial acquaintance or caricature in this approach, but as an aid to teaching and learning, there is much to commend it. In earlier generations, copying and arranging the music of other composers was considered useful training in composition because it enabled the student composer to gain a sense of the physical process of composing. In much the same way, an art student might copy the drawings and paintings of an established artist in order to develop technical skills and understanding of content and structure. Reports of the young J. S. Bach secretly copying a score by moonlight might indicate both his desire to perform the pieces and his wish to learn about their compositional devices (Emery, Wolff, & Jones, 1980, p. 786; Scholes, 1942, p. 34). Performing works by acknowledged masters was not enough; the act of writing enabled Bach to understand something of the intrinsic musical, technical, and structural qualities of a piece of music. Our attention should first be with the *sound* of a composition; however, the visual impact of a score can aid understanding and even prompt compositional ideas and structures.

Professional compositions, paintings, poems, and the natural or constructed environment can be used in various ways to encourage students to compose. If students have grappled with particular compositional problems and devised their own solutions, they may well listen more attentively to professional works where similar challenges are presented and overcome. Such an approach can either be prearranged, where the teacher links the project to a series of planned examples, or treated more informally, in which case the teacher responds to whatever the students present. The latter method requires the teacher to have a wide musical knowledge and repertoire of recorded works, scores, and other materials for illustration.

Alternatively, professional compositions can be used as models to stimulate compositional ideas by providing students with a secure structural framework in which to compose. Essentially, such an approach extends the context of focused listening so that it supports compositional development. A composition such as *Polymorphia* by Penderecki provides a good example of how to work with micro- and macrostructures through exploring different playing techniques (at the micro level) within a context of juxtaposition of blocks of contrasting sounds (at the macro level). The opening movement of Stravinsky's *Petrouchka*, "The Shrove-tide Fair," provides a similar structural model of juxtaposition. In the case of Penderecki, the language is exploratory and textural; in contrast, Stravinsky employs a tonal framework for his ideas, responding vividly to the fairground scene and the different stalls and activities. Employing works to illustrate compositional problems and solutions or to prompt compositional activity allows for variety in the way composing, listening, and performing are encouraged in the classroom.

A consideration of the relationship

between idea, technique, and structure is fundamental to the compositional process. The use of stories, thematic or contextual frameworks (such as a journey), and abstract starting points (such as contrast) provides varying levels of structural control that can usefully be applied to compositional activities. We should be concerned with both musical and technical aspects of the compositional process as we seek to stimulate ideas and provide support for their realization. Our primary responsibility as teachers is to create appropriate contexts that enable students to develop their abilities in this area. Freedom does not come from the absence of guidelines or rules, but through the establishment of clear parameters within which decisions can be made.

Assessment

Professional composers are not always confident in assessing their own output, nor are they always in agreement concerning the quality of other composers' works. Bruckner, for example, exhibited great uncertainty over his own judgment, accepting advice from friends and colleagues to revise his symphonies, while Chausson and Duparc demonstrated a high degree of perfectionism and self-criticism (Cooke & Nowak, 1980; Cooper, 1980; Gallois, 1980). In the case of Duparc, a medical (physical-psychological) condition was at least partly responsible for a hypercritical attitude to composition that led him to destroy many of his works. If experienced composers encounter problems in the evaluation of compositions, this should caution us against adopting simplistic or dogmatic approaches to assessment.

While it might be desirable to involve

professional composers in the process of assessment, teachers must be able to make appropriate judgments themselves. It is they who guide students by setting the context for compositional activities, and it is they who are responsible for helping students improve. Notwithstanding any external requirement to assess compositions, it is important that student composers are satisfied with their work on the basis of their developing critical discernment. Ultimately, this discernment indicates a growing musical sensitivity, the cultivation of which is a fundamental purpose of teaching. Analytical *listening* thus assumes a central position in the teaching and assessment of composition. In language development, our confidence in the correct use of words develops as we listen and speak, while our vocabulary, accent, and dialect are influenced by the context in which we live. A similar process operates in compositional development, where our confidence, skill, and approach mature through observation, analysis, and practice.

Although many teachers have little difficulty in establishing frameworks in which students are encouraged to compose, there are particular problems in the assessment of compositions. Teachers are required both to devise strategies for teaching and learning and to measure successful completion of clearly articulated goals. Moreover, an ability to encourage self-assessment and peer review and to provide formative feedback during the process of composing is essential.[3] The questions we ask are often more valuable than the opinions we proffer, for questions allow the door to remain open to change. In an ideal world, the experience of composing would take precedence over a

societal need to evaluate creative work, with its attendant risk of distorting the nature of composing and the purpose of its inclusion in the curriculum. While the areas of formative assessment, peer review, and self-assessment provide the most valuable arenas for developing thinking and practice in the art of composing, summative assessment seems to present many teachers with the greatest difficulty.[4] Consequently, I offer the following observations on the assessment of compositional products. It is hoped that these guidelines will encourage teachers to pursue the all-important task of developing opportunities for students to engage in compositional processes as a natural part of their musical education.

The Summative Dilemma

Assessment of creative processes and products is fraught with many difficulties, particularly where the approved model is objective, graded evaluation. There is an understandable assumption that such assessment has greater validity than more subjective responses, for collective attested judgment provides a measure of security and observable worth beyond that of individual taste. It is far easier to assess materials and ideas on a correct-incorrect basis, to award marks out of ten, or to allocate grades than it is to provide an acceptable measure where there are no right or wrong answers but, rather, more and less effective solutions. It could be argued that the more qualitative forms of assessment, however, require a higher level of articulation and perception of the quality of student work than is the case in more objective forms of assessment. Such qualitative human judgment is surely to be encouraged as a necessary part of mature, developed thinking, rather than the alternative: to allow education to be dominated by multiple-choice, factual assessments that can be administered by a machine.

The issue is not that we are unable to properly assess creative activities, but rather that the way that much formal education is constructed may not support an appropriate model of evaluation. For many years, we have assessed student understanding of literature, history, philosophy, and a range of the arts and humanities through essays rather than checklists; moreover, students seeking advanced degrees are required to submit dissertations and to debate their ideas with other qualified professionals. Such examples indicate that appropriate forms of assessment are possible within the formal context of school or university. It is not unreasonable to assign grades to student compositions if required, provided that such grading follows the identification of qualitatively based categories and criteria. Where the interpretation of such criteria is further tested against the collective views of other professionals (music educators/composers), it is likely that the result will reflect an acceptable and valid measure of achievement. Such a system of checks and balances ensures a fair interpretation of criteria and minimizes any negative effects arising from assessment based on personal taste.

Familiarity might breed contempt, but it also provides a degree of security. In the area of musical performance, for example, there is a long tradition of graded assessment, with varying levels of specificity concerning musical and technical requirements and stages of difficulty. Depending on our culture, we have a shared understanding that has been built up over time of what constitutes a Grade 5 pianist or a Grade 7 flautist. National and international music performance competitions provide a context where accredited professionals interpret criteria; this model can be applied to the assessment of creative work. Where examination requirements are articulated in clearly defined assessment categories and criteria, it is possible to develop a shared understanding of expectations.

We are at an earlier stage in deciding appropriate levels or stages of development for student compositions than we are in the assessment of music performance. What, for example, precisely characterizes an undergraduate composition or a masters or doctoral folio of works? The temptation is to increase technical requirements concerning length, number of instruments, demonstration of compositional devices, and other aspects, thus creating the "examination composition." How easy it is to fall into the trap Copland (Thompson, 2000) identified of telling composers what they "ought to do with their music or how they ought to do it." Of course, it could be argued that such formal assessment requirements are acceptable because they identify the necessary levels of attainment that all professional composers should achieve. In much the same way, a pianist might be required to play a range of scales, arpeggios, and studies in an examination, both to inform his or her performance and to indicate a standard of technical accomplishment. A developed technique is, after all, an important part of the skill or craft of a performer or composer. It is essential, however, that there is an appropriate relationship between qualitative and quantitative measurement tools—*more* should not be confused with *better*. In a quantitative context, Satie's set of *Gymnopédies* might be considered a Grade 3 composition, and Webern would not be awarded a doctorate because of the brevity of much of his output. Clearly, such simplistic evaluations would not be acceptable to many musicians, even though they might satisfy a school's bureaucratic requirements. Assessment tools should arise out of the substance of compositions and not merely dictate the devices a composer should employ. Moreover, it is important to consider the more imaginative dimensions of a work rather than to focus mainly on its technical aspects.

One way around the problem of defining grades or levels as a means of identifying progress in the skill of composing is to record typical compositions at various stages of student development. Examples of such observations and evaluations of student compositions have been reported in a number of publications over the past 20 years (e.g., Barrett, 1996, 1998; Bunting, 1988; Davies, 1992; Glover, 1998; Kratus, 1989; Loane, 1984; Salaman, 1988; Simmonds, 1988; Swanwick & Tillman, 1986; Tillman, 1989). From such information, it is possible to develop an understanding of capabilities, although any evolving picture of normal expectations has to allow for exceptions. Encouraging individuality—or, as Copland (Thompson, 2000) says, giving "them lots of leeway to do the thing that comes natural to them"—is a fundamental educational consideration that should not be forgotten in a systematized assessment framework.

Categories and Criteria

Intuition often plays an important part in assessment and, when coupled with experience, it may provide an evaluation that is just as appropriate as one based on published standards. Contemporary society, however, demands a common measure for public examinations, with clearly articulated assessment categories and criteria. Such statements have a level of authority that intuitive responses or personal opinion lack, though they are also open to interpretation in those areas of the curriculum where the focus is on appropriate solutions rather than right or wrong answers. While professionals might not always agree in their assessment of a student composition, it is likely that there will be broad agreement on the categories and criteria against which a work is judged. Let us, then, turn to the matter of devising suitable statements for the assessment of composition. Whether or not we consider it appropriate to evaluate compositions in this way, formal education requires proof that teaching and learning have been effective and that students have made progress. Moreover, as Best (1985) and others have reminded us, to withdraw from the assessment of creative work can lead to its devaluation in the minds of politicians and society.

Categories. School and university examination boards have developed various lists of categories and criteria for assessing student compositions and have assigned levels or grade descriptors to guide assessors in their judgment. The articulation of assessment requirements in those areas of the curriculum where qualitative issues are uppermost does not dispense with subjective evaluation or interpretation of statements; rather, such statements guide evaluators, providing a shared context in which consensus takes place.

It is likely that any list of assessment categories in the area of composing will include the following:

- communication of ideas, a sense of identity, shape, and style
- musicianship, artistry, and expressive intention
- technical skills and an awareness of practical considerations.

These areas may be further defined through reference to specific terms such as the following:

- presence, involvement, ability to evoke responsive listening (communication)
- feeling for design and structure, musical character, imagination (musicianship)
- tempo, articulation, balance, instrumental/vocal considerations (technical skills).

The above categories could be expanded (for example, by treating design, structure, and musical character separately) or reduced simply to musicianship and technical skills—as communication informs both musical and technical considerations. Some would include aesthetic involvement as a category, although this could be viewed as something that informs all other areas, either as an overriding consideration or as an aspect within each category. The purpose of these categories is to assist examiners in the analysis of specific aspects of a composition, not to encourage a separation of music into disconnected areas. Even the main spheres of musicianship and technical

skills overlap in a number of regards, for the communication of music requires both musical understanding and technical control.

Criteria. Assessment criteria can be relatively simple (for example, word descriptors such as excellent/exceptional, good, acceptable/satisfactory, minimally acceptable, and unacceptable/unsatisfactory) or qualified by expanded statements within specified assessment categories. Both approaches require interpretation, although the latter has the advantage of clarifying some of the qualities examiners look for. The following phrases provide a useful framework for evaluating compositions and indicate greater specificity than one-word descriptors:

- fully involved and committed; the music is brought to life and communicated clearly (communication)
- well-conceived, artistic work, convincing with a sense of the music's aesthetic significance (musicianship)
- some technical inaccuracies, difficulties, or shortcomings, but competent overall (technical skills)

The above statements can be adapted to reflect a series of levels where required.

A qualitative approach to the assessment of compositions can be adapted to the age and stage of students' work; for example, student work can be compared to the "normal expectation" for a particular stage of development. The work of more able students and those with learning difficulties might be considered against the broad stages of expected development without restricting levels to numerical age.

Discussion of musical and artistic features—such as unity and variety, tension and resolution, musical development and flow, and artistic assurance—can also enlighten the assessment process. Once again, assessment should grow out of the composition itself rather than be imposed upon it; there is little point in judging Ligeti's *Atmosphères* on the basis of its melodic interest or Mozart's Clarinet Concerto for its treatment of serial technique.

In devising suitable criteria, it is necessary to be aware of a natural tendency to become more specific in defining the details of the assessment process and to accumulate ever-increasing lists of descriptive statements. The current emphasis on standardized, competency-based approaches to teaching, learning, and assessment is an example of this tendency. Overprescription in assessment criteria may get in the way of professional judgment. An undue emphasis on particular aspects can misrepresent or even distort the nature and meaning of a subject. The whole is more than the sum of its parts. It is essential, therefore, that we avoid a movement toward an exclusively convergent model of assessment in a more divergent area of the curriculum, a movement that may be characterized by a focus on individual details rather than on the whole.

The growth of an individual voice poses certain difficulties for assessment. At one level, students in a formal composition program might be expected to progress from derivative approaches to a more distinctive musical language. The former is more straightforward to assess; highlighting the latter could encourage an approach that emphasizes originality—or novelty for its

own sake—over musical substance. Once again, it is important to focus on the integrity of a composition and maintain a more holistic approach to creative involvement, rather than to isolate particular aspects of a work. The 1960s and 1970s were notorious for emphasizing novelty and denigrating composers whose musical language appeared to be retrospective. The preferred model was the artist ahead of his time rather than the baroque or classical composer who produced compositions to order and operated largely within established musical styles. Although there would seem to be little point in composing in an older style, there is a sense in which a work should be judged on its own terms, rather than on the basis of historical placing. Fortunately, the passage of time allows us to reassess and appreciate compositions without the distraction of social expectation or historical period.

Conclusion

A basic difficulty in facilitating progress in composing is that of identifying and measuring development in creative activities without adopting a prescriptive approach. In encouraging students to get better at composing, it is important to avoid mechanical, staged approaches and to recognize different types of progression that do not assume neat, linear growth. Musical development may, however, be perceived to follow certain developmental stages even when—as in the case of a prodigy—these are reduced in time. As teachers, we need to understand the internal processes of composing and devise strategies that prompt ideas and encourage individual progress—to release the "songs in their heads." Our primary concern should be to enable students to develop a capacity to select and discriminate between ideas and to make *musical* choices.

My reasons for being convinced of the value of engaging students in a range of compositional tasks go beyond personal predilection. As a teacher, a music educator, and an observer of teachers and students over several decades, I have witnessed the benefits that accompany an approach to music education in which composition assumes a central part. In recent years, technology has enabled many individuals to realize their creative ideas and to take on the roles of composer, listener, and performer in an integrated way. While some fear that a "composition-made-easy" approach devalues the art of composing, the exciting possibilities that technology has created should be seen as an opportunity for music educators to address more qualitative issues in their teaching.

"Music for all" not only involves all individuals in society, but also opens the doors of formal education to a much wider and more diverse range of music than existed in many schools of the mid-20th century. The problem today is not that many more people now have access to music—nor is it how we learn to cope with increased musical genres and assessment requirements. The challenge is to provide a suitable basis for considering the quality of ideas and to encourage appropriate techniques for developing students' musical thinking. If we as teachers do not rise to this challenge, we will have missed a valuable chance to engage students in vital learning opportunities. Fundamentally, the issues facing us in considering the place of composition in

schools are no different from those experienced by pioneers and explorers throughout history. In the words of Christopher Columbus, "Nothing that results from human progress is achieved with unanimous consent ... and those who are enlightened before the others are condemned to pursue that light in spite of others" (as quoted in Scott, 1992). With adequate preparation, commitment, and vision, we can pursue the light as we sail toward a new horizon, confident that we shall not fall off the edge of our familiar world.

Notes

1. The first date listed for these curricula and guidelines indicates the publication of the main documents. The second date indicates the publication of music documents. Some materials have been subsequently revised.

2. Odam spoke about this project at the Fifth International Symposium of the Research Alliance of Institutions for Music Education (RAIME), London, Ontario, 1999.

3. Formative feedback can be defined as feedback that is intended to help students learn.

4. Summative assessment is designed to measure student progress.

References

Barrett, M. (1996). Children's aesthetic decision-making: An analysis of children's musical discourse as composers. *International Journal of Music Education, 28*, 37–62.

Barrett, M. (1998). Researching children's compositional processes and products. In B. Sundin, G. E. McPherson, & G. Folkestad (Eds.), *Children composing* (pp. 10–34). Malmö, Sweden: Lund University.

Bennett, S. (1976). The process of musical creation: Interviews with eight composers. *Journal of Research in Music Education, 24*(1), 3–13.

Best, D. (1985). *Feeling and reason in the arts.* London: Allen and Unwin.

Bunting, R. (1987). Composing music: Case studies in the teaching and learning process. *British Journal of Music Education, 4*(1), 25–52.

Bunting, R. (1988). Composing music: Case studies in the teaching and learning process. *British Journal of Music Education, 5*(3), 269–310.

Buson. (1985). On the temple bell. In K. Koch & K. Farrell (Eds.), *Talking to the sun* (p. 79). New York: Holt, Rinehart, & Winston. (Based on translation from *An introduction to haiku*, by H. G. Henderson, Ed. and Trans., 1958, Garden City, NY: Doubleday)

Campbell, P. S. (1998). *Songs in their heads: Music and its meaning in children's lives.* New York: Oxford University Press.

Campbell, P. S., & Scott-Kassner, C. (1995). The creating child. In *Music in childhood: Preschool to elementary grades* (pp. 246–66). New York: Schirmer Books.

Chagall, M. (n.d.). *The America Windows* [Placard at exhibit]. Art Institute of Chicago. Viewed June 2000.

Cooke, D. & Nowak, L. (1980). Bruckner, Anton. In S. Sadie (Ed.), *The new grove dictionary of music and musicians* (Vol. 3, pp. 352–71). London: Macmillan.

Cooper, M. (1980). Duparc, Henri. In S. Sadie (Ed.), *The new grove dictionary of music and musicians* (Vol. 5, pp. 726–27). London: Macmillan.

Davies, C. D. (1992). Listen to my song: A study of songs invented by children aged 5 to 7 years. *British Journal of Music Education, 9*(1), 19–48.

Dennis, B. (1975). *Projects in sound.* London: Universal Edition.

Department for Education. (1988/1992). *National Curriculum for Schools in England and Wales.* London: HMSO.

Department of Education for Northern Ireland. (1989/1996). *National Curriculum for Northern Ireland.* Belfast: HMSO.

Dolloff, L. (2000). The promise of expertise: Implications for music teacher education. In H. Jørgensen (Ed.), *Challenges in Music Education Research and Practice for a New Millenium: Proceedings of the Fifth International Symposium of the Research Alliance of Institutions for Music Eduction (RAIME)* (pp. 19–31). Oslo: Norges musikkhøgskole [Norwegian Academy of Music].

Elliott, D. (1986). Finding a place for music in the curriculum. *British Journal of Music Education, 3*(2), 135–51.

Ellis, P. (1987). *Out of bounds: Music projects across the curriculum.* London: Oxford University Press.

Emery, W., Wolff, C., & Jones, R. (1980). Bach, Johann Sebastian. In S. Sadie (Ed.), *The new grove dictionary of music and musicians* (Vol. 1, pp. 785–840). London: Macmillan.

Favaro, E. (2000). Preparing students for a career in the music industry. *International Journal of Music Education, 35*, 66–68.

Forster, J. (1983). *Music-lab: A book of sound ideas.* London: Universal Edition.

Gallois, J. (1980). Chausson, Ernest. In S. Sadie (Ed.), *The new grove dictionary of music and musicians* (Vol. 4, pp. 181–84). London: Macmillan.

Gamble, T. (1984). Imagination and understanding in the music curriculum. *British Journal of Music Education, 1*(1), 7–25.

Glover, J. (1998). Listening to and assessing children's composition. In J. Glover & S. Ward (Eds.), *Teaching music in the primary school* (2nd ed., pp. 135–52). London: Cassell.

Harris, R., & Hawksley, E. (1989). *Composing in the classroom.* Cambridge, England: Cambridge University Press.

Hennessey, S. (1998). Teaching composing in the music curriculum. In M. Littledyke & L. Huxford (Eds.), *Teaching the primary curriculum for constructive learning* (pp. 163–72). London: David Fulton.

Howard, J. (1989). *Learning to compose*. Cambridge, England: Cambridge University Press.

Jorgensen, E. (1996). The artist and the pedagogy of hope. *International Journal of Music Education, 27*, 36–50.

Kratus, J. (1989). A time analysis of the compositional processes used by children ages 7–11. *Journal of Research in Music Education, 37*(1), 5–20.

Loane, B. (1984). Thinking about children's compositions. *British Journal of Music Education, 1*(3), 205–31.

Marsh, K. (1995). Children's singing games: Composition in the playground? *Research Studies in Music Education, 4*, 2–11.

Paterson, A. (2000). *Composing in the classroom: The creative dream* (G. Odam, Project Director). High Wycombe, UK: National Association of Music Educators.

Paynter, J. (1982). *Music in the secondary school curriculum*. Cambridge, England: Cambridge University Press.

Paynter, J. (1992). *Sound and structure*. Cambridge, England: Cambridge University Press.

Paynter, J. (2000). Making progress with composing. *British Journal of Music Education, 17*(1), 5–31.

Paynter, J., & Aston, P. (1970). *Sound and silence: Classroom projects in creative music*. Cambridge, England: Cambridge University Press.

Paynter, J., & Paynter, E. (1974). *The dance and the drum*. London: Universal Edition.

Ross, M. (1995). What's wrong with school music? *British Journal of Music Education, 12*(3), 185–201.

Salaman, W. (1988). Objectives and the teaching of composition. *British Journal of Music Education, 5*(1), 3–20.

Schafer, R. M. (1979). *Creative music education: A handbook for the modern music teacher*. New York:

Schirmer. [This is a collection of five earlier seminal texts: *The Composer in the Classroom, Ear Cleaning*, the *New Soundscape, When Words Sing*, and *The Rhinoceros in the Classroom.*]

Scholes, P. A. (1942). T*he first book of the great musicians* (10th ed.). London: Oxford University Press.

Scott, R. (Producer/Director). (1992). *1492: Conquest of Paradise* [Motion Picture]. United States: Paramount Pictures.

Scott-Kassner, C. (1992). Research on music in early childhood. In R. Colwell (Ed.), *Handbook of Research on Music Teaching and Learning* (pp.633–50). New York: Schirmer.

Scottish Office Education Department.(1988/ 1992). *Curriculum and Assessment in Scotland: National Guidelines*. Edinburgh: HMSO.

Self, G. (1967). *New sounds in class: A practical approach to the understanding and performing of contemporary music in schools*. London: Universal Edition.

Self, G. (1976). *Make a new sound*. London: Universal Edition.

Simmonds, R. (1988). An experiment in the assessment of composition. *British Journal of Music Education, 5*(1), 21–34.

Spencer, P. (1993). GCSE music: A survey of undergraduate opinion. *British Journal of Music Education, 10*(2), 73–84.

Stephens, J. (1994). Metamorphosis: Creative and integrated teaching methods in European music education. *British Journal of Music Education, 11*(3), 239–48.

Stephens, J. (2000). Shades of meaning: A consideration of aspects of peer learning and peer assessment in music and the arts. In John Stephens (Ed.), *Proceedings of the International Conference on Peer Learning and Peer Assessment in Music and Cognate Disciplines* (Resource Pack, Part 2, pp. 49–55). Northern Ireland: University of Ulster.

Swanwick, K. (Ed.). (1990). *The arts and educa-*

tion: Papers from 1983–1990. London: National Association for Education in the Arts. [See particularly papers by Rumbold, Swanwick, and Aspin.]

Swanwick, K., & Tillman, J. (1986). The sequence of musical development: A study of children's composition. *British Journal of Music Education, 3*(3), 305–39.

Thackray, R. (1965). *Creative music in education.* London: Novello.

Thompson, D. (Executive Producer). (2000, October 29). *Aaron Copland: American composer: A centenary celebration of the composer* [Televsion Broadcast, BBC2]. London: British Broadcasting Corporation. (A coproduction with WNET, New York)

Tillman, J. (1976). *Exploring sound: Creative musical projects for teachers.* London: Galliard/ Stainer & Bell.

Tillman, J. (1989). Towards a model of development of children's musical creativity. *Canadian Music Educator, 30*(2), 169–74.

Upitis, R. (1992). *Can I play you my song?* Portsmouth, New Hampshire: Heinemann.

White, E. W. (1966). *Stravinsky: The composer and his works.* London: Faber & Faber.

Wiggins, J. (1990). *Composition in the classroom.* Reston, VA: MENC.

Winters, G. (1986). *Listen, compose, perform.* Harlow, England: Longman.

Wolfson, R. (2001, January 6). Pop has learnt from classical: Can classical learn from pop? *The Daily Telegraph*, p.7.

Jonathan Stephens is director of music and head of aesthetic education at the University of Aberdeen in Scotland. He has served as chair of the Commission for Music in Schools and Teacher Education of the International Society of Music Education (ISME) and as president of the Research Alliance of Institutions for Music Education (RAIME), and he is a founding member and currently the Scottish representative of the European Association for Music in Schools (EAS). He has written articles and conference papers and lectured in Europe, the United States, Australia, and Canada on such topics as music education, creativity, improvisation, and contemporary music.

Contexts for Composing

7

A Frame for Understanding Children's Compositional Processes

Jackie Wiggins

To make composition an effective and integral part of teaching and learning in a music classroom, teachers need to understand what students do when they are asked to compose in a classroom setting. Understanding what students actually do when they compose will help teachers know the kinds of compositional problems to pose and the nature of the support students need in order to be successful. The better teachers understand students' compositional processes, the more effectively they can use composing as a means of nurturing musical understanding and appreciation in their students.

Composing is a kind of musical thinking. A musical work is someone's ideas in motion. The process of composing music can be described either as generating musical ideas (motivic material and musical gestures) and setting them into a context or as generating a musical context that gives rise to musical ideas. Either way, a musical composition is just that—a series of interrelated musical ideas that makes a statement of its creator's intent. Because musical ideas are the product of musical thinking, in an educational setting, a composition can show a

great deal about a student's musical thinking and understanding. This makes composing an ideal tool for teaching music and an excellent means for assessing student learning. For the composers themselves, it is also an important vehicle for personal expression.

While children's compositional products can be windows into their musical thinking, the processes through which they create music can reveal even more about the nature of their understanding. As students compose, they are thinking aloud. When students compose with peers, it becomes necessary for them to communicate their ideas for motivic material and musical gestures and for the overall musical work. Studying the conversations and musical interactions that take place while students compose with peers can provide insight into how they understand music.

Studies of the work processes of both novice and expert composers show that there is no one way to compose. There are probably as many variations to the process as there are composers. Research studies of students' compositional processes and products indicate that the nature of the compositional task, the way it is explained and expressed, the tools available, and the setting can affect student composers' work processes. For example, analysis of the work by Kratus (1989, 1991) and Swanwick and Tillman (1986) shows links between the nature of the task and the way it was articulated to study participants and the compositional processes and products that resulted. Further indicators of the influence of task, instructions, tools, and setting are evident in analyses of the processes of individuals composing at a computer or MIDI station (e.g., Bamberger, 1977; Folkestad, Hargreaves, & Lindström, 1998; Hickey, 1995; Younker, 2000; Younker & Smith, 1996) as compared to the actions and processes of those composing with acoustic instruments and/or voice (e.g., Barrett, 1996, 1998b; Burnard, 1995, 1999; Davies, 1986, 1992; DeLorenzo, 1987, 1989; Kaschub, 1997; Marsh, 1995; Miell & MacDonald, 2000; Wiggins, 1990, 1992, 1995, 1998, 2000).

Although compositional processes seem to vary to some degree depending on the nature of the tool, task, and setting, identifying common threads among the ways students compose in classrooms should enable teachers to design and support better music instruction. Teachers need to understand how children function and make meaning in the social and musical contexts that are music classrooms. Finding a way to understand children's experiences in classrooms can teach us about how they think and learn in these settings.

Work in my own elementary music classroom and in the classrooms of others has enabled me to develop a frame for understanding children's compositional processes as they compose with their peers in a classroom setting. I call this description of children's process a *frame,* and not a model or framework, because it represents my own ways of thinking about and understanding the process. It is not my intention to propose a universal model that will hold true for all children in all situations. I share this frame, developed to reflect the processes of children whose work I have studied, in hopes that it may provide a lens through which other music teachers and researchers may better understand what children are doing when they engage in composition in a music classroom.

Roots in Research and Practice

As a practitioner who has composed with children in classrooms since 1971, most of what I know about the ways children operate when asked to compose comes from years of interacting with them during the composition process. In 1990, I began looking at children's compositional processes through the eyes of a researcher as well. I wanted to better understand the strategies and processes of successful students in order to know how to be a better teacher for those who were experiencing difficulty. I realized that, particularly when students were engaged in small-group work, my time was often spent interacting with students who were having problems, while more competent students worked on their own and, by some process unknown to me, produced successful products—successful in that they reflected the parameters of the assignment and often also in the level of cohesiveness and creativity they attained. Since the most competent and independent students did not seek teacher support, I knew very little about how they were going about their work and achieving this success. I thought that if I could learn more about the strategies of successful student composers, I would know more about how to guide those who needed my help to become successful.

Therefore, in 1990, I entered my own classroom as a teacher-researcher, collecting ethnographic data (through videotape and audiotape) in order to learn more about what students were actually doing in my music classroom as they engaged in performing, listening, and creating experiences. I analyzed the data transcribed from these tapes in an onoing process throughout the 5-month data-collection period, which meant that the collection and analysis of data interacted with my decisions as a teacher throughout the process. Consequently, what I was learning about the students' perspective nourished my understanding of my own teaching throughout the experience. Since 1990, I have continued to collect data while children are composing in classrooms where the creative process is an integral part of their learning experiences, and I have encouraged others to do the same. As the work has extended beyond my own classroom, it has done more than my original intent of informing my own practice. In the work of my own students, in work done in the classrooms of other music teachers, and in the work of other researchers, I have found similar characteristics emerging again and again. These patterns of characteristics have led me to propose this frame for understanding children's work.

The frame represents a synthesis of the themes that have emerged through formal analysis of data collected in the elementary general music classrooms of nine different teachers across 10 years, which includes the work of some of my graduate students (Wiggins, 1990, 1992, 1994, 1995, 1998, 2000; Bongiorno, 1998; Cleland, 2002; Meyers, 1996; Ogonowski, 1998). It is supported by more than 15 years of informal conversations with practitioners who teach through composition and 30 years of observing and interacting with students as they composed in classrooms. I freely acknowledge that my researcher's eye is heavily influenced by what my practical experience has taught me about the ways children compose.

The Frame

What has emerged from the data has enabled me to describe what seems to be a consistent modus operandi for students working alone in class, in small groups, and in whole-class settings to compose original vocal and instrumental music as part of a classroom assignment. On the figures representing the frame, I have placed the word *shared* in parentheses to represent both the process of individuals composing alone and the shared understanding of individuals composing collaboratively. The work processes of the students occur within layers of context, all of which impact their path and flow. The frame shows my understanding of the different phases of the students' process as it occurs within and is influenced by its various contexts. Many aspects of the frame overlap to represent the high level of interaction between or among them. This level of interaction makes it difficult to discuss the various elements in isolation, as will become apparent in the discussion that follows. We will explore the frame in layers in order to make these contexts clearer.

The Compositional Work of the Individual: Alone and Within a Group

Let us first consider the processes of individual students as they work alone or with peers to create original music (Figure 1). The compositional process has been represented by a continuous arrow because the process tends to move forward in a progressive manner toward the goal—a performance that marks the social sharing of the finished product. What takes place along the path to the goal is highly interactive and is therefore represented by interconnected circles and arrows within the large arrow. The shading of the large arrow becomes more intense as it progresses to reflect that the students' work becomes more interconnected, refined, focused, and unified as it nears completion. The last

Figure 1. Individual student processes

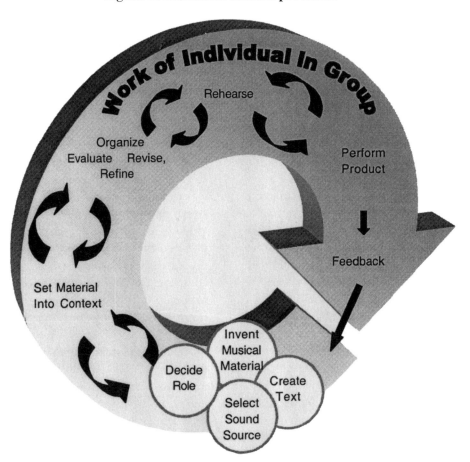

phases in the process are a public sharing of the music and feedback from people who did not create the music (peers, teachers, parents, audience, etc.). The end of the large arrow points back to the beginning of the process because experiences in each compositional project inform students' work on subsequent projects.

In my studies, I have given particular attention to how students begin their work because I have found that to be particularly informative about the nature of their understanding of the process in which they are engaged. Their beginnings tend to be quite complex, reflecting decisions that need to be made about a variety of issues before work can actually begin. These issues are represented by the interconnected circles at the base of the arrow.

Initially, the process begins with the interaction of three or four key decisions. ˜ If instruments are to be used, students need to decide (1) who will play what instrument, (2) what role that person and instrument will play in the overall design of the work, and (3) what music will be played on that instrument. In songwriting, students need to make similar decisions, but their decisions also involve (4) text issues— the subject matter of the song and the creation of lyrics. While these four issues are integrally linked, in order to understand their nature, we need to consider them separately.

Nature of Role, Defined by Group or Individual. When students compose collaboratively, one of the initial decisions is determining each individual's role in the work in progress. This decision is often personal—made by each individual. To some extent, this is an organizational decision

that is sometimes influenced by the nature of the assignment, as when the parameters of the assignment dictate form or other kinds of structure, such as texture. (Such assignments include those that ask students to create a melody and accompaniment, create a piece in ABA form, create a variation on a theme, or create a rap song and a drum track.) There are times, however, when the unfolding of the musical plan (whether determined by the teacher or the students) dictates the role of the individual, as in statements like "You be the A and I'll be the B. You guys be the background. Who wants to be the introduction?" In more open-ended assignments, students working collaboratively need to make similar decisions just to get the project moving forward. To some extent, they need to decide who will be playing what before they begin to think of musical ideas, although there are certainly instances where the invention of musical ideas precedes decisions about role.

When students collaborate, the nature of their independent work within the group is defined not only by their musical role in the piece but also by their social role in the group. That some students emerge as leaders and others as followers can sometimes affect students' role in the musical work. (This will be discussed further in the section dealing with social contexts.) More aggressive students sometimes end up with more significant parts in the piece. However, it is also quite common for students who have interesting musical ideas to emerge as leaders—even if they do not generally seek or assume such a role.

Selecting Sound Sources. Decisions about the role students will play are linked to their selection of the sound sources they will use. In instrumental composition, depending on the teacher's instructions and the classroom routine, selecting instruments sometimes precedes defining students' roles in the piece. Often students' roles are determined by their choice of instrument. Instrument choice is also often related to each individual's role in the social structure of the group or the musical structure of the work in progress (which reflects the nature of the assignment, the extent of the students' understanding of the assignment, and, more importantly, the group's and individual's conception of the overall plan of the work in progress—as will be discussed later). Inexperienced composers sometimes make many trips to the instrument shelf, making a different choice each time. This kind of exploration is not unlike the exploratory actions of a student using a synthesizer for the first time, trying out all 200 sounds. However, in my work, I have found that students who have had more experience with the instruments (especially electronic instruments) and more experience composing rarely do this. If they do, it is with definite intent—to replace a chosen instrument (or sound) with one that the group or individual has decided will be more appropriate for the work in progress, either because of the nature of the musical material or because of orchestration or balance issues resulting from their initial choices.

Text Issues. When students write songs, they often begin with the subject matter of the song or a particular part of the lyrics (e.g., the first line of the text, a catchy phrase, a lyric for the refrain). Some students write lyrics before inventing melodic material, but most experienced songwriters link the creation of text and melodic material quite early in and throughout the process. While most songwriters that I have observed begin by creating at least some of the lyrics before choosing accompanying instruments, some choose to begin with the selection of the sound sources that will be used for accompanying parts, such as percussion parts or drum tracks, bass lines, or chord progressions. It depends on the effect they are trying to create and the nature and level of their prior musical and composing experience. As with the selection of a sound source, some of these decisions might be linked to the role the individual will play in the finished product (soloist, accompanist, etc.).

Inventing Musical Material. The most complex aspect of the initial work is the invention of musical material—the motives and gestures that will be developed to create the piece. This process may be linked to the selection of instruments, the determination of students' roles in the piece, or whether the music is designed for a particular instrument or to fit song text. There are many points of entry. For example, songwriters may start with spontaneous singing of part of the text or the invention of an instrumental part that will eventually accompany or otherwise embellish the song. In instrumental composition, students may select an instrument to fit a musical idea that they wish to play. When students are very accustomed to working with particular instruments, they sometimes do not play them at all before initiating musical ideas. Some sing or chant what they want to play on an instrument before they play it. Initial invention of musical material is also linked to the role the music will be designed to fulfill. Students who are creating the introduction and coda or an accompanying part are apt to seek different instruments from those students who are developing a melodic line. In turn, the music they conceive will have a different character, relevant to the role it will play, the instrument chosen, and the text, if there is one.

The nature of students' conception and invention of their initial musical ideas has been a major focus of my research. I believe that the key to understanding the nature of their conception and invention lies in respecting the breadth and diversity of ideas they bring to the situation. In the instances I have studied, extensive evidence exists that students generate musical ideas that are conceived before they play them. All the students I have observed and recorded originated musical material in chunks—complete with all their melodic and rhythmic aspects. I have no evidence of experienced or even first-time composers building musical material note by note. Initial phases of invention are characterized by a great deal of repetition of musical ideas, reflecting that the students are creating the music aurally and, to some extent, depending on repetition to remember their ideas. When the students develop or vary these ideas, they manipulate chunks. They often refer to the larger plan while developing musical material. There is generally a kind of oscillation between independent work and work with peers during the creation and development of musical material, reflecting the students' need to hear the part within the whole. Students sometimes borrow musical material from other sources (e.g., musical ideas they have

learned in class, parts of pieces they know how to play, music learned from a family member, music from the media), but they do not always identify borrowed material as such. The nature of the musical material is also influenced by the choice of sound source or the nature of the lyrics. Evaluation occurs throughout the process— often against a shared understanding of what the final product will sound like (which will be discussed further in the section on setting material into context).

It is evident that independent work is necessary for the creation of motivic material. Even in collaborative work, conception of motivic material seems to be an individual act. Further, the creative processes of students working alone in classroom contexts seem to be very similar to those of students engaged in collaborative work. This may reflect the fact that students working alone in a classroom are still operating in a social setting and that they have had prior experience with collaborative composing, which may influence their work style.

Through the years, I have captured on audiotape and videotape numerous examples of the first music that students play or sing when they are beginning work on a compositional project in a general music class. An individual's first musical utterance is invariably a whole musical idea that has musical integrity. The student may alter the idea after its initial appearance, but the ideas are produced in chunks of sound that have an inherent logic. As part of a recent study (Wiggins, in progress), I interviewed fourth-grade students after they had worked on a particular instrumental composition project, asking them how they came up with their musical ideas when they were composing. Here are some of their responses:

- "We all knew it in our head—we just couldn't get it on to the instruments."
- "We just do stuff in our heads sometimes, and then we take an instrument and try to find it."
- "You think of an idea and then you try it again and again until you get it."
- "You pick what you want it to sound like and then pick the instruments and try to work with the instruments and try to do the best you can."
- "After you have an idea, you fiddle with it."
- "First we just created some music that we liked, and then we started to just put it together."

Student responses such as these, combined with the instances I have captured on audiotape and videotape, have convinced me that students working on specific compositional assignments in general music classrooms conceive of musical material before they play it. Once they have played their initial idea, they may reject it and replace it with another, or they may engage in a lengthy process of altering, evaluating, revising, and refining the idea. However, I have no instances in any of my data of a student trying to put an idea together by playing or singing note by note. Their ideas are always melodic or rhythmic wholes that contain affective qualities—such as accent, articulation, tempo, and sometimes dynamics—from the outset.

Some other researchers who have analyzed the compositional processes of individuals (e.g., Kratus, 1989, 1991; Stauffer, 1997,

1998; Younker, 2000) have identified a period of exploration as a first step in the compositional process. In the children's work I have studied, I have found that they do not necessarily link exploration of medium with initiation of musical ideas. Therefore, I tend to view this kind of exploration of the compositional medium to determine its capabilities as more of a precompositional act.[1]

Further, when students compose in a familiar setting (i.e., their own classroom as opposed to a research setting) and work with familiar instruments on familiar types of tasks, they do not seem to engage in many exploratory activities. I have hardly ever found student work that I would characterize as "trying out" sounds. In all of my recordings, students play or sing whole musical ideas, which may then be repeated, revised, refined, or rejected, but I would not characterize this process as one of exploration. In the context of the children's work, it sounds more like a purposeful invention of musical ideas than it does exploring. To me, exploration implies that students do not have a preconceived notion of what they will play. The data I have collected clearly show that students' invention of motivic material is intentional and purposeful, often emanating from a preconceived notion of what they want the music to sound like. Evidence of this includes (1) times when children sing or chant what they want to play before playing it, (2) times when they appear to be searching for a starting pitch which, once located, precipitates the playing of an extended, complete idea, and (3) times when they play a phrase and then say "No" and try new phrases or variations until they locate what they seem to have been looking for ("That's it! Listen to this!") and then play the idea in its entirety. This is more than exploration—which, to me, implies that students may not know what they are seeking and may "happen upon" it. In my data, I have no instances of students "happening upon" material.

Setting Material into Context. Once students have thought of a musical idea, they often begin immediately to set the idea into the context of the whole—the next step on the arrow in Figure 1. Sometimes this is done quite feverishly, and when individuals settle upon musical material that they like, they will shout to their peers something like "Come here! Let's try this! I need to try my part with yours." One can see students engaged in small-group composition pulling away from one another to develop their own personal ideas and then excitedly regrouping with some or all of the group members as soon as they have decided that their material is ready to share. This is likely to happen numerous times in the initial stages of group work (as represented by the small circular arrows within the large arrow in Figure 1).

Organizing, Evaluating, Revising, Refining, and Rehearsing. Setting musical ideas into the context of the whole involves organizing, evaluating, revising, and refining. If the product is coming together in a way that is consistent with what the group intends (their shared vision of the whole), the group will move quickly to rehearsing. It is more common, however, for the group to pass again and again through the stages of inventing new material; setting that material into the whole; and organizing, evaluating, revising, and refining until group members finally decide that the

piece has met their intent. (This process is represented in Figure 1 by small circular arrows.) Sometimes, students even return to the very earliest stages and change the sound sources or, less often, roles of individuals within the piece. They will then rehearse until they are pleased with the overall effect, sometimes going back in the cycle several more times and making revisions they feel are necessary.

Performing the Product. The project most often ends when it is time for students to perform the product for others. When work time ends because of time constraints, it is quite common for students to express that they still need time to rehearse or even to revise and refine. When it is possible to give students unlimited work time, such that they are able to decide for themselves that a product is finished, it is more likely to be completed to their satisfaction. When students are given sufficient time to work, they are generally willing to engage in repeated and extended rehearsals with extraordinary patience as they strive to make the music meet their own criteria. This reflects the meaning they attach to both the process and product. It is also important to note that, in general, from the students' perspective, once they have decided that the project is complete, they see it as a finished entity. If students were drawing this frame, they would probably choose to end the large arrow here, with the performance of the work.

Feedback. In a classroom setting, it is common for peers and teacher to provide some sort of feedback or response to students' work. This is part of using composing as a teaching tool. In my experience and in the data I have collected and studied, I have found that once students consider their products to be finished, they have little or no interest in further revision. In fact, they are often quite resistant to such suggestions. After the initial public performance of their work, they sometimes opt to make self-motivated revisions based on their self-assessment of their performance in relation to their intent (e.g., "Can we try that again? We messed up." or "Can we try it with that drum because this one is drowning everyone out?"). However, they are less likely to respond to external critiques with self-motivated revisions. Most often, what they choose to do is to carry what they have learned from one experience into subsequent experiences. This is reflected in conversations during subsequent projects in which students refer to what they or other groups have done during earlier projects. In the frame, this is represented by the large arrow pointing to a new beginning and is emphasized by the smaller arrow within it pointing to the start. For teachers, this is critical because it informs us about one of the important ways that students grow musically through engaging in compositional process.

Context of Meaning and Intent
Connections Between Motivic Material and the Whole Work

Throughout the description of the processes of the individual composer, I have alluded to students' connections between the musical material they are developing and their concept of the whole musical work in progress (Figure 2). One of the most important things I learned from my research is that the work of individuals within the group seems to take place in the con-

text of the group's collaborative vision of what the final product will be. Consistent in the data is evidence that students make all their decisions based on a shared understanding or vision of the character, structure, and intended meaning of the work in progress. When composing alone, children work from their own understanding of the nature of the music they are creating, reflecting their intent; when collaborating, they work from a shared understanding of the work in progress. Often, the music seems to take on a life and image before it actually exists. This is evident from the ways in which children talk about and evaluate their musical ideas as they compose. Their visions of the final product may shift and mutate as the process continues. When students work collaboratively, conflicts of vision and intent often produce new ideas, and the vision may not necessarily be agreed upon throughout the process. The final product may very well be a negotiated compromise or someone's ideas may be excluded. However, what is important is that students' shared vision of where they are headed provides a basis against which all decisions and evaluation are made throughout the process.

Holistic Vision of the Work in Progress

As they work, children's conversations and actions reflect a holistic vision of the work in progress. They often consider or judge ideas against the more holistic elements of the work (such as form or texture) or holistic qualities (such as mood, style, or affective intent). They generally attend to issues of simultaneity, balance, tempo, dynamics, appropriateness of sound source, and other elements that contribute

Figure 2. Context of meaning and intent

to a general sense of ensemble—often throughout their compositional work and even in the earliest phases of the process. Then, as individuals create motivic or gestural material, it is placed within the whole, usually based on the approval of some or all of the group members, with attention to the relationship among existing musical ideas and between individual musical ideas and the whole. As noted in the description of the work of the individual, evaluation occurs throughout the process—often against a shared understanding of what the final product will sound like.

Other researchers have noted the presence of broad, holistic understanding in the compositional process. In a study of problem solving and decision making in

151

professional musicians, Whitaker (1996) asked them to record *think alouds* as they worked. One composer's recording includes the following statement:

> The [composition] process goes on in my head all the time, over a long period of time. When I sit down at a piano, I'm sort of filling in details of forms and styles that have already come to mind and have already developed. (p. 5)

Younker (2000) noted that students' evaluative comments reflected their efforts to make the music sound the way they wanted it to sound. This could be interpreted to indicate that the students were evaluating their work in terms of some sort of master plan or, at least, some overriding image of the final product they were trying to produce.

Many researchers who have collected and analyzed children's spontaneous and planned musical creations note the presence of structural characteristics, which is reflective of holistic conception. In Barrett's (1996) analysis of the form and structure of 137 compositions collected from children aged 5–12, even the work of the youngest students exhibits structural characteristics, indicating a sense of the whole. Davies (1986, 1992), whose work includes similar findings for young children, considers the presence of structural organization to reflect children's holistic vision of the music they are creating and their desire to make meaning. Campbell (1998) also describes children's ability to establish structure in their invented songs. Dowling (1984) recorded young children singing the same invented song over weeks,

maintaining the same general contour but "filling in" the details differently with each repetition. Regarding compositional process, Loane (1987) suggests that "each 'momentary' act of creation is a decision which links a whole structure of other decisions, confirming some, modifying others, but above all generating an overall musical idea, which is the single outcome of the whole process" (p. 33, as cited in Burnard, 1999, p. 65). The students in Burnard's (1999) study practiced silently before performing their work. Since the students in her study did not notate their pieces, she describes their process of preservation of their work as "memorizing imagined forms" (p. 316). Their ability to remember their work and practice silently reflects the extent of their holistic conception of the structure and the extent to which that structure has been realized.

Holistic Conception and Successful Student Work

Although all the students I have studied seem to have been able to initiate musical material at the outset, not all the work I observed produced successful products. In unsuccessful compositions, the place where the process seems to break down is in students' ability to negotiate the path between the motivic material they have generated and the overall product they are trying to create. In general, they are trying to produce "real" music that will fit within their understanding of their cultural norms, fulfill the parameters of the assignment, and be valued by their peers. When students are unable to work out the details of setting their idea into their intended context, frustrations occur. At this point, students sometimes discard motivic material and start again. Interestingly, social conflicts sometimes arise out of these musical frustrations, with individual students suffering blame for the lack of forward motion on the project, even though the problems are more musical than social.

Implications for the Nature of Teacher Support

Understanding that students' lack of success often lies in their inability to fit their motivic ideas into their concept of the whole has led me to lend support to students by talking with them about the larger issues of their work before addressing specific details. Discussion of a student piece needs to start in a place that is meaningful to them, which for them includes the larger issues. They may want their music to sound scary or funny or cool, which usually means that they want it to have some sort of contemporary pop sound. They may want it to sound "real," not like "school music." They may also have visions of the way the piece will be organized—who will play what instrument or what part, which parts or instruments will play together and when, who will play the melody, and who will play the "background." Their understanding of the music of their experience may also tell them what will be acceptable melodically, rhythmically, and/or harmonically. (This will be discussed further in the section on shared understanding of the culture.)

Students are generally much more eager to discuss these larger issues than they are to discuss the specific details of their work. However, understanding their holistic perspective provides the teacher with a doorway in to discussion of details. Students'

frustration at their inability to produce something that is consistent with their vision of what they want is sometimes reported to the teacher as something like "We don't have anything." Experience has taught me to ask "Can you show me the parts that you do have?" Invariably, if they have had some time to work, they can produce quite a bit of music. Most often, the problem lies in their attempts to bring the various ideas together in a way that is consistent with their vision of what they are trying to create. Sometimes this is because of problems with the material they have developed. For example, one student may have created a melody that moves in triple meter while another group member has created an accompaniment for the melody that moves in duple. Sometimes it is a harmonic issue in which individuals have created melodic and accompaniment material that do not work well together in the students' vision of what will "sound good" (which is, of course, culturally influenced). They will be much more receptive to teacher support that enables them to work through these details if they sense that the teacher has a good understanding of their overall intent. A teacher who understands student intent is seen as an ally rather than as an outside advisor.

Implications for Designing Compositional Problems

Understanding and respecting students' holistic vision of their work and the level of meaning these holistic decisions hold for them also provides insight into how to design compositional problems that will enable students to produce the most successful products. If students tend to consider the larger elements first, then we ought to design compositional problems from a holistic perspective. In my experience, I have found that students produce much more successful products when working on assignments based on the broader structural elements of a musical work, such as form, texture, meter, harmonic progression, or when working to produce particular affective or expressive qualities. They seem to produce far less interesting work when assignments focus on specific melodic or rhythmic details. I believe the reasons for this go beyond the holistic nature of student conception of musical ideas. When people think in music, they conceive of melodic and/or rhythmic ideas holistically. They think in chunks of sound that usually include both pitch and rhythmic features—just as verbal thought takes place in chunks of verbal ideas and not in single words. Therefore, asking students to compose a piece that uses only certain pitches or rhythm patterns is like asking a student to write a story that only uses certain words, as in a typical spelling assignment. Assignments of this type do not unleash spontaneous musical or verbal thought. They are cotrived and tend to result in contrived products. If students think holistically in sound and conceive of the process of musical composition holistically, then, as teachers, we need to design compositional problems that are rooted in the more holistic elements of music. Further, understanding students' capacity for holistic conception of music should inform our ways of approaching listening and performing experiences as well. All music education needs to be approached in ways that make it most meaningful to students.

External Influences

In the students' work process, their shared understanding of the character, structure, and meaning of the work in progress is impacted by their understanding of three external influences: (1) the compositional problem, (2) the curriculum, and (3) the musical culture(s) in which they live (Figure 3). In the frame, I have represented these three influences as circles that intersect the context of meaning and intent and the social contexts because they relate to both. They are rooted in social experience, but they also directly influence the students' understanding of the work in progress.

Shared Understanding of the Compositional Problem

Students' processes and products reflect their personal or shared understanding of the compositional problem. This includes the impact of the nature of the teacher's directions and the groundwork laid prior to student work (Burnard, 1995; DeLorenzo, 1987). Shared understanding of the assignment is also affected by curricular issues, instructional-design issues, and teacher effectiveness. Understanding the parameters of the assignment and how to function within them is critical to students' success in carrying it out. For the practitioner, it is important to understand that the focus of any instructional episode is the nature of the problem that is at its heart. Since student work is strongly affected by the nature of the problem they are asked to solve and by their understanding of how to solve it, it would be wise for teachers to give serious consideration to the problems they design and the groundwork they lay to enable student work. Preparatory work for a compositional project must provide opportunities

Figure 3. Shared understandings

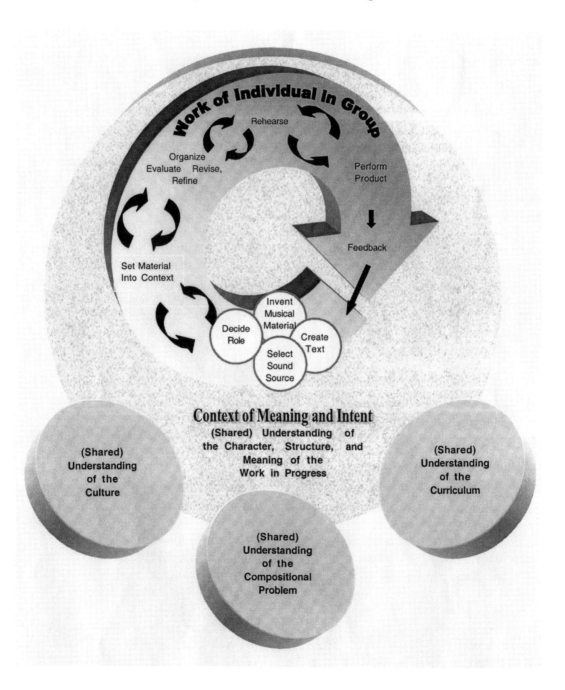

for students to develop sufficient understanding of the concepts being taught to enable them to operate with a reasonable level of independence. Although student understanding of musical concepts grows during composing experiences and they have opportunities to seek help from peers and teacher while composing, students do need to have achieved at least a basic level of independence with the concept in order to contribute to the project.

Shared Understanding of the Curriculum

Students' work also reflects their personal or shared understanding of the curriculum, which generally consists of their understanding of prior classroom music experiences. Their shared understanding of the classroom music experience is influenced by curricular issues, instructional-design issues, and teacher effectiveness. In my data, I have noted that more experienced composers bring a higher level of shared understanding to the situation as a result of their prior experience. Also, when composition assignments are linked to other music-class experiences (i.e., listening or performing experiences), students' products reflect the models they have heard or performed and the ideas they have learned.

Student work can also be influenced by curricular experiences they have outside the music classroom. Stauffer (1999) found that students' experiences playing piano and band and orchestral instruments sometimes, but not always, are reflected in their compositional work. In her study, references to non-music-curricular experiences also emerge in some of the music.

Shared Understanding of the Culture

Finally, students' work reflects their personal or shared understanding of the culture, which includes their understanding of the music of their experience and of the world in general. In my own work and that of Campbell (1995) and Marsh (1995), there is evidence that students composing together make judgments and decisions based on a mutual understanding—drawn from prior experience and cultural influences—of how such a work ought to sound. For example, in their work, students make references to the way the music "has to be" or "is supposed to be." The work of students I have studied and taught has generally been created in duple meter, following basic tenets of Western harmony—unless it is modeled on a film-score-type sound, in which case it may sound quite contemporary. Frequently, this happens with synthesizer pieces, reflecting the influence of the tool on the process and product and reflecting the students' understanding of that tool's typical role in society.

Students' products are heavily reflective of their knowledge of the songs of their musical environment, particularly when they write songs. Students' cultural knowledge of Western songs is reflected in their decisions about form (e.g., verse and refrain, with the refrain relating to the title of the song), their choice of topics for lyrics, their use of rhyme scheme, their use of instrumental introductions and bridges, the nature of their accompaniment styles, and other style characteristics that are typical of the songs of their experience (mostly with the media). Stauffer (1999) also notes the influence of electronic media in the decisions of some students she observed.

It is also important to recognize that student work draws on the musical culture of the music classroom. Students sometimes draw on the previous work of other students, or stylistic commonalities may emerge from a particular class or grade level as a result of sharing of products. Because of these experiences, students working in a classroom that has a rich history of prior improvisation and composition experiences seem to have more ideas to draw on and a much greater sense of possibility. This underscores the importance of incorporating opportunities for creating throughout the curricular experiences of children.

Social Contexts

The outermost contextual layer of students' classroom compositional experience is made up of the social influences that impact their work process (Figure 4). In order to work productively, students need to be able to operate in a *rich, safe, supportive environment* in which they are given *sufficient uninterrupted time*. These aspects of the context are created and mediated by the teacher and the school. From my own practice and from what I have observed in the classrooms of other teachers, I have learned that we need to give students enough time and space in which to think, and we need to structure work time so that we do not interrupt their thought processes while they are working.

Rich, Safe, Supportive Environment

A rich, safe, supportive environment is a classroom in which students' ideas are sought and valued. It is a classroom that belongs to the students—one in which they have a sense of ownership of the contents, materials, and curriculum. They need to feel that what takes place in that classroom is for them and about them—for their learning and about their learning. They need to feel free to explore their classroom (at appropriate times) and to believe that their own ideas, suggestions, hopes, and dreams belong there—whether they are engaged in listening, performing, or creating music. The classroom cannot be teacher-centered or performance-driven; such an atmosphere is counterproductive for students because it tends to stifle individuality and independent thinking.

Sufficient Uninterrupted Time

At a conference on creativity in general music in 1996, Peter Webster talked about the importance of time in the creative process. In his work with students who were composing in small groups, he found that there was a definite relationship between the amount of work time the students were allotted and the nature and quality of their work. His comments connected to my understanding of decisions I had made when planning curriculum. Over the years, limited by the brief time given to general music, I had learned to vary the length of time given to compositional projects. I knew that the amount of time given to a particular project would directly impact the quality and sophistication of the work my students would be able to produce. I therefore chose to determine the allotted time for a project according to the importance in my overall curriculum of the concept it was designed to teach.

When students are given enough time to carry projects through, they are able to

Figure 4. The complete frame

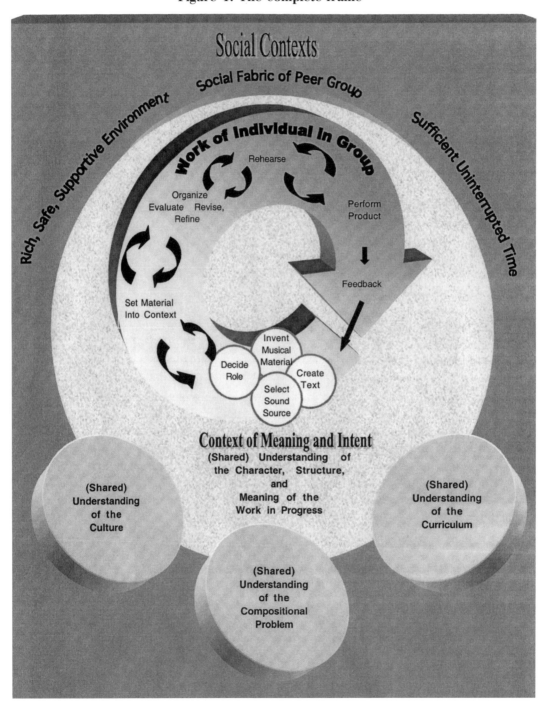

spend time considering aspects that go beyond the original parameters of the assignment and produce highly complex, successful, and meaningful work. The time and effort students spend also generate pride in their work, derived from the attention they are permitted to give their work and the extent of ownership they feel of the project and the classroom itself. In short-term projects, students are usually able to develop some original music that demonstrates their understanding of a particular concept or musical idea, but they rarely produce those moments of silence followed by spontaneous applause that occur when students create excellent musical work. In these short-term projects, composition is often used as a teaching and assessment tool and not for its own ends. In long-term projects, students have time to put more of their own ideas into the project and produce a worthy, expressive musical work that reflects more of their personal perspective. Burnard (1995) talks about freedom and constraint in students' perceptions of the task at hand and the effect that perception has on their products and processes. In her findings, part of what impacted student perception of the task was its conditions and context. Time is one of the contexts that can establish either freedom or constraint in a compositional setting.

As I thought about incorporating the element of time into this frame of the students' experience, I realized that it was not just sufficient time that was important for student productivity; the time provided must be free of interruption from teachers, peers, and the intrusions of the school schedule and environment. I therefore chose to label this context for student work *sufficient uninterrupted time*. As a practitioner, I composed with children in general music classrooms for 20 years before I first entered my classroom as a researcher. Upon entering my own classroom as a researcher, one of the first things I learned about my teaching and my students' learning was that my ever-present monitoring of their work was interfering with their ability to carry it out. As "classroom manager," I would move about the room, listening to students as they worked and offering assistance where I felt it was needed. Every so often, I would blink the room lights (our signal for quiet) so that I could monitor progress by asking group members how far along they were. I did all these things because I believed this was my job; I was supposed to monitor progress and be sure students were working and learning. When I first listened to the tapes of my students at work, I was amazed to learn that my actions were seriously interfering with students' planning and thinking. What I saw as my job was actually interrupting their thought processes and making it more difficult for them to work. When I spoke with my students about this, they smiled sheepishly. They had perceived my actions as what the teacher "was supposed to do," but they also articulated quite clearly that it would be better if I just let them work. From that day on, we agreed that I would not bother them while they worked if they would seek help if they needed it. The change in quality and intensity of work that took place once I learned to stay out of the students' way was substantial. The students I taught in the years following this first research study produced far more sophisticated compositions than any done by the students I had previously taught (See Wiggins, 2001, Chapter 11).

A byproduct of this realization was an affirmation of the importance of ensuring that students understand all the parameters of a compositional project before they begin work. If I was not going to interrupt them once they were working on their own, I needed to be sure that everyone understood all aspects of the assignment before they began. For me, this focused my attention even more on the nature of my directions and the nature of the lesson plans that laid the groundwork for compositional assignments.

Social Fabric of the Peer Group

The last component of the outermost contextual layer is the social fabric of the peer group. The nature of verbal, musical, and physical interaction that takes place within small groups or between pairs who are working together to create original musical ideas impacts both student process and product. When I speak with experienced teachers about planning small-group projects for their classes, they always express concern about the social issues that they anticipate will arise. Experience has taught me that once students become focused on the project itself and learn to value and enjoy the process of creating their own music, social issues become secondary to musical issues. In general, it takes several compositional experiences for students to begin to reach this level of valuing. In the first few projects that students attempt, it is likely that only some groups will succeed. Once students begin to see themselves as active composers, musical

considerations begin to outweigh social concerns. Unpopular or difficult students may become sought-after group members because they can create interesting drum parts. Students who have been unsuccessful working together in the past often seek out different group members in order to become successful and avoid the embarrassment of again being in the group that is unable to produce a successful piece. This hearkens back to the importance of the classroom environment. If students feel that their musical ideas are valued, they will want to succeed and will often take it upon themselves to fix social problems that interfere with their potential for success.

My work as a researcher has taught me that achieving a level of shared understanding and common purpose within the group helps students produce more successful products (Wiggins, 2000). Work in a collaborative setting includes negotiation and evaluation of ideas, which requires individuals to explain, clarify, justify, and "campaign for" their ideas. This sometimes prompts refinement of ideas to make them acceptable to the group, fitting the collaborative vision of the work. Several researchers who have studied students' collaborative compositional processes have commented on the various ways that social interaction impacts the process. Claire (1993/1994) notes connections between the nature of the social interaction and the success of the project. Kaschub (1997) speaks of the ways that student interaction impacts the revision process: "Throughout the revision process in group composition, students challenge each other's musical ideas and often new musical concepts emerge as students defend their original ideas or seek to reach compromise" (p. 15). The social fabric of the peer group also emerges as an important factor when a student composes alone because, even in noncollaborative work, students want to invent something that will be socially acceptable to their peers.

The strong influences of the social aspects of the situation speak to the importance of allowing students to choose their own work partners. In collaborative creating, the importance of familiarity among the people involved may be more important than previously realized. Miell and MacDonald (2000) studied the verbal and musical interactions of pairs of students who had identified themselves as "good friends" and those who had no particular prior relationship (non-friends) as they solved a compositional problem. They found that the nature of the interactions between friends was very different from that of non-friends and that friends seemed to maintain a higher level of mutual engagement. According to Miell and MacDonald, "Pairs of friends were significantly more likely to develop and elaborate on each other's ideas, and to ask questions of each other" (p. 357). Pairs of friends and non-friends produced similar amounts of music, but the friends did "significantly more to build on each other's musical ideas and contribute towards the development of the composition than the non-friends" (p. 361). Further, "the pairs of friends produced compositions that were rated overall as significantly better than the compositions produced by pairs of non-friends" (p. 362). Miell and MacDonald concluded that students who have a prior history are able to get to the production of musical ideas more quickly and easily because

their established shared knowledge and pattern of interacting allows them to anticipate each other's ideas, draw on experiences they have shared or previously discussed. ... Non-friends have to establish a way of working with each other before they can begin to establish a shared view of what the task is and start to compare their views about it. (p. 365)

These findings also reaffirm the importance of shared understanding in the collaborative compositional process.

Usefulness of the Frame

It should be evident from this discussion that the various elements represented in this frame are interactive on all levels. None of these processes or contexts exists in isolation, and each is strongly affected by the others. In my attempts to clarify my understanding of these processes, I have rearranged, redesigned, and reorganized the elements of this frame countless times. I am not sure that a chart on paper can ever represent such a fluid and complex process.

This frame is not intended to be a fixed model or recipe that students should be expected to follow in order to be successful. It merely represents one way to describe phenomena I have observed in the work processes of students. Its use is limited by the individuality through which people experience and understand their world and by the multiple contexts in which the compositional process can take place.

Understanding what the frame tells us about the ways students choose to proceed can help teachers address some of the issues raised at the beginning of this chapter. What kinds of compositional projects nurture and promote musical thinking and creativity? From the perspective of this frame, students flourish when they have the freedom to generate musical material without constraints on their choices of pitch, rhythm, phrase length, melody length, and so on. Freedom of choice in these aspects allows students to think melodically and rhythmically and generate spontaneous motivic material. If teachers set parameters that address broader organizational features, students are free to generate musical ideas to dwell within those structures. The same kind of spontaneity is possible when teachers set parameters concerning affective and expressive qualities. Parameters that deal with melodic and rhythmic details can inhibit spontaneous musical thought because students think in sound—not in specific pitches and rhythms.

What kinds of teacher and peer support are helpful to students? Because all of the students' work, including the invention of motivic material, is done in the context of their understanding of the work in progress, including the contexts of curriculum, culture, and meaning or intent, they are most receptive to support that is rooted in these contexts. In other words, students are more apt to understand and relate to teacher and peer help with the details of their compositions if it is presented in a way that indicates that the helper understands the big picture and the intent.

Do teachers inadvertently make choices that inhibit students or make their work process more difficult? Besides being influenced by the design of compositional problems and the nature of the support of student work, students' ability to compose in the classroom is affected by choices teach-

ers make regarding classroom environment, time allotment, social issues, and groundwork laid prior to composing (including the explanation of the project and the curricular experiences that precede it). Teachers also need to consider the children's musical-cultural experience and what kinds of experiences would be meaningful to them as a result.

The greatest usefulness of this frame, I believe, is to encourage teachers and researchers who work with student composers to (1) look at student work contextually and respect the complexity of its contextuality, (2) respect what students bring to the situation, including their musical and social expertise, (3) learn to interpret student work through the meanings that students intend, and (4) respect and value students' perspectives on their own work.

My efforts to learn more about the processes through which the students in our classrooms work to compose their own music have only increased my respect for the musical knowledge and ability children bring into our classrooms. I think that we often underestimate what our students can do. My work as a practitioner and as a researcher has also taught me to respect the power of allowing students to use music as a vehicle for personal expression and meaning-making. Doing so can transform the music classroom into a place where students actively seek, and sometimes even demand, to learn. There can be no more productive music learning environment.

Note

1. Kratus (1989) defines exploration as a time

when "sounds are tried out which are unlike previous music played earlier" and considers this activity the first step in the compositional process (p. 9). However, Stauffer (1997) points out that the student in her case study seemed to be exploring and experimenting with the software she was using, "discovering how the medium for composing worked" (p. 14). Since Kratus characterizes the students in his study as novices, inexperienced with the medium with which they compose, I suspect that these students also may be exploring and experimenting with the medium during periods he describes as exploration.

References

Bamberger, J. (1977). In search of a tune. In D. Perkins & B. Leondar. *The arts and cognition* (pp. 284–319). Baltimore: Johns Hopkins Press.

Barrett, M. (1996). Children's aesthetic decision-making. *International Journal of Music Education, 28,* 37–62.

Barrett, M. (1998a). Children composing. In B. Sundin, G. E. McPherson, & G. Folkestad (Eds.), *Children composing* (pp. 57–81). Malmö, Sweden: Malmö Academy of Music, Lund University.

Barrett, M. (1998b). Researching children's compositional processes and products: Connections to music education practice? In B. Sundin, G. E. McPherson, & G. Folkestad (Eds.), *Children composing* (pp. 10–34). Malmö, Sweden: Malmö Academy of Music, Lund University.

Bongiorno, C. A. (1998). *Experiences of third grade students in general music class.* Unpublished master's thesis, Oakland University, Rochester, Michigan.

Burnard, P. (1995). Task design and experience in composition *Research Studies in Music Education, 5,* 32–46.

Burnard, P. (1999). *Into different worlds: Children's experience of musical improvisation and composition.* Unpublished doctoral dissertation, University of Reading, Reading, United Kingdom.

Campbell, P. S. (1995). Of garage bands and song-getting: The musical development of young rock musicians. *Research Studies in Music Education, 4,* 12–20.

Campbell, P. S. (1998). *Songs in their heads: Music and its meaning in children's lives.* Oxford, England: Oxford University Press.

Claire, L. (1993/1994). The social psychology of creativity: The importance of peer social processes for students' academic and artistic creative activity in classroom contexts. *Bulletin of the Council for Research in Music Education, 119,* 21–28.

Cleland, L. (2002). *Teacher scaffolding in creative process in a music classroom.* Unpublished master's thesis, Oakland University, Rochester, Michigan.

Davies, C. (1986). Say it till a song comes. *British Journal of Music Education, 3*(3), 279–93.

Davies, C. (1992). Listen to my song: A study of songs invented by children aged 5–7 years. *British Journal of Music Education, 9*(1), 19–48.

DeLorenzo, L. C. (1987). *An exploratory field study of sixth-grade students' creative music problem solving processes in the general music class.* Unpublished doctoral dissertation, Teachers College, Columbia University, New York.

DeLorenzo, L. C. (1989). A field study of sixth-grade students' creative music problem-solving processes. *Journal of Research in Music Education, 37*(3), 188–200.

Dowling, W. J. (1984). Development of musical schemata in children's spontaneous singing. In W. R. Crozier & A. J. Chapman (Eds.), *Cognitive processes in the perception of art* (pp. 145–63). Amsterdam: Elsevier Science.

Folkestad, G., Hargreaves, D. J., & Lindström, B. (1998). Compositional strategies in computer-based music-making. *British Journal of Music Education, 15*(1), 83–97.

Hickey, M. (1995). *Quantitative and qualitative relationships between children's creative musical thinking processes and products.* Unpublished doctoral dissertation, Northwestern

University, Evanston, Illinois.

Kaschub, M. (1997). A comparison of two composer-guided large group composition projects. *Research Studies in Music Education, 8,* 15–28.

Kratus, J. K. (1989). A time analysis of the compositional processes used by children ages 7–11. *Journal of Research in Music Education, 37*(1), 5–20.

Kratus, J. (1991). Characterization of compositional strategies used by children to create a melody. *Canadian Music Educator, 33,* 95–103.

Marsh, K. (1995). Children's singing games: Composition in the playground? *Research Studies in Music Education, 4,* 2–11.

Meyers, M. A. (1996). *Improvisatory experiences in a fifth grade general music classroom.* Unpublished master's thesis, Oakland University, Rochester, Michigan.

Miell, D., & MacDonald, R. (2000). Children's creative collaborations: The importance of friendship when working together on a musical composition. *Social Development 9*(3), 348–69.

Ogonowski, C. (1998). *Quality time in the music classroom.* Unpublished master's thesis, Oakland University, Rochester, Michigan.

Stauffer, S. L. (1997, February). *Composing with computers: Meg makes music.* Paper presented at the National Symposium for Research in General Music, The University of Arizona, Tucson.

Stauffer, S. L. (1998, April). *Children as composers: Changes over time.* Paper presented at the Creativity Special Research Interest Group, Music Educators National Conference, Biennial Conference, Phoenix, AZ.

Stauffer, S. L. (1999, February). Social and cultural cues in the compositions of children and adolescents. In M. S. Barrett, G. E. McPherson, & R. Smith (Eds.), *Children and music: Developmental perspectives: Proceedings of the Second International Music Education Research Symposium* (pp. 294–98). Launceston, Tasmania: University of Tasmania.

Swanwick, K., & Tillman, J. (1986). The sequence of musical development: A study of children's composition. *British Journal of Music Education, 3*(3), 305–99.

Webster, P. (1996, September). *"Here's My Song Teacher! What Now?" Next Steps in Thinking Creatively with Music.* Presentation at the second annual symposium of the Society for General Music, Chicago.

Whitaker, N. L. (1996). A theoretical model of the musical problem solving and decision making of performers, arrangers, conductors, and composers. *Bulletin of the Council for Research in Music Education, 128,* 1–4.

Wiggins, J. H. (1990). *Case study: Musical decisions of two fifth graders.* Unpublished pilot study, University of Illinois at Urbana–Champaign.

Wiggins, J. H. (1992). *The nature of children's musical learning in the context of a music classroom.* Unpublished doctoral dissertation, University of Illinois at Urbana-Champaign.

Wiggins, J. H. (1994). Children's strategies for solving compositional problems with peers. *Journal of Research in Music Education, 42*(3), 232–52.

Wiggins, J. H. (1995). Building structural understanding: Sam's story. *The Quarterly Journal of Music Teaching and Learning, 6*(3), 57–75.

Wiggins, J. H. (1998, May). *Recurring themes: Same compositional strategies—different settings.* Paper presented at the Southeastern Music Education Symposium, Athens, GA.

Wiggins, J. H. (2000). The nature of shared musical understanding and its role in empowering independent musical thinking. *Bulletin of the Council for Research in Music Education, 143,* 65–90.

Wiggins, J. (2001). *Teaching for musical understanding.* New York: McGraw-Hill.

Wiggins, J. (in progress). *Preliminary analysis of data collected in a fourth grade general class.*

Unpublished data analysis.

Younker, B. (2000). Thought processes and strategies of students engaged in music composition. *Research Studies in Music Education, 14,* 24–39.

Younker, B. A., & Smith, W. H. (1996). Comparing and modeling musical thought processes of expert and novice composers. *Bulletin of the Council for Research in Music Education, 128,* 25–36.

Jackie Wiggins is professor of music education at Oakland University in Rochester, Michigan. Known for her work in children's musical creative process, technology, and constructivist teaching and learning, she has been an active clinician, presenter, and author in local, national, and international settings. She holds two degrees in music education from Queens College, CUNY, and a doctorate in music education from the University of Illinois.

8

The African Drum: The Compositional Process as Discourse and Interaction in a School Context

Magne Espeland

In the following vignette, a student is taking part in an event that is important to him. He is about to show his parents, family, and classmates his part in the final musical outcome of a school project in which the class has dramatized fairy tales and composed an overture for each play:

> From his position in the small orchestra, 10-year-old Helge takes a quick look at the audience. His family is there. He can see his little brother eagerly talking to his best friend. He is pretty sure they are talking about him and his drum—the big African one that he can barely manage to hold in his lap and which he is about to use to play his part. It is his group's turn to play its own composed overture and perform the play *The Little Red Hen*, which they have been working on for some time.
>
> Composing was quite difficult this time. There were so many ideas and strong opinions—and they had to accomplish everything in 60 minutes! How could Mrs. L. put such a group

together? He knew at the outset that with Lisa, Sigrun, and Irene in his group it was going to be difficult. Strange, however, that he put so much effort into getting the big xylophone as his instrument in the beginning. Now, having the African drum seemed much better, and he had to admit that Sigrun's opening part on the big xylophone was quite catchy. Some of the other groups wanted to know how she had made that up. But, never mind, his drum part had become really important, too. After Mrs. L. had listened to them the first time, he got a big solo part! He had to make sure to be ready for that one now. Ah, here we go. (Vignette 1)

Helge enjoyed this performance and remembered it with joy. I was not present during the composing process, but I studied the overture and a videotape of the whole composition process along with a number of similar processes. As I examined the videotape from the performance and interviewed Helge, what struck me most is how proud he was. At the time of the performance, I was uncertain about how much Helge enjoyed the whole *process* of composing the overture, including the ongoing interactions that took place during this process. I also wondered whether he recognized the musical ideas of the overture as *his* and whether he would be able to compose something like this on his own. The actions and decisions during the processes of classroom composition are very often concealed from observers— be they audience members, teachers, or researchers— who only listen to the final outcome.

This chapter is about compositional processes in a school context. Based on my own research on the compositional processes of small groups of 9–11-year-old children in Norwegian schools and a review of relevant literature, I will discuss some basic aspects of compositional processes in a school context. I will commence by looking at some conflicting views in research and, from this starting point, suggest a model for understanding compositional processes in schools. Toward the end of the chapter, I will discuss how research into composition can be made relevant to music education practice. The questions that I will attempt to answer include the following:

- In what ways do compositional processes in a school context develop, and how are these processes structured?
- In what ways do musical compositions emerge in such a context?
- What are the connections between the musical piece being created and the context of its creation?
- In what ways do the musical and the social interact when children compose?

Composing in Schools: The Need for a Shift in Research Focus

In a 1998 chapter on his own pioneering research into Swedish children's musical creativity in the 1960s, Bertil Sundin expresses a deep concern about contemporary research on children's composing. Coming from the tradition of educational progressivism, Sundin more than 40 years ago rebelled against research that focused upon what he calls a "normative adult-oriented perspective." He states:

> This discussion continues today. The various opinions are dependent upon several factors: whether product or process is emphasized; whether childhood is seen as a special culture or just as a precursor to adulthood; what is counted as music and what is not; what criteria are used for categorizing and assessing the products, and so on. (1998, p.37)

Referring to Pond's 1981 research on composing, Sundin (1998) reminds us that children work hard to make the world, including the world of music, meaningful. Sundin says, "perhaps they [children] cannot make much meaning out of creativity studies conducted in non-natural settings with highly specific tasks which severely limit their own imagination and also their choices" (p. 53). Sundin argues for shifting the research to a focus on children's interactions in natural settings, commenting that such a direction "might lead to an abandonment of the traditional but artificial dichotomy between process and product" (p. 54).

In my view, the dichotomy between process and product is a result of the concentration of research in music education within the narrow frames of the so-called cognitive revolution, which focuses on development studies and music as cognition (e.g., Hargreaves & Zimmerman, 1992; Serafine, 1988; Swanwick, 1988). In this tradition, there seems to be little emphasis on the importance of situation, process, context, and culture. In a recent survey on research on children's composing, Barrett (1998b) suggests that this research is in its beginnings and that "a number of conflicting views of children's capacities to engage in compositional experience have emerged from the research findings, suggesting that we have still much to learn from the study of children's compositional processes and products" (p. 30). The conflicting views referred to by Barrett have to do with what children are able to *do* musically at different ages and what they are able to *think* about music and composition. Today, we witness an interesting development in the wake of what is called the second wave of the cognitive revolution. Many researchers consider this development to constitute a major shift in the focus of educational research. DeCorte, Greer, and Vershaffel (1996) describe this change as a shift

> from a concentration on the individual to a concern for social and cultural fators [*sic*]; from "cold" to "hot" cognition; from the laboratory to the classroom as the arena for research; and from technically to humanistically grounded metholologies [*sic*] and interpretative approaches. (p. 491)

In the second wave of the cognitive revolution, the situated perspective and the importance of accounting for human sociocultural actions seem to dominate the discussion of thinking, understanding, and learning in a number of research communities. The renewed concern with the situatedness of experience has stimulated the general discussion about such issues as the relationship between the individual and the context, the relationship between the universal and the particular, and the very characteristics of knowledge and learning (Engeström, Miettinen, & Pukamäki, 1999; Lave & Wenger, 1991; van Manen, 1990; Wenger, 1998; Wertsch, 1998).[1] My approach to researching music composition in schools attempts to view this important aspect of music education from a perspective that is focused on activity and learning, as suggested by these writers.

Compositional Processes in Society and in Schools

Sigrun's opening melody really is a good one! As Sigrun plays, Helge recalls how flattered he felt at the beginning of their composition work when Irene and Sigrun asked him to tell them how they were going to compose the piece. He really had tried to explain, but they caught him by surprise. Suddenly, they ran out of the circle to choose their instruments, and, of course, they headed for the big xylophone. He was too slow, and Martin was even slower. When Sigrun suggested that Helge could play the triangle, he really got mad! He decided to stay out of it then. If it had not been for Irene offering him her African drum he probably would have complained to Mrs. L.

Irene was playing the small xylophone right now—he did not quite remember who found that melody or when. Irene was very able. Now is Irene's duet with Martin. Martin would never have been able to do it if it had not been for Irene playing with him and his own whispering as he played.

Helge's own part was rather boring to begin with, but then he had added the stuff with the drum brush, which really made it something. He still remembered Irene's and Lisa's eager nodding when he improvised that. It's his turn now. (Vignette 2)

In the above scenario, Helge is performing his composition for his parents and friends as a member of a group at school. As we will learn later, he has moved through a process of composition that involved conflicts to a full acceptance of his role as composer and performer. This seems in many ways to be different from the situation of a real composer in modern society. Modern composers traditionally work alone and let others perform their creations.

In *The Musical Mind,* Sloboda (1985) puts forth a model for analyzing the compositional processes of composers. He suggests that the compositional process is a four-part structure where the main elements are: (a) the holistic concept of the creation itself, (b) the thematic idea or core, (c) the development of this idea into an intermediate form, and (d) the final form. Sloboda ascribes inspiration to Phase b in this model; development, extension, and change of the emerging piece can be located between Phases b and c; and evaluation and modification of the piece

between Phases c and d. Sloboda's model thus focuses strongly on structure, the musical product, and the composer's artistic decisions about the emerging piece.

The compositional processes of students in schools should be viewed as arenas for artistic and aesthetic decision making (Barrett, 1996). I suggest, however, a model for understanding composing in a school context that includes a much stronger emphasis on student-composer actions and how these actions are related to one another, to the students, and to other elements of the music classroom. Indeed, if musical creations are primarily a result of human action, then it can be argued that human action should be the basic phenomenon to analyze in schools, as well as in society (van Manen, 1990).

This *actional view* is the basis for Wertsch's (1998) method of sociocultural analysis. According to Wertsch, the task of this sociocultural approach is to "explicate the relationships between human action, on the one hand, and the cultural, institutional and historical contexts in which this action occurs, on the other" (p. 24). In this approach, the action is *mediated action,* which can be defined as action that is influenced by agents (i.e., those who are acting) and their cultural tools—both of which are the mediators of action. Focusing on agents and their cultural tools gives the relationship between agent and instrumentality a privileged position. Wertsch states:

> It forces us to go beyond the individual agent when trying to understand the forces that shape human action ... the point is that even when one focuses primarily on the individual agent's role in

mediated action, the fact that cultural tools are involved means that the socio-cultural embeddedness of the action is always built into one's analysis. (p. 24–25)

Wertsch (1998) relies heavily on the writings of Kenneth Burke. The notion of human action as the basic phenomenon to be analyzed is, according to Wertsch, the very link between Burke's ideas and those of such figures as Vygotsky, Bahktin, Mead, and Wertsch himself. Wertsch maintains:

Although there are important differences among these figures, at a general level they all took human action to be their fundamental unit of analysis. In all cases they were primarily concerned with describing, interpreting, or explaining action, as opposed to some other phenomenon such as behaviour, mental or linguistic structure, or attitudes.(p. 12)

My point here is to suggest that, in order to understand research on composition in schools, we must be conscious of the different perspectives of researchers and which aspects of composition have been researched and which have not. Readers should therefore be aware that when I suggest a model for understanding compositional processes in a school context, it is based on observation and analysis through sociocultural lenses.

Toward a Model for Understanding Compositional Processes

Observing and listening to Helge as an active and concentrated co-performer of his group's overture to *The Little Red Hen*

give some, albeit limited, insight into the story behind the work. Being in the audience or watching a video of the event reveals that Helge plays a very visible and audible solo part on the African drum and that he performs with a good sense of time and pulse. Viewing the performance, however, does not tell us why he plays the drum rather than a different instrument or why his solo is in the middle of the piece rather than at the opening. In other words, we lack knowledge of connections between the piece and its creation. To learn more, we need to observe, examine, and understand the discourse, actions, and events that took place during the compositional process.

I suggest that a compositional process and the outcomes of such a process can be best understood and analyzed when *compositional actions, personal actions,* and the interactions between these are considered basic components of the process, as in Figure 1.

The interactions between personal and compositional actions bring about many kinds of outcomes. The outcome we are most concerned with here is the musical piece itself. When a small group composes music, we find the most important hidden knowledge about the piece and its creation in the dynamic relationship of personal actions and compositional actions. The dynamic character of this relationship is indicated by the zigzag arrow in Figure 1.

Compositional actions focus directly on the creation of the musical piece. Such actions could include the following:

- experimenting with musical sounds and ways of producing sound
- applying perceived or invented methods

Figure 1. Basic components of the compositional process

and strategies
- inventing musical ideas
- planning and structuring the work and the piece
- trying out parts of the piece
- revising ideas and structures
- expanding rhythms, melodies, and sounds
- appropriating parts and the whole piece
- performing the whole piece
- leading collective development and competence.

Personal actions focus on a person's social role or intention. These actions may or may not be motivated by the creative tasks at hand, but they can be vital to the outcome of such creative tasks. Personal actions can include the following:

- positioning oneself or others in relation to something
- negotiating ideas and personal roles
- procrastinating
- being passive or active
- participating in discourse with peers and teacher
- cooperating with peers and teacher
- opposing peers and teacher
- counteracting compositional actions.

It is not my intention to argue that there are clear lines between personal and compositional actions, but I do believe that the two types of action are fundamentally different. The relationship between them is dynamic, and it influences the entire composing process. It is, for example, evident that Helge's role in the performance of the overture arose from the interactions between compositional and personal actions that took place as the group composed together. Some of these interactions greatly influenced the final outcome.

Vignette 1 revealed that Helge was too slow to get the musical instrument he wanted—the big xylophone. His next priority, it seems, is the African drum:

> Helge is leaning toward the piano looking at the others.
>
> Irene asks, "Which instrument do you want, Helge?"
>
> "Well … nothing," Helge says slowly while touching the keys of the piano.
>
> "But what do you want to play?" Irene repeats, more impatient now. It is evident that Irene understands that they will get no further until they have solved the problem of Helge's choice of instrument. Helge seems rather depressed and

unwilling to contribute.

Irene says, "We have to begin now. Take the guitar!"

Helge responds, "That is not the sort of guitar we can use in this piece."

Sigrun says, "Go and find a triangle then."

"Or you could take this," Lisa points impatiently to the piano.

"Piano? We cannot bring the piano along," Helge retorts.

"Ooh, choose something." Irene balances herself on the African drum. "We have to get going. Come on!"

"We're never gonna make it!" Lisa shouts in despair.

"Ok!" Irene is shouting too now. "Take this drum then. I will use this one," she mumbles to herself as she picks up the soprano xylophone.

Helge walks slowly and seemingly reluctantly over to the African drum while gesticulating with his arms. He sits down slowly, saying nothing.

"Now we have to cooperate!" says Irene, followed by a loud "Yes!" from Lisa and Sigrun, and all the students get ready to play their instruments. (Video Transcription 1)

The episode above occurred after 20 minutes of group work in which an important compositional action had been "planning and structuring the piece." Helge's personal action with regard to the instrument he wants counteracts the ongoing compositional action of planning. Irene, however, initiates another compositional action that can be categorized as "planning and structuring the *work*." Her initiative brings the constructive compositional

action back on track and leads to another compositional action that we could label "trying out parts of the piece." As Helge succeeds in obtaining the African drum, he is now placed in a position with the potential for controlling and producing music on an instrument that obviously is attractive to other members of the group. This is seemingly a good starting point for influencing the final outcome. However, this is not what happens. Helge's initial position as a *knower* of how to compose is weakened as a result of his personal action, while Irene's position is strengthened.

The short glimpse of the process shown in Video Transcription 1 also illustrates another component in the model, that of the *means*—sometimes referred to by theorists as "cultural tools," "instrumentality," or "artefacts" (Engeström, 1999, p. 30; Wertsch, 1998, p. 24). In this discussion of Helge's group's composing process, the use of the term *instrument* to signify means is appropriate because the group is composing instrumental music. My use of the term *instrument* includes material aspects (e.g., a musical instrument) and nonmaterial aspects (e.g., language).

The episode in which Helge obtains the African drum clearly shows the interactions and tension involved in the relationship between actions and instrument (see Video Transcription 1). This tension can sometimes be observed in verbal and nonverbal discourse (e.g., when Helge, even after he has gained access to the drum, expresses his feelings through gesticulation and slow movements). This episode shows how actions are mediated in that the instrument is involved in the actions and thereby becomes important to the compositional process and its outcomes. This relationship is indicated by the double-pointed arrows in Figure 2.

In addition to being willing to sacrifice personal gain—her possession of the drum—Irene is also able to perform well and to create ideas. She demonstrates this skill when the group engages in another compositional action, "trying out parts of the piece." This "trying out" action is in many ways a musical *outcome,* even if it is a preliminary one. As a preliminary outcome, it influences the interactions and the future personal and compositional actions. A compositional process is made up of a number of recurring processes defined by the ongoing interaction of outcomes and compositional and personal actions, as illustrated by the large arrow at the top of Figure 2.

The Question of Context

The African drum, which seemed to fascinate several of the children, is an influential part of the mediated actions of the

compositional process of Helge's group. The African drum is also an important part of the *relevant context* for the composition process. Sometimes sociocultural theory of mediated action is criticized on the grounds that it seems problematic when used to understand *context.* The essence of this critique is that the theory fails to account for the *whole* context of the human process being researched (Engeström & Miettinen, 1999). In my view, not any kind of context is always relevant—as the proponents of activity theory seem to suggest. In order to be important, the context has to be sufficiently relevant to the phenomenon being analyzed. Relevant context for composing in schools has a special relationship to music, to music education, and to learning. Such context can be of different kinds and exist on a macro, meso, or micro level (Bresler, 1998). According to Erickson and Schultz (1997), "contexts are not given, they are mutually constituted, constantly shifting, situation definitions that are accomplished through the interactional

Figure 2. The relationship of actions, instrument, and outcomes

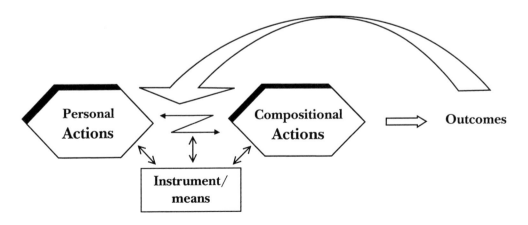

work of the participants" (p. 6).

Even if I agree that dynamism, interaction, and shifting characterize the relevant contexts for composition in schools, some contextual elements—such as teacher input and the organization of the classroom—can be quite static. In many cases, classrooms and schools are stable environments. Having said that, there is no doubt that context might change considerably during a compositional process in a classroom—for instance, when teacher input leads to a change in the students' choice of musical instruments. Relevant context for a compositional process in a school might include the following:

- teacher input (e.g., established methods and strategies, teacher instructions and assignments, and teacher expectations)
- student perceptions of teacher input
- student habitus[2]
- participants' sense of time.

Several of these elements are of vital importance when we try to explain the characteristics of compositional processes and, consequently, of the piece being created. In the compositional process of Helge's group, relevant contextual elements may include the following:

- aspects of the "situation" (e.g., composition in a small group within a time span of 60 minutes, the room and instruments available, the video camera)
- aspects of teacher input (e.g., the assignment itself, teacher visits during the process, the student perceptions of methods and strategies)
- aspects of the student habitus (e.g., previous experience)
- aspects of the students' sense of time available during the process (e.g., when they realize they have to finish in 15 minutes).

Even if it is possible to say *when* a particular contextual element can be observed, the relation and position of context in the compositional process is different from the relationship between actions. There is no doubt that relevant contexts continually influence actions and interactions. Sense of time, for example, is often underestimated when explaining compositional processes and products. When observing Helge and his classmates, I noticed recurrent references to the limitations of time and observed how this awareness sped up the number of compositional actions. In our model, the relationship between context and actions is illustrated by the double-pointed arrows linking context, actions, and instrument in Figure 3.

One contextual element important to the compositional actions of Helge's group proved to be "student perceptions of teacher input." Even though the teacher explained and had prepared a written assignment with a number of suggestions, the children seemed to interpret their task quite narrowly. The assignment looked like this:

> Compose a piece of music that should be an introduction to your fairy tale. We can call it an "Overture." The piece should be no more than 2 minutes long. You can choose your instruments freely, but the music should suit the fairy tale. What is new today is to try and create a composition with several melodies in it. Suggestions:

■ You could start with text (words, sentences, title, dialogue).

■ Write a melody that moves upward or downward, step by step, or by jumping; repetition is also important; try using repetition of phrases.

■ You can make melodies as question/answer.

■ The pentatonic scale is easy to use if you want accompaniment, but you can use any notes.

Special advice: Discuss what texts could be your starting point. Try making small melodies and put them together. If you like, write them down in some way so you can remember. Use instruments you feel are suitable. Remember to make a composition that is interesting to listen to. Practice before performing. (my translation)

Now let us observe some of the group's interpretation of that assignment. In the beginning, the group turned to Helge and asked for his advice:

Sigrun says, "How are we going to make this? Helge, you know how to do this."

Lisa adds, "Yes, Helge, you know this."

Helge clears his throat, "Let's see, let's see, let's see. What we need is to get something fitting in with the text, … but you do understand that, … the question is what, and then we have to think about what fits."

The others say, "Yes."

"Who will mow the corn, who will mow the corn?" Irene chants rhythmical-ly while Lisa chants, "The little red hen, the little red hen."

Irene says, "Martin—you have to join in too."

Martin hesitates, "Me? I don't know what to say." (Video Transcription 2)

When creating melodies later on, the students followed the idea of starting with the text and then using it as the rhythmic foundation for melody making. They even started using the text to decide questions about the form and structure of the piece and the progression and relationship between the rhythms and melodies before they had played a single note. This technique is only suggested as one of many possibilities in the assignment, but it comes through very strongly in Helge's initial interpretation as well as throughout the process, probably because they were used to working in this way in class. This did change considerably during the process; however, "student perceptions of teacher input" remained a very strong influence.

Outcomes

When listening to the final outcome, an awareness of the student perception of teacher input and its relation to actions in the compositional process is crucial to understanding what hides behind the composition itself. Viewing outcomes as part of the compositional process reveals that contextual elements (e.g., student perceptions of a teacher-directed performance) can change as a result of performing. Helge's evaluation of the whole composition project as enjoyable seems to stem from his pleasure in performing for an audience (Vignette 1). His somewhat mixed feelings

Figure 3. A model for understanding the composition process in a school context

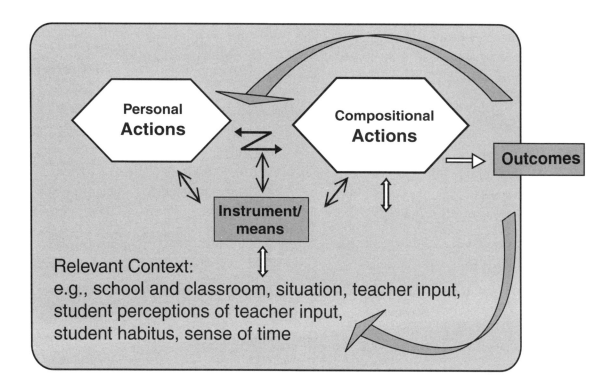

during the early part of the composition process seemed to give way to pride during and after the performance. As a result, his compositional habitus could be changed with regard to future compositional processes. In Figure 3, the arrow linking outcomes and relevant context illustrates this relationship.

Relational and Circular Activity

The dynamic relationship of actions, outcomes, and contextual elements suggests that compositional processes in schools are highly relational and circular by nature. This dynamic relationship creates a kind of circulation that drives the process. It is most evident when we examine composition in small groups, but I believe it is also highly relevant for individual composing in a school context. This suggestion, however, might be more acceptable after we have more closely examined some of the phenomena taking place in this web of relations and actions.

Significant Events in the Compositional Process

As he was waiting for his next part and listening to Lisa, who was playing in the repetition, Helge suddenly realized that Lisa had come up with most of the ideas for melodies on her glockenspiel, except for Sigrun's and his own of course. Lisa's ideas of who should play at the same time and when to come in with the new parts were good too, even if he did not realize that at first.

But the solo part was his—even if Mrs. L. had made it possible by suggesting that they repeat it all and then have

a Coda. There was no time for other solutions by then. No one protested when she suggested Helge could make a "bridge," as she called it, to the repetition. Some kind of bridge! Helge smiled to himself. Coda and all together now! (Vignette 3)

Within the intricate web of relations and actions in a compositional process, it is possible to identify some *significant events*— events that are more important than others. These events have an impact on whether the group members successfully produce a composition together. Significant events can be constructive or destructive. Such events can include the following:

- *Breakthroughs*
  - when a convincing musical or structural idea comes forward
  - when the performing of parts or the whole piece works well
- *Focus Episodes*
  - a period of intense collective focus on moving on
  - a period of peer teaching and leadership from a competent participant
  - a period of constructive student-teacher dialogue
- *Blockages*
  - when no ideas are around
  - when no one sees any solutions to a problem
  - when personal actions hurt someone
  - when compositional actions are counteracted by a personal action.

The episode describing how Helge got the African drum (Video Transcription 1) is an example of a *focus episode*. Irene is leading and controlling this episode, and she shows competence as a participant in a group when she gives Helge the drum. At the same time, this episode nearly becomes a *blockage* through Helge's personal action of refusing to move forward until he has the drum. A *breakthrough* can be observed in the following incident:

> They try again from the beginning. Martin comes in at the right place, but stops, saying "No, it doesn't …"
>
> "Yeeeeeeeeeeeessss!" Lisa cries out. "We have to play it together or it won't be music."
>
> In the meantime, Irene tries an alternative melody for Martin's part, seemingly just in case Martin will not be able to play his rhythm. Then, Sigrun asks Martin to join in with the rhythm on Irene's alternative motif.
>
> Then Lisa, gesticulating, suddenly says, "The two of you [Irene and Martin] can do this [play the motif] all the time, and then, then, then," very eagerly now, "when you have started, then Helge can come in with his part … and then Sigrun and I can come in again and then," shouting now, "we can change back and forth!" (Video Transcription 3)

Lisa, with some help from the other two girls, is sketching the structure of an important part of the composition. This idea can easily be identified in the finished composition; therefore, Lisa's activity here is quite clearly a breakthrough. What is interesting to notice is that this breakthrough and the artistic and aesthetic decisions that go with it seem to result from the interaction of compositional actions and Martin's personal action of withdrawing and being passive.

Focus episodes can also involve the teacher. I have already pointed out that teacher input and student perceptions of teacher input are very important parts of the relevant context. The teacher can also be an important part of a focus episode, especially with regard to solving a personal or compositional problem or being part of a constructive student-teacher dialogue. There is no doubt that this is the role of the teacher in the following episode:

> "Should we only be repeating and repeating here?" Lisa asks.
>
> "What you can do," Mrs. L. answers, "is to keep what you have got, because that is a very nice part—"
>
> "And how can it end then …," Lisa interrupts.
>
> "And then," Mrs. L. continues, "you can play it twice or three times."
>
> "Two!" Lisa and Irene call out together.
>
> "And then you can find a new small part to end it with."
>
> "Yes," the two girls chant together.
>
> "For instance a Coda … and then," Mrs. L. ends her counseling, "you, Helge, could do the interplay as a drum solo. Would that be Ok?"
>
> Helge nods his head.
>
> Then there is some discussion about the Coda. Everybody searches for a suitable melody for this part for a while. "I don't know how to do it," says Irene, but then Lisa comes up with a melody on the glockenspiel and Sigrun joins in singing it.
>
> "Maybe everyone can play that melody together as an ending," Mrs. L.

says, "because there isn't more time."
(Video Transcription 4)

It is important to know that the group was having a compositional problem when Mrs. L. entered the scene. The students did not know how to finish their composition. There was a blockage. The teacher's guidance solves this problem, and the two girls who have been most active in the preceding compositional actions support her suggestion. Seemingly unknowingly, the teacher also restores Helge to a stronger position in the group, probably not for a social reason, but for a musical one, as Helge is in possession of an instrument well suited for a solo and interplay. During this focus episode, teacher input becomes more than an underlying element. She enters the web of interaction through a compositional action of leading the group toward a better outcome. This is, in my view, a classical example of what Vygotsky (1934/1986) calls the *zone of proximal development,* which, put simply, is the difference between what a learner can do independently and what can be accomplished with scaffolding from others who are more knowledgeable.

Focus episodes and breakthroughs can be vital to a successful compositional process, just as blockages can be damaging or can slow the process down. To understand the nature of such a process, however, it is not enough to analyze the actions, instrument, relevant context, focus events, breakthroughs, and blockages. It is also necessary to understand some of the underlying and seemingly hidden aspects of the process that are operating whenever human beings are involved in the production of knowledge. These aspects have to do with authority, legitimacy, and power relations.

Power and Knowledge in the Composition Process

Composing in schools operates primarily within the broad concepts of learning and education, but composing is clearly also the production of knowledge. The process and the final outcomes are expressions of children's knowledge that can be observed, appreciated, and discussed (Reimer, 1992b). In a 2000 study on music teacher practice, Krüger maintains:

> What seem to be simple acts of classroom practice in fact contain certain profound and complex principles of authority, legitimacy, and power relations … power/knowledge aspects are implicit in the ways authority relationships are constituted, in the way positions are established with regard to who should regulate the discursive space, and in ways of communication and negotiating. (p. 178)

Krüger (2000) builds his analysis on Michel Foucault's theory of power and knowledge. Some basic ideas in Foucault's theory link power quite closely to knowledge. According to Foucault (1980), there is a close relationship between certain aspects of power and the development and production of knowledge. Knowledge is the basis for power, and power produces knowledge—these two cannot be studied separately (see Ball, 1990; Marshall, 1996).

Power relations and their connection to knowledge can easily be identified in the composition process, and it is apparent in other fields of education (see Espeland, 1998–1999). The relationship is most obvious if we take a closer look at group leadership, peer teaching, and participation. These issues will directly or indirectly determine the speed of actions and events in the process and, consequently, will affect the outcome—the piece of music. The following incident depicts a power relation that influences the compositional process:

"Then we have to [play] 'no, not me, no, not me,'" Irene says and leans over to the African drum, playing the rhythm of the text on the drum with her beater. "You have to take this part, Helge."

"I don't want to play that!" Helge answers back.

"Ok, then Martin can play it," Irene continues and looks at Martin. She has moved closer to the two boys. Irene plays the "no, not me, no, not me" rhythm on Martin's hand drum and then moves back to her place in the ring.

"Martin, can I borrow your drum?" Sigrun says suddenly, and Martin gives her the hand drum. Everyone is playing a little bit now. Irene looks at Sigrun and plays the "no, not me" rhythm with her beater on the floor. Helge has turned away from the rest of the group, seemingly quite uninterested in what is going on.

"I think you can do like this Martin," Sigrun demonstrates Irene's rhythm. "Three times and not very hard," she says, handing back the drum.

"In the middle of the drum?" Martin asks for confirmation.

"Yes," Irene says, "you have to play it two times."

"Two times?" Martin asks again and then does as he's told.

"That's it," Irene says, "a little softer."

"You must stop complaining," Irene turns towards Helge.

"Complaining?" Helge retorts.

"Come on Martin, play it," Irene says, and Martin tries.

"Two times?" he says.

"Yeeees!" Lisa shouts. She has been watching with increasing impatience.

"Let's try everything again … and then you have to be ready," Sigrun says to Martin.

Helge ignores it and does something for himself. "Never mind him," Sigrun mumbles and starts playing. (Video Transcription 5)

In this episode, Irene tries to exert leadership. She acts according to a plan, and Helge is the only one not accepting her leadership. The others accept and support it, even though Martin seems a little confused and uncomfortable as he is sort of stuck in between the power exchanges of Irene and Helge.

The situation is not a happy one. In fact, Lisa finds it frustrating. It is easy to point to Helge as the villain here because he refuses to be directed, but, in the beginning of the process, Helge was looked at by the others as the *knower* of composing (Video Transcription 2). Irene is so eager to make progress that she invades his territory by playing on his instrument a rhythm that he does not want to play.

The importance of power in this act of producing knowledge (i.e., creating a piece of music) can be seen primarily in the relationship between Irene and Helge. It can only be understood, however, if we look beyond this particular event. The dynamics of this relationship to a great extent define what does and does not happen. Helge resists the invasion of Irene's rhythm and is happy to play something very different in the final outcome. The power relation between Helge and Irene in this episode prevents efficient peer teaching from taking place with regard to Helge. Peer teaching can be observed recurrently in compositional processes, but it is a delicate thing, because personal actions can prevent it from happening. Even in the rather tense atmosphere of this episode, however, peer teaching takes place between Sigrun and Martin.

Participation

The episode in Video Transcription 5 also illustrates certain aspects of learning and composing as *participation*. In viewing the episode above as a process of learning, it is evident that some children are participating more fully than others and that one participant, Helge, is at times quite peripheral to the compositional actions. Lave and Wenger build their learning theory around the concept of *legitimate peripheral participation* (LPP) (Lave & Wenger, 1991; Wenger, 1998). They suggest that learning is a process of participation in communities of practice; such participation is at first legitimately peripheral, but it increases gradually in engagement and complexity. Lave and Wenger (1991) explain the relationship between LPP and power:

> Furthermore, legitimate peripherality is
> a complex notion, implicated in social

structures involving relations of power. As a place in which one moves toward more-intensive participation, peripherality is an empowering position. As a place in which one is kept from participating more fully—often legitimately, from the broader perspective of society at large,— it is a disempowering position. (p. 36)

It is possible to regard Helge's travel through this process of composition as a move toward different levels of participation in the making of a composition, but it is certainly not an even, quiet, one-way journey. Rather, it can be described as a movement in opposite directions, from full participation in the beginning, to very peripheral participation at certain times in the middle of the process, to full participation again toward the end of the process and in the performance of the final outcome. In this particular compositional process, a power/knowledge connection to Helge and his relationship to the African drum can explain this journey and a number of the other interactions.

Process and Product Revisited

The overture to *The Little Red Hen* for parents and family was a successful performance of what can be considered a stand-alone piece of music. As a composition, it can be subjected to analysis and speculation about the composers' cognitive processes, such as their musical and aesthetic thinking and decision making; their ability to deal with form, structure, melody, rhythm, closures, and personal expression; and their use of compositional strategies. However, such an analysis of a piece of music that intends to give reasonable answers without a deep understanding of the compositional process would be a bold venture.

Looked at through musicological lenses, this overture can be described in a musically accurate way. It is very likely, however, that *my* description will be colored by my knowledge of the process behind the composition. When I describe the overture, I *can* respond to it musicologically, but I find it very hard to say something about the cognitive processes of the composers that is more than speculation without relying heavily on my knowledge of the process. I am not saying that such speculation is not worthwhile or that it is uninteresting or irrelevant to the creation of knowledge about children as composers. What I *do* question is to what extent knowledge that is primarily based on the analysis of children's compositions is useful to the *practice* of composing in schools. To me, knowledge about children's mediated actions in a composition process and the way they interrelate with relevant context is far more relevant to compositional practice in schools.

Compositional Practice in Schools and Research in Music Education

At the beginning of the 21st century, composing is firmly established in music curricula all over the world (Odam, 2000). Academic research that is relevant for this area of music education can boast of a more than 40-year history (Barrett, 1998b). Barrett's (1998b) survey, *Researching Children's Compositional Processes and Products,* recounts a substantial amount of research on the product and process of composing. There can be little doubt that the great majority and the most influential of this research relies on studies of children's compositions. Swanwick and Tillman (1986), for instance, build their well-known theory of musical development on the analysis of 745 child compositions. In later writings, Swanwick (1988) bases his advice for curriculum development and musical practice in schools on his earlier work with Tillman. Connections to practice have been a recurrent theme in music education research (e.g., Espeland, 1994; Mark, 1992; Reimer, 1992a).

A major reason why I study children's composing in schools is that I hope to influence and inform this area of music education. I believe that my initial training as a music teacher and my viewpoints on composing in schools lie at the bottom of a number of the choices I make as a researcher. Such choices have to do with the arena for research, the questions I pose, the concepts and language I use, the literature I read, and the theories I develop. In a 2000 study, Krüger comments on the connections between research and one's own agenda and priorities:

This aspect, so self-evident that it is usually not reflected upon, also has implications for how we deal with issues of knowledge, such as how the agenda for discussion is set, and how the discussions of knowledge in music education are organised ... One also often forgets that the languages of didactics and music aesthetics enable one to categorise and classify events in ways that involve predispositions towards those solutions we see as appropriate. (p. 181)

The research literature on children's composing covers a wide range of methodologies, age ranges, and arenas. Overviews often group the research into studies of products and of processes (e.g, Barrett, 1998b, Hargreaves & Zimmerman, 1992; Webster, 1992). A somewhat different categorization could be to group the research according to the arenas where data are collected. Are the phenomena being studied taking place in a natural setting (e.g., as part of a regular educational music program), or are they occurring in a laboratory setting? The two methods of categorizing

together create a different kind of overview, with options for identifying research by a richer set of criteria.

In my view, the model in Figure 4 offers a more comprehensive opportunity to understand, discuss, and evaluate the relevance of music education research to practice. Because this chapter is about compositional process in a school context, I suspect readers will expect me to argue that research situated in area W should be our first priority if we wish to improve and inform practice. Indeed, I do think that research conducted in the W area has a better chance of informing musical practice, especially if such research simultaneously

Figure 4. Research categorization by setting and focus

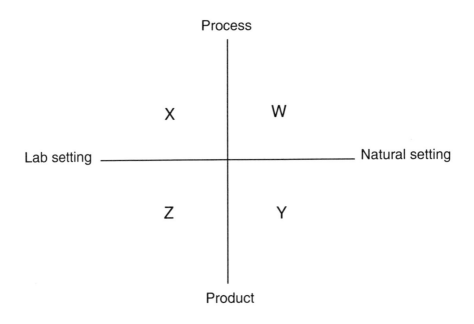

focuses on the *Y* area in order to improve our understanding of the relationship between the two main elements of children's composing—process and product. The vast majority of research over the past 20 years seems to be within areas *X* and *Z*. However, one should remember that concepts like natural and laboratory setting and product and process are constructed conceptions with numerous possible interpretations.

It is interesting to study how contemporary researchers on children's composing position themselves in relation to these concepts, how these concepts seem to shape their ways of collecting and dealing with their data, what kinds of findings they choose to focus on, and how they account for the purpose of their studies. I have chosen to examine how some recent studies based in "natural" educational settings relate to the study of compositional process.[3]

Burnard's recent study (2000b) involves 12-year-old children in a London comprehensive school whom she observed in over 21 weekly music lessons over a 6-month period. In a preliminary report on the study, Burnard says that these sessions are part of an extracurricular lunchtime activity, the reason being that it then "would not be regulated by the demands of a school curriculum" (Burnard, 2000a, p. 230). Burnard (2000b) relies heavily on child interviews, as well as on observations of compositional processes and interpretations of the children's music, and she uses her findings to argue for rethinking pedagogy in music education. Burnard (2000b) seems to pay equal attention to products and processes. The examples she gives from children's interviews are especially

rich with references to compositional actions. In commenting on one of her interviews, Burnard (2000a) maintains that the working process

> includes externalising decisions, feeding back opinions, reinforcing ideas, and making explicit the musical plans. The planning is made explicit by a process Sidin described as "confirming" whereby they [the children] play and then purposively stop in order to share with each other feedback on the worthiness of an idea. As a revisionist strategy, "confirming" appeared to be central to the formative process of composing. (p. 237)

What Burnard describes in the comments above looks to me like a combination of personal and compositional actions with a strong emphasis on circular and relational activity—feeding back, reinforcing, and confirming.

Barrett's (1996) work focuses on children's aesthetic decision making, as evidenced in their original compositional products. Her research arena is the regular classroom music program and a great number of compositions produced by children from preparatory class to grade six. In addition to the compositions, she relies on her observations of classroom practice. In justifying why she wants to research children's aesthetic decision making by examining children's products, Barrett (1996) states:

> Form and structure are integral to music and the communication of musical meaning. To place one sound after another is to make a number of structural decisions: how soon after the first

sound will the second sound appear; will the second sound be the same or, shorter, longer, higher, lower, louder, quieter? Even in the most simple of compositions, these decisions are made. (pp. 147–48)

Barrett is correct that composing involves a number of important decisions about structure. What I question, however, is how an examination of the outcomes of compositional processes—the musical pieces—can give sufficient information about something that I would consider an actional activity, namely decision making and the making of a composition.

Wiggins' (1992) work on composing is a study of compositional activity in her own fifth-grade general music classroom. She studied the musical experience of two target children within the class. Wiggins deals with data collected from a broad spectrum of composing activities over 5 months, with an emphasis on small-group composition. Her findings draw on products as well as on process. She underlines "the importance of looking at process in addition to product" (Wiggins, 1994, p. 70). In Wiggins' reports, one can find numerous examples of the dynamism of the compositional process:

> Sam: I have an idea. Matt, listen! I have an idea.
> Michael: Well, that's for your part. Now for me and Matt … I know … "A" will be very light and then "B" will be like strong. All right?
> Sam: But I have an idea for "B!"
> Negotiation began. When peers work together, it becomes necessary for individuals to express, clarify and justify their ideas and to evaluate one another's ideas

before they can be assimilated into a unified work. (Wiggins, 1995, p. 65)

Wiggins' reports (1992, 1995) include descriptions of significant events and personal and compositional actions. Wiggins' (1992) main agenda, however, seems to be to argue against the findings of cognitive researchers who suggest that children of this age are not capable of dealing with structure and holistic planning.

To me, this argument is not the most interesting part of her (1992) study. I find the descriptions and interpretations focusing on the dynamic nature of relations among actions, instrument, outcomes, and contextual elements in the compositional process to be of greater relevance for informing compositional practice in schools.

In Folkestad's (1996) Swedish study, the focus is on musical learning as cultural practice. Folkestad (1996) examined composition through computer-based music making. He deliberately chose an out-of-school setting in order to be closer to what he calls "real life," and he collected his data through interviews and through having the young composers continually save the MIDI information from the creative process, "from the first idea until the completed piece of music" (1998, p. 111). Folkestad (1998) refers to Swanwick (1988) and argues that *process* can be defined as "products over time" and that "process and product are coherent, two sides of the same coin, in an intertwined relationship" (p. 107). He adds:

> Studying the process focuses our attention on the creator's perspective; his or her thoughts, acts and understanding of

the activity become the basis of their description. In contrast, studying the product implies a shift in focus, where the music is separated from its creator and is regarded as an independent object and analysed from the perspective of the observer. Thus, the observer's, not the creator's criteria, thoughts, musical praxis and musical theory, become the basis for the analysis. (1998, p. 108)

By examining a great number of saved computer files, Folkestad (1996) seems to claim that he has access to the compositional process of the computer-based pieces of music. Even if this undoubtedly gives a richer collection of data, I would still question whether the definition of process as "products over time" holds water. To me, a retrospective examination and a focus on the preliminary outcomes of a composition process cannot fully account for the interrelated, dynamic aspects of such a process. The creators' "thoughts, acts and understanding" are highly relational and circular in a compositional process, especially when one of the components is such a strong instrument as a computer.

All of the fine studies highlighted above have similarities and dissimilarities. All of the researchers collected their data in natural or close-to-natural settings, in classrooms and in out-of-school activities. They differ, however, in their description of and in their relationship to the compositional process. It is not accidental, of course, that I have chosen four studies situated in the natural-setting area—*W* and *Y*—of the matrix in Figure 4. This does not mean that I think research conducted in laboratory settings is useless or irrelevant to music education, but such research is highly questionable if the intent is to inform practice in education.

Group, Whole Class, and Individual

One of the many questions that remains is to what extent my actional and sociocultural conception of the compositional process is relevant for understanding all such processes in school contexts. Based as it is on the observation of small-group composition in a natural setting, it is very relevant to ask whether a description of an *individual* compositional process should put a similar emphasis on relations and actions.

My answer to such a question will have to be yes, but with some important reservations. I believe that any compositional process in a school has to be conceived of as a process of learning within a community of practice (Wenger, 1998). Even if children compose individually, they will rely on and interact with their context and their cultural tools—a computer, a xylophone, or their voices. They will also interact with other human beings—teacher, classmates, and others.

However, any artificial conception of something so complex as a composition process has to be modified in terms of the actual situation to be analyzed. Figure 5 illustrates how the model I have presented could be modified with a view to an individual child. This model would suit a researcher or teacher who wants to pay special attention to the relationship between the child (agent) and the instrument, as in Folkestad's (1996) study of the interactions of composing students and a powerful cultural tool—a computer. In my view, any such conception

Figure 5. A model for understanding an individual's compositional process

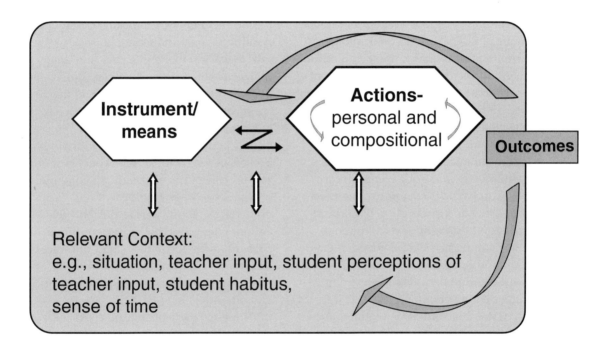

should reflect the relational and dynamic character of a compositional process. These aspects of composing in schools need research in order for teachers to better understand what is going on and in order for teachers to give children better conditions for learning and artistic expression.

Even if tempted to do so, I will not enter into a comprehensive discussion here about the balance of different ways of organizing composition in schools.[4] I would like to express, however, that any program of composing in schools needs to recognize composing as musical *and* social learning, as well as a vehicle for artistic *and* personal expression.

Summary

I have suggested and discussed a conception for understanding compositional processes in a school context from an actional and sociocultural perspective. The main components of this model are compositional and personal actions, outcomes, instrument, and relevant context. This conception of composition in schools is highly relational and circular in nature. Relationships are important during the creation of a composition, and the dynamic nature of relations among actions, instrument, outcomes, and contextual elements create a kind of circulation that drives the process.

I have sought to identify significant events in such a process (e.g., breakthroughs, focus episodes, and blockages), and I have tried to account for how power relations in the composition process can influence participation, group leadership, and peer teaching. By paying a short visit into recent research that has been conducted in natural settings, I have tried to dis-cuss these researchers' relationship to such issues as the process-product debate.

The final outcome of a compositional process, the piece of music, is, in my view, an integrated part of the process; the implication being that a cognition-centered interpretation of the music in isolation from the process behind it is speculative to such a degree that it runs the risk of being irrelevant to compositional practice in school contexts. Composing in schools needs research in order for teachers to give children better conditions for musical and social learning and artistic and personal expression via African drums and other cultural tools.

Notes

1. Etienne Wenger (1998) maintains that theorists of "situated experience give primacy to the dynamics of everyday existence, improvisation, coordination, and interactional choreography. They emphasize agency and intentions. They mostly address the interactive relations of people with their environment" (p. 13). In education, Wenger lists Dewey (1922) and Schön (1983) as representatives.

2. *Habitus* is a concept introduced by Pierre Bourdieu (1977). In the context of this discussion, I am using his description of habitus as "a system of lasting, transposable dispositions which, integrating past experiences, functions at every moment as a matrix of perceptions, appreciations and actions" (p. 83).

3. I am well aware that I am running the risk of wild speculation here because I have neither interviewed these researchers nor observed their working processes. I have only studied some of the final outcomes of their work as presented in articles and dissertations.

4. My advice to the practical field of composing in schools can be found in a 280-page book, *Komponering i klasserommet: en praktisk metodikk.* [Composing in the Classroom: A practical methodology]. The methodology presented in this book is based on constructivist and social learning theory and has a Vygotskyian perspective.

References

Andersen, V., Espeland, M., & Husebo, B. (1997). *Komponering i klasserommet: en praktisk metodikk* [Composing in the Classroom: A practical methodology]. Bergen, Norway: Fagbokforlaget.

Ball, S. (Ed.). (1990). *Foucault and education*. New York: Routledge.

Barrett, M. (1996). *Children's aesthetic decision-making: An analysis of children's musical discourse as composers*. Unpublished doctoral dissertation, Monash University, Victoria, Australia.

Barrett, M. (1998a). Children composing: A view of aesthetic decision-making. In B. Sundin, G. E. McPherson, & G. Folkestad, (Eds.), *Children composing* (pp. 57–81). Malmö, Sweden: Malmö Academy of Music, Lund University.

Barrett, M. (1998b). Researching children's compositional processes and products: Connections to music education practice? In B. Sundin, G. E. McPherson, & G. Folkestad (Eds.), *Children composing* (pp. 10–34). Malmö, Sweden: Malmö Academy of Music, Lund University.

Bourdieu, P. (1977). *Outline of a theory of practice* (R. Nice, Trans.). Cambridge, England: Cambridge University Press.

Bresler, L. (1998). The genre of school music and its shaping by meso, micro, and macro contexts. *Research Studies in Music Education, 11*(3), 2–18.

Burnard, P. (2000a). Examining experiential differences between improvisation and composition in children's music-making. *British Journal of Music Education, 17*(3), 227–45.

Burnard, P. (2000b). *Into different worlds: Children's experience of musical improvisation and composition*. Unpublished doctoral dissertation, University of Reading, Reading, England.

DeCorte, E., Greer, B., & Vershaffel, L. (1996). Mathematics learning and teaching. In D. C. Berliner & R. C. Calfee (Eds.), *Handbook of educational psychology* (pp. 491–549). New York: Macmillan.

Dewey, J. (1922). *Human nature and conduct: An introduction to social psychology*. London: Allen and Unwin.

Engeström, Y. (1999). Activity theory and individual and social transformation. In Y. Engeström, R. Miettinen, & R. Punamäki. (Eds.), *Perspectives on activity theory* (pp. 19–38). Cambridge, England: Cambridge University Press.

Engeström, Y., & Miettinen, R. (1999). Introduction. In Y. Engeström, R. Miettinen, & R. Punamäki (Eds.), *Perspectives on activity theory* (pp. 1–18). Cambridge, England: Cambridge University Press.

Engeström, Y., Miettinen, R., & Punamäki R., (Eds.). (1999). *Perspectives on activity theory*. Cambridge, England: Cambridge University Press.

Erickson, F., & Schultz, J. (1997). When is a context? Some issues and methods in the analysis of social competence. In M. Cole, Y. Engeström, & O. Vasquez (Eds.), *Mind, culture, and activity: Seminal papers from the Laboratory of Comparative Human Cognition*. Cambridge, England: Cambridge University Press.

Espeland, M. (1994). Formative research in Norwegian primary schools: A collaborative endeavor. *Bulletin of the Council for Research in Music Education, 122* (Special issue), 83–93.

Espeland, M. (1998–1999). Curriculum reforms in Norway: An insider's perspective. *Arts and Learning Research, 15*(1), 172–87.

Folkestad, G. (1996). *Computer based creative music-making: Young people's music in the digital age*. Unpublished doctoral dissertation, Universitatis Gothenburgensis, Göteborg, Sweden.

Folkestad, G. (1998). Musical learning as cultural practice, as exemplified in computer-based creative music-making. In B. Sundin, G. E. McPherson, & G. Folkestad (Eds.), *Children composing* (pp. 97–134). Malmö, Sweden: Malmö Academy of Music, Lund University.

Foucault, M. (1980). Two lectures. In C. Gordon (Ed. & Trans.), *Power/knowledge: Selected interviews & other writings: 1972–1977* (pp. 78–108). New York: Pantheon.

Hargreaves, D., & Zimmerman, M. P. (1992). Developmental theories of music learning. In R. Colwell (Ed.), *Handbook of research on music teaching and learning* (pp. 377–91). New York: Schirmer Books.

Krüger, T. (2000). *Teacher practice, pedagogical discourses, and the construction of knowledge: Two case studies of teachers at work.* Unpublished doctoral dissertation, University of Wisconsin, Madison.

Lave, J., & Wenger, E. (1991). *Situated learning: Legitimate peripheral participation.* Cambridge, England: Cambridge University Press.

Mark, M. L.(1992). A history of music education research. In R. Colwell (Ed.), *Handbook of research on music teaching and learning* (pp. 48–59). New York: Schirmer Books.

Marshall, J. (1996). *Michel Foucault: Personal autonomy and education.* Dordrecht, The Netherlands: Kluwer.

Odam, G. (2000). Teaching composing in secondary schools: The creative dream. *British Journal of Music Education, 17*(2), 109–27.

Pond, D. (1981). A composer's study of young children's innate musicality. *Bulletin of the Council for Research in Music Education, 68,* 1–12.

Reimer, B. (1992a). Toward a philosophical foundation for music education research. In R. Colwell (Ed.), *Handbook of research on music teaching and learning* (pp. 21–37). New York: Schirmer Books.

Reimer, B. (1992b). What knowledge is of most worth in the arts. In B. Reimer & R. Smith (Eds.), *The arts, education, and aesthetic knowing* (pp. 20–50). Chicago: NSSE.

Schön, D. A. (1983). *The reflective practitioner: How professionals think in action.* New York: Basic Books.

Serafine, M. L. (1988). *Music as cognition. The development of thoughts in sound.* New York: Columbia University Press.

Sloboda, J. (1985). *The musical mind.* Oxford: Clarendon Press.

Sundin, B. (1998). Musical creativity in the first six years: A research project in retrospect. In B. Sundin, G. E. McPherson, & G. Folkestad (Eds.), *Children composing* (pp. 35–56). Malmö, Sweden: Malmö Academy of Music, Lund University.

Swanwick, K. (1988). *Music, mind, and education.* New York: Routledge.

Swanwick, K., & Tillman, J. (1986). A sequence of musical development: A study of children's compositions. *Journal of British Music Education, 3*(3), 305–39.

van Manen, M. (1990). *Researching lived experience: Human science for an action sensitive pedagogy.* Albany, NY: State University of New York Press.

Vygotsky, L. (1986). *Thought and language* (A. Kozulin, Rev. & Trans.). Cambridge, MA: MIT Press. (Original work published 1934)

Webster, P. (1992). Research on creative thinking in music: The assessment literature. In R. Colwell (Ed.), *Handbook of research on music teaching and learning* (pp. 266–80). New York: Schirmer Books.

Wenger, E. (1998). *Communities of practice, learning, meaning and identity.* Cambridge, England: Cambridge University Press.

Wertsch, J. (1998). *Mind as action.* New York: Oxford University Press.

Wiggins, J. H. (1992). *The nature of children's musical learning in the context of a music classroom.* Unpublished doctoral dissertation, University of Illinois at Urbana–Champaign.

Wiggins, J. H. (1994). Children's strategies for solving composition problems with peers. *Journal of Research in Music Education, 42*(3), 232–52.

Wiggins, J. H. (1995). Building structural understanding: Sam's story. *Quarterly Journal of Music Teaching and Learning, 6*(3), 57–75.

Magne Espeland is associate professor of music education at Stord/Haugesund University College in western Norway, where he specializes in curriculum studies, music methodology for the general classroom, and research methodology for music education. He has made presentations at International Society of Music Education (ISME) conferences and was the chair for the 2002 ISME World Conference. His work has been published in numerous journals, including the *British Journal for Music Education,* the *Bulletin of the Council for Research in Music Education,* and the *Arts Education Policy Review.* He is currently researching the secrets of the general music classroom and the role of indigenous music in music education.

9

The Birth of Song: The Nature and Nurture of Composition

Brian Moore

"Know what, Mr. Parker?" Debbie asked with a touch of excitement in her voice and a slight twinkle in her eye. As a first-year music teacher, Justin Parker welcomed any opportunity where a seventh-grade middle school student showed a little enthusiasm for anything during music class. Of course, he was also excited that any of his students actually thought he knew something!

"What's that, Debbie?"

"Did you know that orchestra is my favorite class at school?"

Five years of undergraduate course work had finally paid off! Mr. Parker beamed with pride and responded in his best "friendly teacher voice."

"Well, I didn't know that, Debbie. Tell me—why *is* orchestra your favorite class?"

Mr. Parker was already forming the appropriate selection of responses: "Maybe I'm her favorite teacher. After all, I think the kids like me—better make sure there's not a crush here." Or perhaps, "Debbie is realizing, in her own way, the great quality of teaching she is receiving, how hard I am trying."

Debbie looked Mr. Parker right in the eye. "It's because it's the last class of the day."

The puzzled look on Mr. Parker's face was Debbie's cue to go on.

"In all of my other classes, like history and English, all we do is sit at desks and do the same stuff all the time. Orchestra is so different—there are no desks, we don't sit in straight rows, and we don't have any books. I like ending the day that way."

There was a moment of silence before Mr. Parker replied, "Well thanks, Debbie. Thanks very much. That was ... quite helpful."

Though the names have been changed to protect the guilty, this conversation between a seventh-grade orchestra musician and first-year music teacher actually did take place many years ago. Mr. Parker needed to learn that there was more to music education than having a teacher, some students, and a subject or ensemble. There was a place and a time—a context—in which learning occurred. In some cases, the context is the most significant aspect of learning. The words of Marshall McLuhan still ring true: "The medium is the message" (as cited in "McLuhan," 2000).

We are all naturally creative, wired to be curious, and desirous of self-expression. While we all share to some degree these common characteristics, each one of us has a distinctive voice, an individual thumbprint, a unique perspective. It is human nature to want to create and express. To teach is to nurture this creative ability and expressive desire.

The medium of our message is music. Music as an art form continues to be an engaging form of human expression and perception. Young children are especially drawn to music as a *complete* experience. They desire to participate not only as listeners or performers but also as composers and creators.

Both the creative product and the creative process are fundamental to music composition. The nature of composing is the heart of this chapter. Our ability as educators to help learners musically express and create is powerfully influenced by the environment(s) we create, adapt, and find ourselves in. I hope that by viewing technology as such an environment, we will be better equipped to perceive the various contexts for composition and thus gain understanding of how to make intelligent, intuitive, and even inspired choices toward nurturing the song in ourselves and our students.

The Nature of Style
Educational Stages

Teaching and learning in school is based, both formally and informally, on stages of development. The goal is to promote a first grader to second grade, to prepare a middle school student for high school, to graduate a high school senior into college or career. Educational psychology provides important developmental theories. Piaget, Maslow, Dewey, Bruner, Seashore, Petzold, Gordon, Zimmerman,

and many others have helped educators in general and music education to understand the maturation of the learner. Stages of development, taxonomies of domains, and goals and objectives all involve a sense of a hierarchy and direction. Labels such as middle level, beginning band, pre-algebra, and first-grade teacher all imply a sense of direction and development in an educational context. Considering ages and stages helps us identify the kinds of learners we have, the nature of our content, the instructional approaches to take, and even our own identity as teachers.

Musical Styles

Music embodies many characteristics and elements that parallel those in other arts. We speak of the form of a dramatic play, the color of a poem, and the texture of a painting. A piece of music also has form, color, and texture. What brings these elements together into an aesthetic is style. If a piece of music in a jazz style is contrasted with one in a baroque style, words such as form, color, and texture are used to describe, compare, and contrast the styles.

The idea of style can also describe the entire music experience for the three types of participants: composer, performer, and listener. A composer creates a piece of music that has certain style characteristics. A performer or performers re-create the piece by adhering to performance practices within the style. The listener's appreciation of and aesthetic reaction to the work and its performance are enhanced when style issues are understood. The roles of the participants are intertwined as

the composer, the performer, and the

listener are in a certain sense collaborators in a total musical experience, to which each makes his individual contribution. ... not only are the performer and the listener, in a real sense, re-experiencing and re-creating the musical thought of the composer, but they are, also in a real sense, adding to it. We might even say that, according to the various gifts involved, the three functions sometimes overlap, with the performer supplying whatever for him is missing in the work of the composer, the listener hearing the composition sometimes beyond the performer, and the composer, to a very important degree, visualizing (with his ears and not with his eyes, be it understood!) his work in terms of both performance and sounds heard. (Sessions, 1950, p. 107)

Music education acknowledges both educational stages and musical styles. This balance and blend of stage and style will give focus to the nature of the compositional product and direction to the nurturing of the composing process.

Music as Art

Figure 1 presents the interaction between performer, listener, and composer in a theoretically symmetrical view. The shaded area in the center of the figure represents a "perfect" musical experience. Such balance does not occur in actual practice, because the influence of musical style varies in strength. Very often, the work of the composer is misunderstood or is not understood at all. Music is a temporal art and thus is perceived in a linear fashion. A listener cannot hear the entire song at once—a 45-second tune still takes 45 seconds to perceive. The composer, on the other hand, has to work at times with the entire composition in mind. The product (i.e., the finished tune) is not equal to the process of its creation.

Often, an audience is drawn to a performance because of the performer rather than the music. The style becomes more important than the specific piece of music. People often attend rock concerts to *see* (and not just hear) a particular band. The style of performer and the accompanying style of music become the greatest influences in this particular music experience. The message is not a specific piece of music; rather, the message is the medium—a style that has extramusical characteristics. Figure 2 attempts to represent this "imbalance."

As we all participate in music as listeners, performers, and composers, we may be more realistically called *consumers, makers,* and *producers.* Furthermore, especially with the influence of technology, the lines between these roles have become blurred, as the producer may also be the maker and consumer

Figure 1. The "perfect" music experience

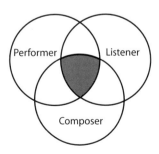

Figure 2. Interaction of style within the music experience

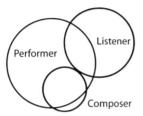

Figure 3. "New" labels for the music experience

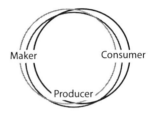

(see Figure 3).

The role of musical style is central to the idea of maker, consumer, and producer. Style gives shape and meaning to each of these musical roles. With the tremendous increase in availability of music through electronic and digital means (CD, radio, television, and Internet) as well as traditional means (live and personal performance), we are surrounded by more musical styles than ever. Is any one style better than the rest? No. We do not view musical style as developmental or hierarchical. Is any one style preferred above the rest? Often. We do view musical style as a matter of preference or taste. The goal of music education in developing more informed consumers of music requires a breadth and depth of experiences with a variety of styles.

Learning as Art

If the music experience can be viewed as the interaction of maker (performer), producer (composer), and consumer (listener), the learning experience shares a parallel model (see Figure 4). In every learning experience, a perceiver and listener—*a*

learner—exists. Someone must also be there to present the information, to make content come alive, to serve as the *teacher.* There also has to be something to teach and learn—a *curriculum.*

There is no perfect learning experience where the three components exist symmetrically and in complete balance with one another. Often, traditional learning experiences, especially those at the college level, are teacher-directed rather than learning-oriented. For example, a lecture by a professor has the teacher as the primary force. The teacher selects and organizes the content (curriculum) and directs the presentation (teaching) with little or no interaction with the learners (see Figure 5). This scenario serves the curriculum well in terms of coverage—getting content delivered to the highest number of learners possible. However, it places great demands upon learners, who have little opportunity for success if they lack listening skills. The learner is at the mercy of the teacher and the environment for learning (i.e., lecture hall and lecture format) as little flexibility exists.

When models of the music experience (Figures 1 and 2) are compared to models

Figure 4. The learning experience

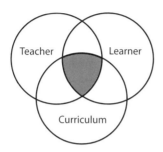

Figure 5. The learning experience model applied to the lecture environment

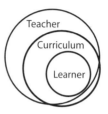

of the learning experience (Figures 4 and 5), a connection can be made to the concept of style. The educational literature abounds with discussion of the differences in how we perceive and process information (see Colwell, 1992, section D). Some of these differences are noted in the construct of learning style (Moore, 1988). While we all, for example, can process information via our senses, some of us prefer visual learning, while others are more comfortable and successful with auditory or kinesthetic perception. Learning style is a nondevelopmental concept in that it focuses more on learning strengths and preferences. This parallels music style.

A model of learning based upon style characteristics has implications for the teacher and the curriculum. If the curriculum is music performance, with the context being a large ensemble, the teaching style will involve directing and leading, primarily through conducting. Even our labels suggest this: we speak of an *ensemble director* and not an *ensemble educator* or *ensemble lecturer.* If the context for music performance is an individual instrument, the style of teaching becomes more one-on-one in a studio envi-

ronment. We now think in terms of mentoring, coaching, and teaching.

Learning style suggests teaching strategy. The content to be learned and the context for this learning have inherent style characteristics. Teachers will not only teach the way they were taught but, more importantly, *the way they learn.* A teacher who is a highly visual learner will naturally lean toward teaching methods and styles that rely upon visuals and perhaps even mental imagery. A teacher with a strong multidimensional, random processing style will engage students in trial-and-error experiences where getting it right the first time is not important.

Our curriculum and content also have style implications. The places where we teach and learn are influenced by content. A classroom, a rehearsal hall, a practice room, and a multimedia lab are all spaces designed for teaching and learning specific content. The area of composition in music education has historically lacked a sense of curricular organization, instructional methodology, or pedagogy.

In order to nurture the musical creativity of learners, we need to understand the nature of composition. Methods of teaching can be discussed in terms of the styles involved in the process of composing. Materials for teaching can be viewed when styles of composition are perceived. Technology as a part of music curriculum can provide specific examples of contexts for the teaching of composition.

Nurture via Technology
Curricular Contexts

Many music educators find themselves with a lack of experience and understanding of composition as curriculum. The adoption of technology in a music curriculum also can seem overwhelming due to its complexity and the lack of the time to learn the "ins and outs" of hardware and software, let alone their educational applications.

Just as a solid philosophy or mission statement can direct us when unaccounted for issues arise, consideration of stage and style can provide a rationale in the identification, selection, and evaluation of music technology. Technology can serve as a tool—a part of the music-learning and music-teaching environment. A process approach to its use helps educators to be more responsive to the rapid change inherent in technology.

In order to be as useful as possible, this discussion of technology does not name specific software titles or hardware configurations. As soon as a new keyboard, computer, or software version is released, it is almost immediately out of date. Manufacturers of computer hardware and music technology engage in rigorous research and development cycles where products have been known to be declared no longer

in production even though retail channels still have ample supply. The approach here will be to identify and discuss categories of technology with specific implications for music education. See Table 1 for a listing of technology categories and their relationship to music education.

Notation. This first category of music technology includes computer software that notates music for display on screen and on paper. Additional resources would include musical keyboards or other instruments that can be connected to computers via a Musical Instrument Digital Interface (MIDI) in order to input the desired music notation. The primary purpose of notation technology is to represent music so it can be used in other situations, usually performance. Seldom is the ultimate goal to view notation on a computer screen. The printing of the music score or its parts characterizes this technology as a tool. When the technology is used as a compositional tool, several assumptions are in place. First, the user must understand the notation system(s) being used. These systems go beyond traditional notation to include tablature, fret symbols, and graphic/iconic systems. The intention is to use, not to teach, the notation systems. If the user is not literate in the notation, the technology is of little value. Second, this technology uses a *symbol-before-sound* approach. Music is entered and edited by manipulating symbols rather than sounds. Third, the end user of the notation does not have to be versed in the technology. The music is usually shared on paper. In many situations, composers use notation technology to communicate their musical efforts with others who lack technological skills or resources.

Table 1. Categories of music technology

Category	Musical Role	Style of Thinking	"Person"
1. notation	composition	critical (rational) thinking	producer (composer)
2. sequencing	improvisation	creative (intuitive) thinking	maker (performer)
3. digital audio	multiple styles	manipulation	consumer (listener)
4. Internet	reference & research	collaboration	all of the above

Notation technologies, with their heavy reliance on visual perception, are tools for critical and rational thinking in music. According to Marzano et al. (1988), "Critical thinkers generate ways to test assertions" (p. 17). Such problem solving and thinking via notation focus heavily on music theory and orchestration rather than performance and interpretation. For example, in notating a jazz swing style, the visual representation of a swing feel would be even eighth notes. What is seen is not actually what is desired in the performance. Many new users of notation technology find it difficult at first to "think" at the screen. Rather, they use the technology as an electronic typesetter, printing music of already created works. Creating and composing from scratch while looking at a computer screen takes practice. The ability to use notation software does not guarantee creative composing, just as the ability to type and to use a word processor does not guarantee that creative writing will occur.

Sequencing. The term *sequencing* origi-nated in the 1940s and 1950s when pieces of electronic music were created by taking bits of magnetic reel-to-reel recording tape and splicing them together to create longer sounds and phrases. These lengths of tape were strung together, or sequenced, to yield a recording of a new piece. The term now applies to both software and hardware used to digitally record, edit, manipulate, and play back music. Typically, a piece of music is conceived as a series of parts called *tracks*. Each track is usually associated with a particular timbre or voice. Each staff on a full conductor score could be represented by a track. However, sequencers do not require that tracks share the same length, content, structure, or form. Each track could even have different lengths and meters. From a composition viewpoint, sequencing represents a fundamentally different way to manipulate sound. Cut-and-paste techniques from word processing are applied to the editing of music, making it easy to brainstorm and test ideas that can then be easily kept or discarded. This method of working fits Perkins's (1984) definition of creative thinking: "Creative thinking is thinking patterned in a way that tends to lead to creative results. This definition reminds us that the ultimate criterion for creativity is output" (p. 18).

If notation technology parallels the traditional idea of composition, sequencing parallels that of improvisation. The focus is *not* the notation, but the sound.

As with notation technology, sequencing brings its own set of expectations to the music environment. First, the user is expected to be able to generate musical ideas. Tracks begin as empty placeholders for musical information. Musical ideas must be entered before they can be edited, copied, and otherwise manipulated. Second, a broad view of the elements of music is assumed. Pitch, rhythm, and timbre are only starting places. Virtually every sequencer available today allows the manipulation of acoustic and musical effects such as balance, vibrato, panning (location of the source, either left, right, or center), reverberation, and chorus. The musical palette is greatly increased. Third, anyone can improvise music because sequencers can record music at one tempo but play it back at any other. Musical performance ability is not a prerequisite for making music with a sequencer. Intuitive thinking finds a place in musical environments involving sequencers. In fact, sequencing can both assist in the making of music and enable music that is *only* possible with the technology. A piece of electronic music can only be re-created with sequencing technology. The technology now becomes not only tool but also technique. The process is also a product.

Digital Audio. Digital audio encompasses technology that records both analog (acoustic) music and electronic instruments in a digital format. Such a format is completely foreign to human perception. The sound is digitally encoded and can only be realized if similar technology decodes it. Common examples of digital music are compact discs (CD), digital video discs (DVD), and computer sound files. It is common, and often necessary, for personal computers to be able to write to CDs and DVDs. While it is difficult to predict what the future might hold in terms of format, the digital encoding and decoding of music is here to stay.

Digital-audio technology includes microphones (to get analog sound into a digital format) and format converters (referred to as DAC and ADC—digital-to-analog converter and analog-to-digital converter). Software and hardware are also used to compress and edit the information, as well as to record this digital information to some physical media, such as a computer's disk drive or a CD-ROM.

The current state of affairs for digital audio assumes that the user is more comfortable with recording-studio metaphors than with musical metaphors. Digital-audio software has the look and feel of an engineer's console where the sound is viewed as a waveform—what would be seen on the screen of an oscilloscope. Manipulation of the sound requires practice and experience in acoustics and sound design. Novices can certainly tweak by trial and error, but, just as notation software is useful only if one can read notation, digital-audio technology is best used with an understanding of the science of sound.

Most consumer users of digital audio re-create CDs by copying or *ripping* (copying a track or portion of a track to a computer hard drive) and then *burning* (recording) a collection of music onto a blank CD. The original source of this copied track does not have to be an audio CD. A digital recording via a microphone and DAT (digi-tal-analog tape) recorder, an MP3 file (Internet format for recorded sound), and other types of digital sound information can all be moved back and forth between various physical media. Multiple styles of music can be collected by anyone, making the consumption of music a most personal experience. What began with the cassette tape recorder in making music accessible at the desire of the listener is finding maturity in digital audio.

It should also be noted that digital audio is not limited to music, but includes any sound or collection of sounds. Sequencer technology can also be used to include digital audio in the tracks of a piece. A composer can create a MIDI accompaniment and sing over it, blurring the distinction between music producer and music maker. Music on demand is also media on demand. Personal musical choic-es multiply as the producer, maker, and consumer can be the same individual. Negroponte (1996) states:

> The real opportunity comes from the digital artist providing the hooks for mutation and change. ... the point is, being digital allows the process, not just the product, to be conveyed. That process can be the fantasy and ecstasy of one mind, or it can be the collective imagination of many, or it can be the

vision of a revolutionary group. (p. 224)

The technology of digital audio, coupled with its delivery at the speed of light, has yielded an enormous repertoire of music from nearly limitless sources. Musical styles from different countries and cultures, forms of musical expression that never before could find an audience, and the ability to manipulate sound have vastly increased our awareness and potential as consumers of music.

Internet. The Internet has grown to become not only commonplace but also necessary for many. Digital audio is the native format for sound on the Internet. This global communication is due to the moving of electronic bits and bytes of digi-tal information (text, video, and audio) at the blink of an eye. While few understand the technical intricacies of the Internet, millions make use of its power. It is not nec-essary to understand the technology in order to use it, but it is exactly this technol-ogy that is allowing collaboration and cre-ativity never before possible. According to Negroponte (1996),

> We are entering an era when expression can be more participatory and alive. We have the opportunity to distribute and experience rich sensory signals in ways that are different from looking at the page of a book and more accessible than traveling to the Louvre. (p. 224)

The inclusion of the Internet as a tech-nology category for music education is rooted in the need for musicians to collab-orate. From chamber groups to large ensembles, music making is a collaborative effort. The Internet simply extends that collaboration beyond the boundaries of time and space.

Internet technology allows MIDI instruments in different places and time zones to perform together in "real time" with each musician hearing what the others are playing. The Internet as a distribution network has already exploded with millions of Web sites. It has never been easier to find an audience for one's musical expressions.

Making Connections

Education has taken various approaches to the organization of content and the context in which instruction and learning occur. In making connections between the nature of composition and the nurturing of it through technology, three views or models for curricula are presented (see Table 2).

Discipline-Based Model. The primary question this model asks is "What are the concepts, structures, and skills that create the content discipline?" In this view, a body of knowledge (a subject) exists. This knowledge is made up of interconnected ideas and is often associated with specific skills. Music theory is usually taught using a discipline-based approach. Music has elements that work together with a given piece of music (e.g., pitch interacts with harmony). Conventions, rules, structures, concepts, and specific skills (e.g., ear training) exist within the discipline of music theory.

Teaching, Learning, and Curriculum. The work of the teacher is to present content. The work of the learner is to master this content. The curriculum is ordered in a formal way that generally involves structures, hierarchies, or taxonomies.

Creativity. Creativity within a discipline-based model can be seen in the work of an artisan and apprentice. The master artisan exhibits a body of knowledge and a specific set of skills. Craftsmanship and inventiveness allow the skills and concepts of the discipline to be applied not only in a technical sense but also in a creative one. The silversmith who produces a spoon that is both useful and beautiful and the carpenter who designs and builds a piece of furniture with aesthetic qualities are both examples of a master artisan. The apprentice is taught through demonstration, mentoring, and one-on-one training. The student shadows the teacher, engages in guided practice, and follows a specific sequence when being trained.

Technology. Notation technology requires discipline-based approaches when it is used to encourage musical creativity. In order to be musically creative when using notation software, a student needs notation-reading skills and knowledge of how the software presents and edits the notation. In contrast, notation technology is less effective if the student is asked to engage in discovery learning. An apprentice who lacks understanding of how glass is made and lacks skill in the techniques of glass blowing will find it virtually impossible to create a useful, let alone beautiful, glass object.

Expert-Thinking Model. This model asks "What is the work of the expert within the discipline?" In this model, curriculum is based upon the work of experts in the field. The learner is encouraged to think and act like an expert. The difference between a discipline-based and expert-thinking model is demonstrated by comparing traditional approaches to the teaching of mathematics and chemistry. The specific concepts and skills of mathematics are usually presented in the artisan/apprentice model (e.g., "Here is what you have to know. Let's practice, then move to the next topic."). The intent is to learn mathematics—a discipline that is needed throughout life. In contrast, chemistry is taught in a laboratory setting where students do the work of chemists. The scientific method becomes an important objective. The goal is to develop a way of thinking, doing, and problem solving within the field of science.

Teaching, Learning, and Curriculum. The role of the teacher is to model the work of the expert. The role of the student is to think and act like an expert. The curriculum, because it is based on what experts do, is more adaptive to change. Innovations in the field that find their way into actual practice are quickly assimilated into curricular programs. The use of technology in education is an excellent example of this. The way computers are employed in the "real" world in many cases determines the direction of school technology programs.

The training of physicians is an example of the expert-thinking model because the student doctor learns by being an intern. The intern is viewed by patients as a "real" doctor, is even addressed as "doctor," and, while working under direct supervision, has full responsibility for certain tasks.

Creativity. Creative thinking and activity on the part of experts include intuition and sometimes inspiration. As experts create new knowledge and develop new approaches, innovation and invention are used. Those experts who work in inspired and intuitive ways emerge as creative leaders.

Technology. The use of most sequencer technology falls into the expert-thinking model. Very often for sequencing software, the metaphor at work is that of a recording studio. The graphics in the software that depict mixer knobs, sliders, EQ meters, and the like have the look and feel of the audio equipment found in professional recording studios. The process of recording a piece of music via software tracks imitates the techniques used in sound-on-sound recording.

The effective use of sequencers requires the ability to create short musical ideas that can be further manipulated. As noted earlier, improvisation is a great resource for cre-

Table 2. Summary of curricular models

	Discipline-Based	Expert-Thinking	Interdisciplinary
Teacher	Artisan	Doctor	Multimedia Developer
Learner	Apprentice	Intern	Content Specialist
Technology	Notation	Sequencer	Internet
Creativity	Craftsmanship Inventiveness	Intuition Inspiration	Creative Thinking Imagination

ating these germinal sources for sequencing. The best way for young musicians to become better improvisers is simply to improvise—to do what experts do. Sequencing technology empowers improvisers to get many ideas down quickly and efficiently and then experience them as listeners by immediately playing them back.

Interdisciplinary Model. This model asks "How does the subject matter in question relate to other areas of the total curriculum?" What are the common threads—the connections between different topics, concepts, and content in the total curriculum? Interdisciplinary teacher and curriculum development require knowledge and skills from diverse areas to be brought together to yield a new whole. Topical or thematic teaching would also fall into this category.

Teaching, Learning, and Curriculum. The work of the teacher is intertwined with the work of the school. Middle-level education is especially fluent in cross-curricular and interdisciplinary development in which teams of teachers are often asked to plan instruction together and coordinate their instructional efforts. Difficulties arise when teachers, steeped in a specific content area, lack the ability or time to see and develop connections to other areas of the curriculum. The connections made can be extended to not just concepts, but skills as well. The skills used in one content area can often be applied directly to others. For example, composition in language arts and composition in music share similar processes (see Table 3).

Creativity. For learners, especially those who enjoy multisensory experiences and discovery learning, an interdisciplinary

approach is very appealing and powerful. The interdisciplinary model allows learners to feel they are creating new knowledge because they are making connections between different areas. In fact, the various disciplines represented are not always cut-and-dry. Skills from unrelated areas might be required for a specific task. An example of this situation is that of the multimedia developer who has the goal of creating content for delivery on the Internet.

Multimedia developers have to work with visual images, sound, and text. The ability to tell a story, to convey meaning through pictures, and to create an aesthetic through music are all creative skills drawn from literature, art, and music. Multimedia also requires knowledge of computer programming, networking, and Internet technologies. The work of such a developer of content requires imagination, as well as critical and creative thinking.

A multimedia developer often oversees a team of content-area specialists and has responsibility for managing a project. The individuals working on a particular feature (e.g., the music track for a multimedia CD-ROM) may lack the total view of the project. A "big picture" global view is required of the manager. Such a global perspective is also helpful in building interdisciplinary curriculum. Individual concepts do not exist in isolation; they are part of an interconnected network of ideas, connections, and constructs.

Technology. The Internet itself is a technological example of such a model. Web pages are created and located across the globe. The user of an Internet browser creates meaning by navigating, selecting, and making connections among these sources of information. Some Web pages are visited once, while others are returned to time and time again. As various sites are navigated, connections are made.

For the student musician, the Internet becomes a source for reference and research in answer to individual questions and needs. The greater power of the Internet, however, is in allowing students separated by time and space to share ideas. The ability to create harmony from varied content and to form organization out of chaos is required when diverse musical styles are used in composing.

The Creative Process

A balanced music experience holds the work of the composer, performer, and listener in symmetry; and a balanced music curriculum holds the work of the teacher, learner, and curriculum in symmetry (Figures 1 and 4). Creativity in the music curriculum is realized, in part, through improvisation and composition. The implementation of technology for fostering composition empowers both the learner and the teacher. The categories of technology

have particular styles that "fit" with specific creative actions and behaviors. A process to assist in developing a model for composition as curricula is outlined in Table 4.

Music is an amazing creation. It is a form of expression that can capture the imagination, challenge the mind, and nourish the heart. The process of helping others create a piece of music is an accomplishment that celebrates the art of teaching. The use of technology as tool and technique in the music-creation process has also elevated that technology. "Music has proven to be one of the most important shaping forces in computer science" (Negroponte, 1996, p. 221). May we continue to engage in creative music education as a way of nurturing the mind as well as the machine.

References

Colwell, R. (Ed.). (1992). *Handbook of research on music teaching and learning.* New York: Schirmer Books.

Marzano, R. J., Brandt, R. S., Hughes, C. S., Jones, B. F., Presseisen, B. Z., Rankin, S. C., et al. (1988). *Dimensions of thinking: A framework for curriculum and instruction.* Alexandria, VA: Association for Supervision and Curriculum

Table 3. Improvisation/composition and language arts

Improvisation and Language Arts	Composition and Language Arts
"Through-composed"	Pre-conceived
aural communication (conversation)	written communication (poetry)
intuitive	rational
focus on process (action and reaction)	focus on product (intended audience)

Table 4. A process for the creative product

Process	Skills	Questions/Comments
1. Find an interesting problem to solve.	• Musical thinking and problem solving • Open-ended vs. clearly defined • Internal vs. external	• Identify the situation. • What's the current state of affairs? • What is needed? • Is there a problem that needs solving? • Who will be the audience?
2. Create something (the germinal idea).	• Initial idea(s) • Elements of music (a chord, a phrase, a form) • Emotion of music (a mood, a feeling, an image) • External to music (a poem, a story, a video)	• Create something—anything. • What you create may not have been done before! • You don't need to worry about labels, structure, etc. Think outside the box!
3. Develop "first draft."	• Brainstorming • Connections • Variations • Relationships • Balance	• Put your creation in context. • Did it fill the need or solve the problem?
4. Evaluate.	• Function as listener rather than composer. • Decide what works and what doesn't. • Try to hear with "new ears."	• What do you think? • Can you view your creation as if perceiving it for the first time?
5. Revise? (May need to go back to #3 or 2)	• You may want or need to go back to try again or just make some changes.	• You might need to rework ideas. • You might need to throw away ideas. • You might need new ideas. • You might need to say "It's Done!"
6. If done, analyze for future use.	• What did you create? • What labels and vocabulary would you use?	• Now figure out what you did! • How did you do it? • Why does it work?
7. Share.	• Live performance • Technology (recordings) • E-mail and Internet	• Let your creation be shared and enjoyed!

Development.

"McLuhan, (Herbert) Marshall." (2000). *Microsoft Encarta online encyclopedia 2000.* Retrieved January 14, 2001, from http://encarta.msn.com.

Moore, B. (1988). Perception and process: A look at learning styles. *The Instrumentalist, 42*(9), 16–19.

Negroponte, N. (1996). *Being digital.* New York: First Vintage Books.

Perkins, D. N. (1984). Creativity by design. *Educational Leadership, 42,* 18–25.

Sessions, R. (1950). *The musical experience of composer, performer, listener.* Princeton, NJ: Princeton University Press.

Brian Moore is associate professor of music education and coordinator of music field experiences in the school of music at the University of Nebraska–Lincoln. His teaching area includes music education and music technology. He has degrees in music education and music composition/theory from the University of New Hampshire and graduate degrees in music education with conducting emphasis and in curriculum and instruction from the University of Wisconsin–Madison.

The Role of the Teacher

10
Responding to Student Compositions

Sam Reese

Nearly all parents have faced the dilemma of what to say when their child, smiling broadly with crayons in hand, exclaims, "Look at the new picture I made." Naturally, mothers and fathers want to encourage their children but are uncertain whether it is better to just say, "That's nice, honey" or to make more comments or ask questions to better assist the budding artist. This is especially true if the work is abstract or unfamiliar, which increases the challenge of discussing it in constructive ways.

Likewise, music teachers who are beginning to involve students in composing activities face doubts about how to respond to students' original music in less superficial ways than "Nice work. Sounds good" or "That's going to take more work." This chapter is written for practicing teachers seeking to grow in their ability to respond in constructive ways to their students' original pieces and for teacher educators who are introducing novice teachers to the strategies and skills of teaching music composition. I will concentrate on one aspect of teaching composition—the teacher's verbal and musical responses to student compositions. First, I will describe the unfamiliar challenges of teaching composition and derive some lessons from how great com-

posers, art and writing teachers, and experienced school music teachers have approached their teaching of creative work. Next, I will articulate a continuum of teacher responses to compositions, analyze actual teacher responses, and offer structured approaches for responding. A final section describes experiences that teacher educators can offer to novice teachers to help them learn the skills of responding effectively.

Scenario: The Young Teacher's Uncertainty

Anne, a young middle school teacher, was pleased when Kevin eagerly approached her and said, "Ms. Benson, I just finished my composition for our last assignment. Would you listen to it and tell me what you think?" Anne had recently acquired a computer and MIDI keyboard so her students could begin composing with sequencing and notation software. Although she had little prior composing experience herself, she was committed to helping her students make progress in meeting the National Standards, which include composing and improvising. "Great, Kevin. I'm pleased to help," she said. "Let's have a listen."

As Kevin's piece poured forth, the smile

gradually faded from Anne's face. Kevin's piece was rhythmically complex, but it seemed poorly organized and did not make a good first impression. Dominating the piece was an apparently random, loud tympani with occasional bell and snare drum notes. Beneath the percussion, she could make out a repetitive six-note, C-major melodic motive played on piano, accompanying C-major and D-minor block chords played on vibraphone, and occasional statements of the motive on a marimba. The melody and chords were not played in the same tempo or meter but were rhythmically independent of each other.

As the long piece continued, Anne's mind was filled with a whirl of confusing thoughts and questions: "Oh my, this has so many problems, which ones should I point out first?" "How do I encourage him but still be honest?" "Should I just tell him that this is too complicated and have him start over?" "Why does he have that tympani banging away?" "Why aren't the melody and chords rhythmically aligned?" "Is there any part of this worth working on? Should he just keep the melodic motive and get rid of his other parts?" "Would it help if I played his motive and chords for him so he could hear them played with better rhythm?"

When the piece finally ended, she said, "Kevin, you have so much going on here that I think I better listen to this again another time. I'll be able to help you more after I get to know your piece better." Anne sensed some disappointment from Kevin as he walked away. "If I had been working with my choir on a new piece, I would have had so much to say to help them," she worried. "Why is this so much harder?"

The Unfamiliar Challenges of Teaching Composition

Anne's circumstance illustrates some of the challenges our profession faces as we strive to better integrate composing into our choral, general, and instrumental programs. Perhaps most apparent is the stark difference between the roles of the teacher when directing performance ensembles and when teaching composition. It is not unusual to hear teachers say "Composition cannot be taught, in the strict sense of the word" (Beck, 2001, p. 55). What these teachers are sensing is that during a band, choir, or orchestra rehearsal, the teacher knows clearly what the ensemble members should change in their playing or singing and can give direct instructions on what students should do to improve. Teachers of composition, however, are more like facilitators. They can never be sure what students will compose in response to an assignment, and they cannot know how students' pieces ought best to be further developed. There are many ways to fulfill a composing assignment and unpredictable composing problems and possibilities to take into account with each student.

Teaching composition might be thought of as providing a structured environment in which students teach themselves or each other. Most practicing music teachers today have little prior experience guiding such an open-ended process. How forcefully should a composition teacher direct a student in developing composing techniques or skills? How much should a teacher "keep hands off" of students' original ideas and allow them to follow their own course of musical development?

Scenario: "Teach and Tell" or "Help Her Find Her Voice?"

The following scenario, as told by a composition teacher, illustrates the enigma of when to take a didactic approach and when to be more heuristic:

A few years ago I was giving private composition lessons to Erin, a bright and very talented high school student. One lesson, she brought in a melody in response to an exercise that I had asked her to complete. It was messily written and had five beats in some of its measures (the meter she had chosen was 4/4). Looking past the surface clutter, I noticed that if one or two minor pitch and rhythm adjustments were made the melody worked as a fugue subject. More private work with it revealed that her idea could support various degrees of stretto. I wrote out a countersubject and then composed an exposition and episode based on the revised version of Erin's subject and my countersubject.

At our next lesson, Erin said she had heard the term fugue before, but could not explain what it was; she had never heard of subjects or countersubjects let alone stretto. I showed her the various steps I went through in the process of reworking her melody and composing the opening of a fugue, using appropriate terms as I went. All along, I stressed that Erin was free to use or reject these ideas as she worked on her piece. Erin said she had not realized how much her melody could benefit from the process of revision and was pleasantly surprised at the potential her music contained.

Some people might think I inter-vened too much in Erin's work. But would I really have been furthering Erin's growth as a composer if I had not used my own experience to point out that, with a little more work, her initial idea could be developed into a much more than passable theme? Would I have been doing my job as a teacher if I had not explained what fugue and stretto are?

Knowing exactly when is the right time "to teach and tell" and when is the right time to "help students find their own voice" is frequently not easy. But if I hadn't told Erin about what I had noticed, I would have been guilty of withholding useful information. And how would that have helped her? (T. J. Bowlby, personal communication, January 17, 2001)

Student Use of Teacher Critiques

Another marked contrast between the role of the teacher in the rehearsal and in the composition class is the difference in how students use critiques from teachers. During a rehearsal, the teacher states what the students need to change and expects students to apply these directions in the next playing of the passages. Such statements include "More crescendo" and "Keep your tone round and warm and use more legato attacks." During a composition class, however, teachers are more likely to respond to students with questions or open-ended suggestions rather than directives. Examples include "How do you feel about that transition between your sections?" and "You might consider using fewer instruments so your melodic line is more noticeable above the accompaniment." In these cases, students need time to think, consider options, and try out ways of assimilating these guiding questions and suggestions from their teacher. Later, the teacher may see little or no direct evidence of the students' applying these suggestions, even when students say they incorporated the teacher's ideas. This situation is illustrated in this statement from a composition teacher to a student:

> I'm going to give you some ideas, and I hope you will try them out. But when you leave I know you're going to do whatever you want with them, and I probably won't recognize my own ideas in your piece when you bring it back. (T. J. Bowlby, personal communication, September 15, 2000)

Bunting (1987) relates a similar incident in his intriguing case studies of teaching composition to Barry, a secondary student:

> Barry was unhappy with the transition to the slower section [of his piece]. ... I suggested a rising sequence of chords ending in an abrupt cut-off—leaving a musical "question mark" to heighten the surprise of the change in texture to come. In his next version [of the piece, I could] see Barry trying to realize my suggestion, but perhaps not very convincingly; I felt uneasy at imposing this idea, ... because I knew ... that such a sophisticated concept would not be properly absorbed. (p. 34)

In a second study, another student said, "I like it ... but I don't think it's coming from my brain" after considering a suggest-ed change that Bunting had made (Bunting, 1988, p. 36).

Teachers' Limited Experience with Composition

Adding to these challenges is the generally limited experience most music teachers have as composers themselves. Teachers might rightfully worry, "I haven't worked with musical ideas myself as a composer, so I don't have many ideas to suggest to my students." As John Kratus has pointed out, asking most music teachers today to teach composition is analogous to asking Spanish teachers to teach French when they do not speak the language (personal communication, June 14, 2000). If teachers have taken composition lessons, they were most likely private lessons in a university composition studio. Teaching composition in school music programs, however, must occur in the very different group-oriented classroom setting, where composition is often done by small groups of students; or a single teacher may have to guide 15 to 25 students who are all working simultaneously, as usually occurs in a middle or high school music-technology lab.

Lessons from Experienced Teachers

Lessons from Great Composers as Teachers

To seek guidance on some of these issues, we might turn to the little that is known about how great composers approached teaching composition. Moldenhauer (1979) has provided extended descriptions of how Anton Von Webern taught composition, based on reports from his students. Webern's lessons began with a "prolonged, silent reading of the music" (p. 508) that helped him get to know the student's composition as well as possible before he offered any critique. In offering comments on what he had seen during the reading of the piece, Webern would play an altered portion of the student's music and ask "Was this not what you really had meant?" in order to "help a basically good idea towards its appropriately clear and comprehensible formulation." His students reported that he tended to refrain from pointing to specific solutions to musical problems, leaving students to find solutions for themselves once problems had been identified. He would make references to how composers like Beethoven might have approached a similar problem and cite a Beethoven sonata as an example. At other times, he would develop "an entire series of variations on a theme furnished by the student, masterfully exemplifying the concept of the variation form" (p. 507). Webern's teaching style was never authoritarian, and he was quick to show contagious enthusiasm for the work being critiqued.

Drawing from Mozart's letters and manuscripts, Mann (1987) relates how Mozart, like Webern, began with the student's musical ideas but then edited and incrementally added to them in order to illustrate the possibilities inherent in the student's music:

> Mozart went through the [student's piece], added a natural sign where it had been forgotten, and rewrote a passage to avoid parallel octaves, but then he started afresh and wrote a completely new version. As his own teacher had done fifteen years earlier, he followed

the student's conception; in fact, he [accepted] the outline of the piece completely. He "merely" loosened the four-part fabric while he tightened its thought. (p. 52)

Mann (1987) also describes how Mozart handled the common problem of a student who is stuck and cannot generate new musical ideas. In a letter to his father about a lesson, Mozart reported:

> Now it occurred to me that she was only at a loss of how to start. I began to vary the first measure [of her piece] and told her to continue along the same lines. This worked after a fashion, and when she was finally finished, I asked her to take up a new melody. ... Well, she deliberated for a quarter of an hour—yet nothing came forth. In the end I wrote four measures of a minuet and said to her: "look, what a fool I am; I have started a minuet and cannot even complete the first section—be so good as to help me out." (p. 51)

To help with the familiar problem of how to get started with a new piece, it appears that Mozart gave students an incomplete beginning idea and asked them to continue it.

We can draw the following lessons from these descriptions of Webern and Mozart as teachers:

■ Get to know students' music well before offering critiques.
■ Encourage students to find solutions to musical problems on their own.
■ Help students discover how other composers may have addressed problems simi-

lar to ones they are having.

■ When changing or adding to students' music, offer incremental changes based directly on their musical ideas.

■ Help students who are stuck by varying one of their ideas or by offering incomplete portions of music to extend.

Lessons From Teachers of Visual Art and Creative Writing

Teachers of our sister arts have much more experience in guiding creative work than we do. In their domains, it is more natural for students to create original works than it is for them to re-create (perform) or study existing works, as we do in music education. Perhaps we can learn from their experience. Engel (1995, 1996) offers guidance to teachers and parents for learning to look at and respond to children's art. First, she believes that we must learn to look more carefully at children's work than we often do: "It is advisable not to leap to interpretation, certainly not to summary judgment. ... Usually the most useful approach is description: start with—and possibly end with—what is there, visible, and describable" (Engel, 1995, p. 27). As a strategy to guide this careful observation and description, Engel (1996) suggests following a systematic approach based on answers to six questions about the student's work: (a) What is it made of? (b) What does the observer see? (c) What does it represent? (d) How is it organized? (e) What is it about? and (f) Where does the idea come from? She points out that almost any thoughtful response to students is valuable simply because it indicates that others take their work seriously, and the time spent considering it validates their work as both a product and a process (Engel, 1996).

In his discussion of how teachers can respond to student poems, Bizzaro (1993) stresses the difference between a directive, didactic approach to guiding students and a facilitative, heuristic manner. He believes that over the longer term students benefit most from the facilitative approach and makes his point by quoting William Stafford:

> First suppose you had a chance to work with someone who would correct your writing into publishability. This person would be efficient, knowing, memorable, valid: an accomplished writer. In the company of this person you ... would quickly learn what brings success in the literary scene. Now suppose another kind of associate. This one would accompany you as you discovered for yourself whatever it is that most satisfyingly links to your own life and writings. You would be living out of your own self into its expression, almost without regard to the slant or expectation or demands of editors and the public. Let there be no mistake about it: a large and significant ... group of writers today would prefer the second kind of company. (p. v)

Bizzaro (1993) recommends that the best way for teachers to learn to respond to students' poems in a facilitative manner is to write poetry themselves. Teachers need to experience firsthand the thinking and feeling process that their students are undergoing in order to give constructive, useful responses. Examining their own processes of writing, reading, and revising is the most authentic way for teachers to improve the range and usefulness of their responses. Also, Bizzaro says that teachers need to write so that students can "sense their teacher's excitement and involvement not only with their [students'] writing but also with his or her own writing as well" (p. 15).

We can learn these lessons from our colleagues who teach art and poetry:

- Observe students' work carefully before critiquing it.
- Use a systematic approach to describing the work, and delay interpretation or judgment.
- Validate students' work through genuine responses because these are inherently valuable, even when they do not contain detailed comments.
- Use a facilitative approach, which helps students find their own composing interests, in addition to a didactic approach, which gives direct suggestions on changes that could or should be made in the music.
- Get involved in the creative process in order to experience what your students experience.

These lessons share similarities with the lessons derived from Webern and Mozart as teachers.

Lessons from Expert Practitioners of Teaching Composition in School

The profession has created a body of research on how children, novice learners, and professional composers think and work through the compositional process (e.g., Daignault, 1996; Hickey, 1995; Kratus, 1989; Levi, 1991; Wiggins, 1994; Younker & Smith, 1996). We also have narrative descriptions of how con-temporary composers have approached their teaching (e.g., Ball, 1970; Gyokeres, 1983; Keane, 1979; Lockwood, 1955). Most of what we know about the teacher's role, however, comes from the work of expert practitioners (i.e., teachers who have many years of experience in guiding music composition in school programs). From their experience, we can draw four general lessons that are most relevant to responding to students' works.

First, these teachers stress the importance of initially responding to the student's whole work and trying to grasp the overall expressive character, or musical meaning, that the student is creating. This is in contrast to immediately giving appraisals on the details of the student's melody, rhythm, harmony, and so forth. Wiggins (2000) advises:

> You have to talk about student work in ways that are most meaningful to them and show you understand their overall intent. In my experience, it is more important to talk with students in relation to their larger plan for the whole work. Feedback on details—either wonderful or troublesome—should be given with their intent in mind.

Deutsch (2000), after more than a decade of teaching composition to elementary students, concurs:

> I begin my interactions with students around expressive ideas, not techniques or rules. Our emphasis is on how music conveys feeling, and as I work with students, I try to find the musical world the

kid is living in, then make it a bigger world. Later, we can turn to techniques and skills.

Mellor (1999) reinforces this emphasis on the expressive whole in her research on how teachers respond to student compositions. She found that the personal value of music for students is enhanced when the teacher avoids acting as an expert who perceives and discusses music in technical terms. Rather, we should retain the intuitive approach of novices who discuss music in more holistic, global terms.

Second, these experts recommend sensitivity to students' readiness to receive critiques, which differs for each individual and at different points in their composing process. This requires judgment on the part of the teacher about whether or when to offer suggestions and responses. Bunting (1987) relates an incident when he decided to be more directive, after working with a promising student for some time: "I did not feel this was a very promising start [to a new piece] ... I decided to intervene and ask Barry to look for more interesting materials with which to develop his initial impulse to compose a powerful chord-based piece" (pp. 31–32). It is wise to remember that students do not often encounter the process of reflection, critique, and revision in traditional school instruction. Instead, the norm is for students to complete an assignment and then have it graded by the teacher, not to revise their work based on teacher or peer reviews. Perhaps the best way to honor the student's readiness for critique is to trust the student and ask, "How can I help you best?"

A related, but different, issue is the student's willingness or interest in revising compositions at all. Younger students often resist the prompting of teachers to refine pieces that the students consider to be finished. Stauffer points out that many students prefer to "revise" their pieces by simply composing a new piece in a similar style or medium, trying to apply what they learned from one piece to a new one (S. Stauffer, personal communication, June 12, 2000). Even though we, as teachers, want our students to experience the composition process, which is inherently a reiterative process of trial and revision, we should be sensitive to the possibility that many students might practice this kind of musical thinking by creating whole new pieces. This method is more like how children approach learning to draw or sketch by doing new drawings, not by erasing or "fixing" finished ones.

Third, experienced teachers understand that neither a primarily directive, didactic approach nor a heavily facilitative, heuristic manner is adequate on its own. Instead, the relationship with students is a true give-and-take through extended dialogue. Bunting (1987), based on his extensive time teaching composition to secondary students, summarizes:

> I have come to believe that neither approach is completely adequate ... [T]he pupil seeks to develop his own values and purposes—often with great determination—but always looking for guidance and clarification from the teacher.
>
> Meanwhile, the teacher feels the need to pass on the knowledge and values he has acquired—but sensitive all

the time to the individual development of the pupil. This model is based on an interplay ... between the viewpoints of teacher and pupil. There are risks of confusing, overwhelming or alienating the pupil, but there is also the chance of real communication, and of personal development that is at the same time true technical discipline. (pp. 25–26)

Our colleagues who have long experience in teaching creative writing tend to support this dynamic, dialectical view of the student-teacher relationship. Sperling (1990), in her research on the teacher-student writing conferences often held in English classrooms, found that these conferences are a collaborative, shifting process shaped by specific circumstances of the writing. They are best understood as being on a continuum, from didactic to heuristic. They vary from student to student and also vary with the same student at different times.

Fourth, veteran teachers recognize that appropriate responses to student compositions are strongly related to the purpose of the composition within the larger music education of the student. Many teachers give relatively restricted parameters for composition assignments that are intended to help students understand a concept and develop a technical skill, even as they strive for an expressive result. Here, composing is a means for teaching or assessing understanding of melody, harmony, rhythm, form, and so forth. For example, an assignment might ask students to develop variations on a melody by using sequence, inversion, retrograde, augmentation, and diminution. Teacher responses to these compositions will be tightly focused on these skills and how they are applied to the expressive whole. These responses can be formalized into structured assessments of student skill and knowledge using rubrics that provide students with detailed criticism of their work (Hickey, 1999a). The extent to which students will invest real commitment and personal interest in these assignments is an issue. When the purpose, however, is for students to think creatively, apply a range of musical skills and sensitivities, and compose a piece that they think of as uniquely their own, teacher responses will focus much more on helping the students derive their own musical ideas and generate their own solutions to musical problems.

A Continuum of Teacher Responses

To summarize the preceding discussion and provide more concrete guidance, Table 1 lists 11 types of teacher responses to student compositions, along with example statements. These types are certainly not discrete, and they are often combined in practice. For clarity, however, they are listed separately here and presented in order generally from least directive (heuristic) to most directive (didactic).

While the majority of responses to students are positive, it is necessary at times to "push" students when the teacher is confident they are capable of better results. As an instance of Response 2, Bunting (1988) tells how he set higher expectations for an advanced student:

[Peter] could have given more thought to his overall strategies. To extend the scale of the piece merely by tacking on

219

Table 1. A Continuum of teacher responses to compositions from least to most directive

No.	Response	Example Statements
1	Acknowledge, recognize, and/or verify students' work.	"This is your best work so far."
2	Encourage, motivate, and/or set expectations.	"Keep working. This section has real promise."
3	Describe salient characteristics and successful aspects of the piece. Be a "mirror" to increase awareness of what others are hearing.	"I like the way you broke away from your repeating rhythm pattern." "That's a neat effect when everything stops except the bass."
4	Provide explanations and definitions of unfamiliar musical material	"The lower part is a good start on a counter-melody (i.e., a second melody played at the same time as the main melody)."
5	Point out composers and compositions that students might find interesting based on the type of music they are composing.	"You might want to listen to how Phillip Glass solved the problem of ending a section with many repeating figures."
6	Ask students to describe their piece and to explain the feedback or help they are seeking. Ask about the student's intentions.	"What things do you need help with?" "Is your piece working out the way you hoped?"
7	Facilitate critique and reflection by questioning and probing about the piece or the composing process. Prompt students to do their own thinking, decision making, and self-appraisal.	"What parts would you change if you could start this section over?" "Have you tried improvising to get some new ideas for your B section?"
8	Point out musical problems and potentials in the piece.	"You have so much rhythmic and harmonic energy built up, it will need a strong ending."
9	Encourage students to experiment—to extend, alter, and develop.	"Try making your two-bar melody into four bars by varying your motive."
10	Provide suggestions for changes, additions, or deletions to students' music.	"I think your melody would stand out better if you transposed it up an octave."
11	Play or sing musical examples and possibilities.	"Listen to how I added longer notes to your melody to give it a more clear ending."

two quite unrelated episodes—to double its length merely by repeating everything an octave higher—and to finish so abruptly—seem to me naïve solutions: not wrong or inadequate, but superficial. (pp. 277–78)

When questioning to prompt students to think more carefully or creatively, as in Response 7, we should use a range of questions from closed to open and from broad (about the whole piece) to specific (about one portion of the piece). One experienced teacher said, "If students need help or aren't making progress, I keep asking more and better questions to help them arrive at their own solutions" (B. A. Younker, personal communication, June 14, 2000).

At times, teachers suggest ideas by playing or singing specific musical examples, as in Response 11. An important question is when these can best be offered within the student's composition process. Musical examples can be used to illustrate a verbal explanation without necessarily intervening too much in the student's musical material. For example, after asking "Have you thought about substituting some short notes for some of the long notes in your melody?" a teacher might first improvise a melody with many long notes and then replay it with passing tones or arpeggios in place of some long notes without replaying the student's melody itself. This leaves the student free to assimilate or reject the idea. One technique for helping students through times of indecision is to offer three different musical examples from which students might choose one to imitate. For example, a teacher can accompa-

ny a student's melody with three different chordal or rhythmic styles and suggest that the student emulate the style he or she likes best. Giving musical examples is a good opportunity to model risk taking and the process of "playing" with musical ideas. A teacher might suggest possibilities by improvising on a student's idea.

Hickey and Leon-Guerrero (2000) found a variety of responses to student compositions in their study of actual written responses by university music-education students, composers, and public school teachers to student pieces. Based on a qualitative analysis, they developed a list of both the type and content of verbal responses. Table 2 shows the types of responses they identified and gives examples. Hickey and Leon-Guerrero also categorized the content of the responses, or the aspect of music that is the focus of the response. Drawing upon research about how college-student mentors responded to writing by ninth-grade English composition students, they labeled the responses as focused on the whole piece, on idea development, on organization, on mechanics, or on "word choice" (analogous to "note choice"). These analyses offer other frameworks by which teachers can reflect on their responses to students and add to their repertoire of helpful reactions.

Analysis of Actual Teacher Responses to Compositions

It will be informative to analyze some actual responses to student compositions that provide concrete instances of how teachers have used the types of responses described above. These examples are

Table 2. Types and examples of written responses to student compositions by music education students, composers, and teachers

Type	Example
Comment	"The rhythms that you use make your composition very exciting."
Suggestion	"Try making it a bit softer and adding another track to it."
Question	"What do you want to do with the second half of your piece?"
Interpersonal	"Nice job." "Good luck." "Congratulations."
Definition	"The way you organized your melody is called a sequence (repeating patterns on another scale step)."
General	"Are you in a music group like the jazz band?"

drawn from two on-line mentoring programs in which university music-education students and professional composers provided written guidance to elementary and secondary students who were creating original music compositions (Hickey, 1999b; Reese, 2000a). These students composed pieces using MIDI technology (sequencing and notation software) as part of their school music classes, then sent their music files to the university mentors, who listened and replied with written constructive critiques. Mentors also sent music files to the students in order to illustrate one of the points they made in writing. Although the responses are written, they are approached informally and in a supportive manner, rather than as formal critiques. Since they are written, however, they are different from spontaneous conversation with students that would take place in traditional classrooms. For the purposes of this analysis, numbers in brackets have been added. These numbers refer to the type of response listed in Table 1 that the sentence preceding the number represents.

Example 1

The first example was written by a professional composer and experienced composition teacher, Professor Dana Wilson of Ithaca College, New York. He is responding to a middle school student, Lynsay, who has composed a 28-measure melody for clarinet. The piece is in 4/4 meter with a moderate tempo and is in the key of E minor. Here is Dr. Professor Wilson's message to the young composer:

Dear Lynsay,

The clarinet piece is terrific. [1] It has a very nice shape, beginning in the middle register and rising gradually—to concert G in the first phrase and then later to A and then B. This affords the piece a good sense of growth and increased energy. You also descend into the darker, rich register of the clarinet for contrasting color. The ending has a very satisfying cadence. [3] You might think about two things. First, think about the clarinet and what draws you to it enough to write for it. What's special about it? What can it do very effectively that other instruments don't necessarily do as well? [7] Listen to clarinet playing in different contexts, and notice the ability to play turns (ornaments), fast notes, long notes moving from one extreme dynamic to the other. Those things that excite you about the instrument will help make it a special piece for clarinet in that it's idiomatic and coming from your own experience with the instrument, though each piece doesn't have to (and shouldn't) use all the things you like about the instrument! [variation of 5] You might also think about musical phrases. Music works somewhat like verbal language in that they both have phrases, sentences, and paragraphs of sorts. If you're writing for a large group, it can be easier to make the punctuation clear: the drum can play the periods and the cymbal can play the exclamation points! But a solo piece needs to use rests or longer or shorter notes (or some combination) to help the audience hear the groupings. [7] Even though your piece is

for clarinet, you should sing as much of the piece as possible, because I think you'll find yourself breathing and shaping the line in a naturally vocal way; then, just put those indications (rests, longer notes, etc.) in the clarinet part. [8] So Lynsay, I hope this is helpful. You've written a very effective piece and I hope someday I'll hear it performed LIVE! [1]

Best wishes, Dr. Dana Wilson

Dr. Wilson's response is facilitative in tone and conveys respect for Lynsay's ability to think through possibilities and problems on her own. He offers information and advice to stimulate Lynsay's thinking but stops short of suggesting specific changes to the piece. His language has plenty of descriptive detail, and his analogy that compares phrases in music to the familiar structure of phrases, sentences, and paragraphs in language is an effective way to make his point clear.

Example 2

This response is written by Anne, a university music-education major with no special preparation in composing or teaching composition. She is responding to Kevin, a high school student doing his first sequencer-based composing. Her response is about the piece described in "Scenario: The Young Teacher's Uncertainty" near the beginning of this chapter. It is the written assistance she actually gave Kevin after getting over her initial bewilderment and listening further to his piece. Kevin's piece uses vibraphone, marimba, piano, tympani, and other percussion. It is 124 measures long, is in 4/4 meter with a moderate, varying tempo, and centers around the key of C major. The piece does not make a good first impression because of its rhythmic complexity and loosely played, loud tympani. Here is Anne's response:

Hi Kevin,

Here are my first impressions on your composition. Right away I could hear your first motive, the c, e, d, b, c, a, b theme. Also, I heard its reoccurrence several times, m. 66, m. 71, m. 113, etc. It seemed to me like you fragmented some of the main theme so that only part of it appeared in certain places. [3] Is that right? [6]

I have a bigger question for you, though. What role does the percussion play in your piece? Is it supposed to be accompaniment and support for the melodic parts, or is it supposed to be an independent, main part? [7] The reason I'm asking this is because you have so many complex rhythms in the percussion that it makes the piece sound busy and cluttered to me. It often covers the development of your motive. [3] Is this what you hoped for? [6] If not, why not try using simpler rhythms or eliminating that part altogether? [10]

Between the statements of your motives, you played chords—something like a C major and G^7. It sounded to me like you were doing a bit of improvisation there, then returning to the main motive. [3] Can you fill me in on what your intent was with those sections? [6] If you want to work further on the chordal sections, you might try using different octaves to get more variety and keep the listener interested. If you want

to work more on the melodic improvising, you could try improvising with fewer notes, or even just outline the chords in an arpeggiated way. [10]

Here's the most important question.

Do you like the sound and feeling of your piece? Would this be something that you would enjoy listening to at a concert, in your car, or playing on the piano at home? [7] I can say whatever I think of the composition, but when it comes right down to how the piece makes you feel, you are the only one who can know that. So think about my question and write back and tell me what you think you would change if you had this piece to do over again. [9] If this were my piece, the things I would try reworking first would be the percussion and the improvised section.[10] You, of course, are free to do your own thinking, and I look forward to hearing what you decide. Thank you for this first composition. I hope you are having fun with it. [1]

Ms. Benson

Anne avoids false praise as she begins her difficult task of responding to Kevin without discouraging him, even though his piece is problematic due to its ambiguous intent and technically inept use of rhythm in the tympani. She follows a strategy of describing the main features she is hearing and then questioning to see if she is hearing what Kevin intended. She offers suggestions but is careful to convey that Kevin can accept or reject the suggestions. She finishes by trying to engage Kevin in stepping back and thinking about the expressive effect of the whole piece, and she summarizes the two aspects that she thinks could use most attention.

Structured Approaches for Responding to Student Compositions

Teachers may find it helpful to use a structured approach—a planned set of steps or actions—to anticipate possibilities for responding. Engel (1996) suggested a method for talking with children about their art work that can be adapted as a process for responding to student compositions. She poses six questions, moving from concrete description to interpretation, for the teacher to answer in order to ensure a thorough description of all aspects of the student's work. Table 3 shows how these questions might be adapted for music compositions. It is interesting to note that in her responses to student work Engel focuses on descriptions, or what Hickey and Leon-Guerrero (2000) call "comments," and questions. Her emphasis is on seeing fully what is in the art work before forming opinions, and the examples of responses that she offers do not include suggestions for changes, only questions to prompt the student to think further. For instance, Engel (1996) proposes this response to Question 4: "The parts of the paper that

Table 3. Engel's questions about student art works adapted for music

Art question	Music question
1. What is it made of (e.g., size, tools, medium)?	What instruments, voices, or sound sources are used?
2. What does the observer see (e.g., lines, angles, shapes, symmetry, colors, overlaps)?	What elements are most readily heard (e.g., melodic, harmonic, rhythmic, textural features)?
3. What does it represent (e.g., design, story, scene, symbol)?	Does the music refer to something else (e.g., the lyrics of a song, a quote from another piece, a story, or a program)?
4. How is it organized (e.g., perspective, composition, action, view, completion)?	What is the form of the piece (e.g., phrases and sections)?
5. What is it about? What is the nature of involvement (e.g., violence, peace, love, sadness, experimentation)?	What is the overall expressive quality or mood?
6. Where does the idea come from (e.g., imagination, observation, literature, imitation, TV, conversation)?	Was the piece inspired by something else? Does it have a specific purpose?

you didn't paint at all look almost like a frame around the parts you did paint. Do you see what I mean?" (p. 76). One explanation for this tendency not to offer suggestions is that adding lines or shapes to a student's art work could alter it permanently. In music, however, we have the flexibility to add or remove notes without irreversibly affecting the piece. Engels' type of step-by-step descriptive process provides a helpful model for careful listening that fosters thoughtful, beneficial critiques, which might include suggested changes. The fast pace of classroom activities can make this kind of thorough listening quite difficult, however. Frequently recording students' works may be a partial solution.

Deutsch (2000) described a set of common problems that students face as they compose and suggested tactical responses for helping students find solutions to these problems. Table 4 lists these problems and briefly describes how teachers can assist with them. When teachers can anticipate likely problems, they can more quickly provide useful ideas for students.

Experiences for Developing the Skills of Responding

How can teachers, especially novice teachers, improve their ability to respond constructively to student compositions? The primary need, of course, is for many opportunities to listen to a wide range of student compositions and then to think about how to assist the student through verbal and musical responses. These skills are challenging to acquire because of the open-ended, indeterminate nature of student compositions. Because we cannot know what students' music will be like, we cannot

follow a formula, recipe, or template when responding to it. The lessons, guidelines, and types of responses described above, however, provide a helpful repertoire from which to draw when practicing these skills.

One way to provide frequent opportunities to practice responding is to develop partnerships with local music teachers who are having their students compose. If student compositions are recorded or notated, music-education students can study these pieces and provide constructive feedback to students in written form or, ideally, in face-to-face interactions. A promising development is the use of on-line Internet forums for exchanging compositions and written guidance among elementary and secondary students, university music-education students, composition majors, professional composers, and practicing school music teachers (Cosenza & MacLeod, 1998; Reese & Hickey, 1999). Because these programs make it relatively easy to exchange music and communicate in writing, music-education students get many chances to listen to student compositions. They can write responses to actual students who are currently composing and compare their ideas to those being written by other participants in the project. Reese (1999, 2000b, 2001) has shown that on-line programs are technically, instructionally, and organizationally feasible; that preservice teachers can improve significantly in their ability to write constructive verbal responses to secondary students about their compositions; and that on-line mentoring has a moderate effect on the quality of preservice teachers' written responses to compositions when compared to responses written by a control group.

Ideas for Teacher Educators

The following are six activities that teacher educators can use to help novice teachers (referred to as mentors) learn the skills of responding.

Presentation: How Composers Develop Musical Material

In a presentation, demonstrate and explain a few ways that composers develop musical ideas. Enlist the help of a composer if possible. To demystify the act of composing, show examples of how established composers have taken basic material and used simple, easily understood and applied techniques to transform it. One informative example is found in a treatise by Hiller (1778/2001), an eighteenth-century com-

Table 4. Deutsch's tactical responses to common problems faced by students when composing

Problem	Response
The student creates too many unrelated ideas.	Encourage the student to select only one, two, or three favorite ideas for development through repetition, sequence, etc.
The student's music is prosaic or formulaic.	Improvise for the student and show willingness to make "mistakes." Appeal to real-life emotions and stories, myths, or folktales to stimulate the student's imagination
The student is stuck.	Play a complete phrase and ask the student to sing something that might sound good after it. If more is needed, offer a gradually narrowing set of musical possibilities to choose from.
The student's music is odd or difficult to understand.	Ascertain the student's intentions before offering suggestions (i.e., if the student is trying to create something unusual or is unsuccessful at something more "normal"). Tape record the piece to have more chances to listen before responding.
The student has trouble hearing coherent ideas.	Help the student create simple patterns to manipulate to build symmetrical phrases.
The student has exceptional abilities.	Challenge the student with theoretical or compositional concepts. Introduce the student to older students who may perform his or her music or provide peer support.

poser and voice teacher. In it, he shows the original melody from an operatic aria and provides a variation on this melody printed immediately below the original. His variations use simple devices such as scales, neighboring and passing tones, and rhythmic variation to ornament the composer's original line. Mentors can recommend these same techniques to their students as they suggest possible changes.

Judging: Study Helpful and Unhelpful Guidance

Another activity can help mentors identify what characteristics make responses more or less helpful to students. Ask mentors to listen thoroughly (i.e., more than once) to a student composition, then read an example of a written response that you consider ineffective. Repeat this with an example of a more helpful response. In discussion, identify the features of the responses that make them weaker or stronger. Finally, provide a third response and ask mentors to judge its quality using a formal rating scale. Hickey and Reese (2001) have developed a valid and reliable rating scale for judging written feedback that contains these eight items with a response scale from 1 ("Not Evident") to 7 ("Evident in Depth or Detail"):

■ Praise or positive feedback is related to a specific feature of the composition or composition process. It is not general or "empty."
■ Critique of any weak areas in the composition is specific.
■ Feedback includes clear analysis/description of the important musical elements of the composition.

■ Feedback provides musical (and/or technical) terms that are appropriate for the age level of the composer.
■ Feedback contains specific suggestions for change.
■ Suggestions for change are musically appropriate for this piece.
■ Suggestions for change are appropriate for the age level of the composer.
■ The writer uses effective devices to communicate imaginatively about suggestions or the piece as a whole (e.g., humor, metaphors, analogies, expressive language).

The following additional criteria may also be used to judge feedback:

■ The writer asks appropriate questions of the composer (e.g., related to intention, purpose, or plans).
■ The writer effectively refers to related styles of music, composers, or specific pieces to support suggestions or musical ideas.
■ Messages are concise and contain two or three specific suggestions.

Revision: Edit an Existing Written Response

Extend the activity above by asking mentors to rewrite an existing written response after analyzing it using the listed criteria. To prepare for this activity, have mentors study an example you have prepared that shows (a) the original writing, (b) the original writing with comments about its weaknesses, and (c) a more informative rewritten version. Examples of these follow:

Original writing. The motive did tend to get repeated a lot. You might think about less repetition of the actual motives and adding in more development. Maybe modulate the motive over several bars or fragment it. You could also do both: Fragment the motive, put some development in, and modulate into another fragment of the motive. I think this would make it much more interesting.

Original writing with comments. The motive did tend to get repeated a lot. You might think about less repetition of the actual motives and adding in more development [Does the student know what development means?]. Maybe modulate [Does the student know what modulate means?] the motive over several bars or fragment it. [Does the student know what fragment means?] [a suggestion for change, but not specific enough for the student to know how to try alternatives.] You could also do both: Fragment the motive, put some development in, and modulate into another fragment of the motive. [difficult to follow] I think this would make it much more interesting.

More informative rewritten version. The motive did tend to get repeated a lot. You might think about less repetition of the actual motives and adding in more development (small or gradual changes in the motive's rhythm or pitches). For example, over several bars, repeat the motive but begin each time on a higher or lower note (this is called a melodic sequence—the same pattern repeated higher or lower). You could also fragment it (i.e., break the motive into even smaller pieces and repeat just a part of it). You might try this order:

1. Fragment the motive.
2. Repeat the fragment once or twice, but begin on a higher or lower note for each repeat.
3. Use the remaining portion of the motive.

I think this would help keep the rhythmic and melodic interest going through the repetitions.

Discussion: Analysis of Problematic Compositions

A common challenge is how to respond to problematic or weak compositions. These might be compositions that (a) do not apply the criteria of the assignment, (b) do not reflect the composer's stated intentions, (c) are technically inept or seem to ignore the effect on the listener, or (d) include musical choices that seem to be made for no apparent reason. In a group, listen carefully to the composition and ask mentors to make written notes about possible problem areas and suggest responses to those problems. Discuss these notes and debate the pros and cons of various approaches to the composition. Next, ask the mentors to read a written response to this piece that you have prepared ahead of time and discuss the types of responses that you used. Finally, to make the verbal explanations clear, listen to a musical example that you prepared ahead of time to illustrate one of your suggestions.

Peer Critiques: Rating Written Responses

After mentors have practiced writing responses, they can assist each other by doing peer critiques of their writing. The mentors read a peer's response to a student's piece, then rate that response using a formal rating scale such as the one by Hickey and Reese (2001) described above. Then, peers share the results of the rating with each other and discuss possible improvements to their responses.

Conference: Review with Experienced Composer/Teacher

To receive one-on-one assistance with their responses, mentors can hold a conference with experienced teachers or composers to talk about how they guide their students. Mentors may bring examples of their writing for review and seek help with particularly challenging student pieces.

Importance of Teachers' Attitudes and Beliefs

In this chapter, I have tried to stimulate careful thinking about our verbal and musical responses to students and to provide some practical guidelines, lessons, and tips to help teachers improve the breadth and depth of their responses to students. Teach-ing composition and responding with perceptive, imaginative assistance to students' compositions is a new challenge for many practicing music educators. This kind of challenge can cause us to examine some of our traditional, perhaps unexamined, attitudes and beliefs about student learning. Teaching composition requires us to adopt a disposition that emphasizes inquiry and creativity rather than to seek closure and judge by strict criteria. It requires that we relax our tendency to be rule-oriented and learn to be more open-ended in our expectations. It requires us to develop greater respect for the musical awareness and skills that students bring to

school. It teaches us to temper our tendency to underestimate what our students can do musically. Finally, it reminds us to approach each learner with the awareness that all people learn in different ways and must thoroughly process ideas through their own sensibilities.[1]

Note

1. The author wishes to express sincere appreciation for the advice and resources provided by composer Dr. Timothy J. Bowlby and the insightful critique of this chapter by Dr. Eve Harwood.

References

Ball, S. (1970). Murray Schafer: Composer, teacher, author. *Music Scene, 253*, 7.

Beck, J. (2001). Discovering the composer within. *Teaching Music, 8*(4), 54–57.

Bizzaro, P. (1993). *Responding to student poems: Applications of critical theory.* Urbana, IL: National Council of Teachers of English.

Bunting, R. (1987). Composing music: Case studies in the teaching and learning process. *British Journal of Music Education, 4*(1), 25–52.

Bunting, R. (1988). Composing music: Case studies in the teaching and learning process. *British Journal of Music Education, 5*(3), 269–310.

Cosenza, G., & MacLeod, S. (1998). Vermont MIDI distance learning network: A model for technology in classroom music. In S. D. Lipscomb (Ed.), *Proceedings of the Fifth International Technological Directions in Music Learning Conference* (pp. 137–38). San Antonio, TX: IMR Press. (Information on the project is available on-line at http://www.webproject.org/midi)

Daignault, L. (1996). Children's creative musical thinking within the context of a computer-supported improvisational approach to composition. *Dissertation Abstracts International, 57*, 11B.

Deutsch, D. (2000, September). *New directions in the school composition program*. Paper presented at the conference New Directions in Music Education: Teaching Composition and Improvisation, East Lansing, Michigan.

Engel, B. (1995). *Considering children's art: Why and how to value their works*. Washington, DC: National Association for the Education of Young Children.

Engel, B. (1996). Learning to look: Appreciating child art. *Young Children, 51*(3), 74–79.

Gyokeres, N. (1983). Views on teaching composition. *Music Scene, 333*, 4.

Hickey, M. (1995). *Qualitative and quantitative relationships between children's creative musical thinking processes and products*. Unpublished doctoral dissertation, Northwestern University, Evanston, IL.

Hickey, M. (1999a). Assessment rubrics for music composition. *Music Educators Journal, 85*(4), 26–33.

Hickey, M. (1999b). *MICNET*. Retrieved June 30, 2002, from http://collaboratory.acns.nwu.edu/micnet/.

Hickey, M., & Leon-Guerrero, A. (2000, November). *A collaborative Internet music composition project: Lessons learned from a two-year study*. Paper presented at the annual meeting of the Association for Technology in Music Instruction, Toronto, Canada.

Hickey, M., & Reese, S. (2001). The development of a rating scale for judging constructive feedback for student compositions. *Journal of Technology in Music Learning, 1*(1), 10–19.

Hiller, J. A. (2001). *Treatise on vocal performance and ornamentation* (S. J. Beicken, Ed. & Trans.). Cambridge, England: Cambridge University Press. (Original work published 1778)

Keane, D. (1979). Beyond technique: Teaching

the unteachable in composition. *Canadian Association of University Schools of Music Journal, 9*(2), 70–90.

Kratus, J. (1989). A time analysis of the compositional processes used by children ages 7 to 11. *Journal of Research in Music Education, 37*, 5–20.

Levi, R. (1991). Investigating the creative process: The role of regular musical composition experiences for the elementary child. *Journal of Creative Behavior, 25*(2), 123–36.

Lockwood, N. (1955). Composition can be taught! *Music Journal 13*(2), 16, 28–30.

Mann, A. (1987). *Theory and practice: The great composer as student and teacher*. New York: Norton.

Mellor, L. (1999). Language and music teaching: The use of personal construct theory to investigate teacher's responses to young people's music compositions. *Music Education Research, 1*(2), 147–57.

Moldenhauer, H. (1979). *Anton von Webern: A chronicle of his life and work*. New York: Knopf.

Reese, S. (1999). Potentials and problems of Internet-based music composition mentoring. *Southeast Journal of Music Education, 11*, 1–11.

Reese, S. (2000a). *NETCOMM. Network for technology, composing and music mentoring*. Retrieved June 30, 2002, from http://www-camil.music.uiuc.edu/netcomm/Default.html

Reese, S. (2000b, November). *The effect of online mentoring of student compositions*. Paper presented at the annual meeting of the Association for Technology in Music Instruction, Toronto, Canada.

Reese, S. (2001). Integration of on-line composition mentoring into music teacher education. *Contributions to Music Education, 28*(1), 9–26.

Reese, S., & Hickey, M. (1999). Internet-based

music composition and music teacher education. *Journal of Music Teacher Education, 9*(1), 25–32.

Sperling, M. (1990). I want to talk to each of you: Collaboration and the teacher-student writing conference. *Research in the Teaching of English, 24*(3), 279–321.

Wiggins, J. H. (1994). Children's strategies for solving composition problems with peers. *Journal of Research in Music Education, 42,* 232–52.

Wiggins, J. H. (2000, September). *Compositional process: The search for common understanding.* Paper presented at the conference New Directions in Music Education: Teaching Composition and Improvisation, East Lansing, Michigan.

Younker, B. A., & Smith, W. H., Jr. (1996). Comparing and modeling musical thought processes of expert and novice composers. *Bulletin of the Council for Research in Music Education, 128,* 25–36.

Sam Reese is associate professor of music education at the University of Illinois at Urbana–Champaign. His publications include a book, *Strategies for Teaching: Technology,* and over 25 articles in music education journals. He has 24 years of public school music teaching and administrative experience and six years of university teaching experience.

11

The Nature of Feedback in a Community of Composing

Betty Anne Younker

Imagine a classroom in which teacher and students are engaged in reflective discussions and demonstrations while they create original works. In one-on-one situations and in small groups, students reflect on what they hear, provide feedback, compare descriptions, and make decisions about others' suggestions.

Feedback involves interplay between student and teacher, as well as between students. In compositional settings, it consists of reflective comments, descriptions, and suggestions about original works that are being created; thus, it involves generating, analyzing, and evaluating multiple possibilities for the music that is being composed. This interplay can contribute to the growth of students' understanding of music and of composing as they find their voices as composers. It can also increase their understanding of the role feedback plays during the process of composing and why it is essential. Quite often, students will view the first attempt at a composition as a finished product and not know what to do with any feedback that may be given (Hickey & Reese, 2000). Involving students in the process of dialoguing can increase the probability of their knowing when, why,

and how to use—or not use—feedback.

The purpose of this chapter is to address the possible multidirectional and dynamic nature of teacher- and student-directed feedback in compositional settings where the growth of students' innate musical capacity is valued. To understand the nature of feedback, we need to examine it in the kind of environment that facilitates feedback, and we need to examine the role feedback plays as one form of assessment and as part of the learning process. First, I will examine how we can facilitate feedback in compositional settings, and then I will address the nature of assessment. From this discussion, I will narrow the focus to one form of ongoing assessment, specifically teacher- and student-directed feedback. I will then examine the interactions that can occur between students engaged in composing activities and their teacher and classmates. Next, feedback will be viewed in the context of different approaches. Finally, I will offer insight into how feedback can contribute to students' musical growth as composers.

Definitions

Throughout this chapter, references are

made to students framing and solving problems while composing. Problem framing and problem solving, within the creative-thinking process, involve dynamic and, at times, nonlinear stages. These stages include sensing, defining, clarifying, or understanding the problem; moving between divergent and convergent thinking while generating and evaluating solutions; and converging on a final solution that may be used in other situations (Davis, 1986; Guilford, 1977; Sternberg, 1988; Webster, 1987a, 1987b). For the purpose of this chapter, *problem framing* is identified as recognizing and defining a problem, and *problem solving* is identified as generating, evaluating, and refining solutions.

Teacher-directed and student-directed feedback are also referred to throughout the chapter. *Teacher-directed* feedback refers to feedback given by teachers in the form of actions and words that direct the processes of framing and solving problems while composing. Such feedback identifies teachers as the sources for recognizing and defining the problem and for generating, evaluating, and refining solutions. *Student-directed* feedback refers to feedback given by students in the form of the actions and words as previously described. When students direct the feedback, they have ownership over framing and solving problems, increasing the aesthetic appeal of the composition, and refining the craftsmanship of the details.

The Classroom: A Community of Music Making

Many factors can prevent students from being active learners in the classroom. One is the role teachers and students adopt in

the classroom (Richardson, 1998). When teachers view themselves as sources of all information, they promote a safe environment for, and attribute power to, themselves. Conversely, in an environment where students are encouraged to acquire and cultivate knowledge for themselves, the power shifts from teacher-based knowledge and teacher-framed problems to shared knowledge and student-framed problems. This requires a shift in roles for teachers and students. One shift would consist of moving from a relationship of masters and apprentices to one of listeners and respondents. The former relationship identifies teachers as sources of information and exemplary models while the latter encourages interactive dialogue in which both students and teachers frame and solve musical problems. The master-apprentice relationship requires teachers to structure the compositional task, assess what students create, suggest solutions for deficiencies in a composition's expressiveness or craftsmanship, provide reasons for those solutions, and guide students as they choose the best solution. The listener-responder relationship empowers students to be involved in all aspects of the composing process, thereby gaining understanding about why and how compositions are structured from the beginning stages to completion. Teachers who recognize, understand, and value students' roles in an interactive relationship will offer insight only when asked or needed, thus minimizing their input about compositional problems and solutions.

As students begin to frame and solve musical problems through composing, the music educator can intercede by answering questions, describing student compositions, offering suggestions, and asking questions to motivate further thinking. As students continue to develop their compositions, they may ask for feedback on what they have done or for suggestions of what could be done next.

The amount of intervention will vary, depending on students' invitations and needs. Howard and Martin (1997) found that while some students may be motivated to work independently, others may need closer, more systematic supervision and intervention. VanErnst (1993) found that students involved in composing activities should be given autonomy to make their own musical decisions and that the teacher's role should be to facilitate and guide. While the appropriate amount and type of feedback depends on the situation, a long-term goal would be to increase opportunities for students to independently make and assess their own musical decisions while composing. How this can be done and what those opportunities would consist of are issues of concern when constructing an environment in which students can compose and, thus, will be further explored throughout this chapter.

Assessment

Interacting with music involves organizing music materials while drawing on knowledge about musical elements, musical styles, composers, musical types, functions, and aesthetic issues (Reimer, 1989). One aspect of this interaction involves assessment, which can be provided formally and informally through various approaches and techniques. When we assess students, we can determine their strengths and weak-

nesses in terms of how well they have developed the skills and knowledge that make meaningful experiences in music possible (Colwell, 1991).

Formal assessment can range from designing "particular activities to seek specific information about the level and extent of students' understanding of a particular concept" (Wiggins, 2001, p. 72) to providing opportunities for students to frame and solve problems. Activities of the former type include performing selections from required repertoire, composing music utilizing a specific form, aurally identifying the style and genre of a musical selection, or showing through movement the contour of a melodic line. Activities that allow students to frame and solve problems include participating in ensembles where students identify and solve musical problems; composing without any given parameters, thus framing a composition and the problems that arise while composing; and analyzing and evaluating the craftsmanship and expressiveness of specific musical selections.

Informal assessment of students' understanding occurs on a continuous basis during the music class. Once teachers have assessed the level of students' understanding, they must make decisions about the next step. These decisions are based on strategies developed in preparation for the class, successfully utilized in previous classes, or suggested by students in past and present classes.

Formal and informal assessment should not be a one-directional process but a multidirectional one in which teacher and students offer feedback to each other and reflect on and respond to the given feedback. Assessment, then, is an ongoing process that occurs during and after the completion of the project.

The "what" and "how" of assessment are directly linked to goals and objectives of the overall curriculum and, more immediately, the lesson and the activity. What is the purpose of the composing activity? Is it to display knowledge about traditional music symbols? If so, then the accurate use of crescendos, time signatures, key signatures, and notation should be assessed as students use the Western symbol system to represent their musical ideas and in performances of their compositions. Is it to demonstrate understanding of a musical line? Then students' ability to shape a musical line while performing should be assessed. Is it to understand relationships between harmony and melody within a specific style and genre? If so, then the assessment should involve examining how students compose melodies over given harmonic progressions, how they compose harmonic progressions under a given melody, how they interweave harmony and melody while exploring possible relationships between the two, or how they utilize their knowledge of style and genre while composing a harmonic and melodic line. The purpose of the activity must be clear in order to guide how the activity is realized and assessed.

Feedback

One form of assessment is feedback, which can be delivered verbally or nonverbally in the form of answers, descriptions, suggestions, and questions. The focus of feedback is on what has been done, what needs to be done, and what can be done. When providing feedback, teachers and students can articulate what they heard, provide suggestions for correcting inaccurate use of specific elements and expressive details, and provide possible solutions for musical problems that have been identified.

Teacher- and Student-Directed Feedback. Teacher-directed feedback is appropriate when a teacher's enhanced composing skills and musical knowledge can contribute to students' music-making experiences. The teacher may (1) provide information about a theoretical concept, a musical style, or a composer's style; (2) suggest recordings of the style in which students are composing or of a contrasting style; (3) model a compositional technique that might provide ideas for possible solutions; or (4) model how problems can be framed and solved by talking out loud while composing. The first three processes will broaden students' knowledge and techniques and further equip students with materials with which to work. The fourth process will allow students to view how compositional problems are framed and solved, become aware of strategies to use throughout composing, and observe the role that feedback plays during the assessment process. All of these processes can contribute to students' understanding, which can in turn be put into action while composing and may give them confidence to generate and respond to feedback.

After the teacher has modeled how musical problems can be framed and solved while composing, students need opportunities to put what they observed into action. This can be facilitated by presenting students with a situation or set of parameters as a stimulus for identifying and solving problems in ways of their choice (Atterbury & Richardson, 1995). Students first identify the problem within the given situation, and then they draw on previous knowledge to explore and sort out possible answers. To sort out the answers, students try out each answer to see if any are desirable. These opportunities differ from ones in which students complete teacher-framed composing tasks that have right and wrong answers and solve teacher-framed composing problems.

When students are expected to initiate feedback and converse about how their compositions sound in relationship to how they want the compositions to sound, they have opportunities to take full ownership of targeting problems and providing possible solutions for those problems. If our desire is for students to experience musical growth and develop their musical understanding through composing, then we need to provide opportunities for composing experiences that involve framing and solving problems.

Other interactions involve student-directed feedback (i.e., feedback generated by students and given to students). Teachers need to be sensitive when students are interacting and providing feedback to each other and realize when their input is not needed or desired. A community of learning in which musical ideas are exchanged and assessed can develop when student-directed feedback is emphasized. Students can learn from one another as they construct understanding in a social context and use that understanding in subsequent projects that are completed individually (Wiggins, 2001). The variety of musical encounters experienced by students within the group

can provide alternate views of how to frame and solve musical problems. One person, because of previous composing experiences, may encounter a musical problem for which a solution is evident and integrated immediately. Another may encounter the same situation and, because of a lack of composing experience, require time to generate and assess possibilities (Bereiter & Scardamalia, 1993). By working together, students can learn from each other and acquire possible strategies for subsequent compositional problems.

Questions as Feedback. Effective questions are one form of feedback that can encourage students to think about musical decisions. Generally, questions should focus students' thinking on how they might proceed, what they want to do with the materials, and how they want their compositions to sound. Questions such as "As you begin to play with the sounds, what melodic or rhythmic ideas interest you?" "What do you want the audience to hear at the beginning of your composition?" and "How could you provide contrast in the next section?" require students to think about how their compositions sound and can initiate comparisons between what they are hearing and what they want to hear. This process of thinking about musical decisions is a step toward thinking musically while composing. Students think about compositional decisions and then think in sound as they realize their decisions while working with the musical materials.

Different questions can involve students in different kinds of thinking. Some questions require students to identify, recall, and distinguish while others require them to analyze, synthesize, evaluate, create, and transfer (Bloom, 1956). When deciding what kind of questions to ask, it is important to identify the purpose of the composing activity and then make thoughtful decisions about the content and formation of the questions. If the goal is to assess students' knowledge about facts, the music educator should ask questions that require students to identify or recall musical information. These questions are direct and require correct answers.

When the desire is to have students uncover answers, as opposed to recalling or identifying information, then questions should follow the Socratic method of questioning. Here teachers ask questions of students who, in turn, provide answers that can guide them to correct responses. These questions can help students develop reasoned thinking about musical choices.

An example in the context of composing would consist of questions that would guide the students to the right—or most appropriate—musical solution, depending on the style or genre. Such questioning could occur in a situation in which the student is composing a piece of music for a middle school band based on a folk song from a particular culture and representing certain aspects of that culture. When making decisions about the melody, dynamics, and tempo, a line of questioning could be as follows:

The teacher asks, "What line in the folk song represents the climax of the piece?" The student will identify either the correct or incorrect answer. To justify a correct answer or allow the student to evaluate an incorrect answer, the teacher could ask, "What in the folk song provides evidence that this line is the climactic part of the

song?" The student answers, confirming the first answer or seeking out another answer.

In terms of making decisions about tempo, the teacher offers the following in response to a melodic line that maintains a consistent tempo throughout the entire folk song: "What kinds of movements accompany the song and are realized by the singer while singing the song?" The student offers answers. The teacher continues, "Explain how your tempo choices, or lack of, reflect those movements." The student offers explanations and possible justifications. The teacher asks, "How might tempo chang-es reflect the movements more accurately?" The student explores possibilities, evaluates, and understands why the first choices did not accurately or expressively portray the movements that accompany the song.

The point of such questioning is to have the student uncover the best solution through exploring and evaluating without being told what the best solution is.

Questions that allow students to make musical decisions within teacher-framed problems do not evoke correct answers but possible solutions. In this case, students can independently make musical decisions for their compositions while exploring possibilities and converging on desired outcomes. When making decisions, students should be encouraged to provide musical reasons to justify those decisions, which requires them to analyze and evaluate and, if necessary, generate further solutions and then choose and justify those new solutions. This recursive process continues until decisions are made about the final product—if there is a final product. This gets students beyond responses that are based on snap decisions and initial likes and dislikes. Situations that call for these questions are those in which teachers frame the problem and students generate, assess, and evaluate multiple solutions. These questions are open-ended and have no "right" answers, but rather they permit the student to have full ownership over musical choices. Questions of this nature within a composing context would include "How could the melody come to closure on the tonic?" "What dynamics are needed for your composition?" "How can you make the rhythm less complex?" and "What makes that instrument appropriate for that musical line?"

Questions that encourage students to frame and solve musical problems throughout the composing experience are open-ended, have no right answers, and provide focus for the larger and more immediate goals of the composition (Richardson, 1998). Questions such as "What do you want the audience to hear?" keep the overall goal in sight and provide structure for the more immediate decisions. Questions such as "What would you like to do next?" and "What do you think needs to be done next?" place students in the position to frame problems and generate possibilities. "What do you hear?" demands that students analyze what they have heard and prepares them for the next step, that is, framing what is to be done next. "What was most and least effective and why?" allows students to reason musically about what they heard and to justify changing or keeping what was composed. The focus could be on one element, and the question, which may be asked by the teacher or the student's peers, could include the following:

- "Describe the complexity or simplicity of the rhythm. Is it effective, and if so, how? What is the level of effectiveness? If not, how could it be effective?" These questions require student composers to identify the complexity or simplicity of the rhythm and assess its effectiveness. During this process, students begin to frame, if necessary, the musical problem—for example, how to make the complexity or simplicity of the rhythm more effectively enhance the overall expressiveness of the composition.

- "What is the relationship between the rhythm and the melody? On what do you want the listener to focus?" Thinking about this relationship requires students to assess foreground and background issues regarding rhythm and melody and frame what rhythmic or melodic changes are needed to achieve what is desired.

- "How does the tempo affect the melodic line?" Assessing how the tempo affects the melodic line, if at all, allows students to explore whether or not the effect is desirable and empowers them to frame how the issue will be addressed.

- "What contributes to variation in your piece of music? What contributes to unity?" These questions direct students' attention to issues of variation and unity, and they empower students to identify areas that could be altered to provide variation and unity. They would then begin to frame how this could be done, generate possible solutions, and assess.

- "Describe the overall form in terms of the beginning, middle, and end." Questions that allow students to think musically about the composition as a whole can guide decisions about specific aspects of the piece, giving students ownership over the complete composition.

Regardless of the kinds of questions, it is important to remember that closure is not always necessary, nor is it always possible. We need not summarize after each discussion in an effort to offer a single correct solution that is endorsed by the teacher (Richardson, 1998). Furthermore, students need to realize that not all questions are immediately answerable and that some may require further exploration, reflection, and assessment. When deciding what questions should be asked, teachers need to think about the following: What question is appropriate and necessary and why? At what level of thinking does it involve students? How do we assess students' level of knowledge, and more importantly, their understanding of the knowledge? How can students exhibit knowledge of content while being involved with content or, as Richardson (1998) states, "thinking in the musical content" (p. 119)? Questions that involve students in the various levels of thinking can be effective at all stages of learning and growth.

The Contribution of Feedback to Musical Growth. The ultimate goal of music education is to develop students' innate musicality (Atterbury & Richardson, 1995) so that musical experiences, including composing experiences, can be more meaningful. We can contribute to this development by offering opportunities for students' musical understanding to be heightened while they compose. Such opportunities allow students to make musical decisions and judgments and apply musical knowledge and skills while they shape musical materials— as in musical composition. To assess stu-

dents' understanding, we ask them to do something with the knowledge, that is, to put the understanding to work (Perkins, 1998). Assessing musical understanding in compositional settings would involve asking students to make musical decisions and judgments.

Further insight to students' understanding may come from having them respond to feedback given by teachers and classmates. Asking students to respond to descriptions of their compositions; suggestions for extension, refinement, and development; and questions about their compositions requires them to reflect, test, and refine. Students may or may not agree with the descriptions, integrate the ideas, or find the questions relevant. Once they have articulated their responses to feedback, they need to justify their decisions. This allows for growth in critical understanding of music.

Providing opportunities for students to use their knowledge—and to transform and enhance it— allows them to grow as composers. They are doing what composers do—working with musical materials while creating, evaluating, trying out possibilities, refining, and deciding. This does not mean using knowledge to solve problems quickly and easily, but it does involve using knowledge efficiently to target viable solutions and acquire new knowledge. At this point, students are experiencing the "growing edge" (Bereiter & Scardamalia, 1993, p. ix) of expertise as they work at the edge of their competence, and, as a result, they are increasing their knowledge. When students work harder and on their edge of capacity, extend their limits, and rely less on routines, they are extending their knowledge—

as opposed to exploiting their knowledge (Bereiter & Scardamalia, 1993). Our feedback, then, needs to progressively challenge students' musical understanding and their growth as composers as they work on their compositions.

Understanding is doing something with materials of music, in this case, composing. One aspect of teaching for understanding is assessing what student composers do with musical materials as they compose. This assessment can be achieved by observing them as they compose, listening critically to their compositions, and examining their responses to feedback from teachers and students.

Conclusions

If students are to grow as composers, feedback is essential for a variety of reasons. Deciding what, how, and when involves reflective decision making. Reflective decision making consists of determining the problem, generating solutions, testing and refining those solutions, and converging on the most appropriate choice. Decision-making processes can be richer and more meaningful if feedback is provided in the form of questions, answers, descriptions, and suggestions. Feedback allows student composers to think about what they are attempting to do musically, and it broadens the quantity and quality of their musical knowledge.

Teachers should be careful to not be the only source of feedback. Teachers can do a variety of things to encourage students to provide feedback. As teachers, we can model how and when to provide feedback and involve students in analyzing what occurred. This interactive process can shift the power from teacher to student and

result in moving from teacher-directed feedback to student-directed feedback and from teacher-framed problems to student-framed problems. Shifting the power can contribute to the growth of independent musical thinkers who have ownership of all decisions that are made while composing.

References

Atterbury, B. W., & Richardson, C. P. (1995). *The experience of teaching general music.* New York: McGraw-Hill.

Bereiter, C., & Scardamalia, M. (1993). *Surpassing ourselves: An inquiry into the nature and implications of expertise.* Chicago: Open Court.

Bloom, B. (Ed.). (1956). *Taxonomy of educational objectives: The classification of educational goals.* New York: Longmans, Green.

Colwell, R. J. (1991). Evaluation. In R. J. Colwell (Ed.), *Basic concepts in music education, II* (pp. 247–78). Niwot, CO: University Press of Colorado.

Davis, G. A. (1986). *Creativity is forever* (2nd ed.). Dubuque, IA: Kendall/Hunt.

Guilford, J. P. (1977). *Way beyond the IQ.* Buffalo, NY: Creative Education Foundation.

Hickey, M., & Reese, S. (2000, March). *Integrating internet-based music composition mentoring into music education methods.* Paper presented at the annual meeting of the Music Educators National Conference, Washington, DC.

Howard, J., & Martin, J. (1997). Developing musical creativity: The Singapore young composers' project as a case-study. *Research Studies in Music Education, 8,* 71–79.

Perkins, D. (1998). What is understanding? In M. Wiske (Ed.), *Teaching for understanding: Linking research with practice* (pp. 39–57). San Francisco: Jossey-Bass.

Reimer, B. (1989). *A philosophy of music education* (2nd ed.). Englewood Cliffs, NJ: Prentice Hall.

Richardson, C. P. (1998). The roles of the critical thinker in the music classroom. *Studies in music from the University of Western Ontario, 17,* 107–20.

Sternberg, R. J. (Ed.). (1988). *The nature of creativity: Contemporary psychological perspectives.* Cambridge, England: Cambridge University Press.

vanErnst, B. (1993). A study of learning and teaching processes of non-naive music students engaged in composition. *Research Studies in Music Education, 1,* 23–39.

Webster, P. R. (1987a). Refinement of a measure of creative thinking in music. In C. Madsen & C. Pickett (Eds.), *Applications of research in music behavior* (pp. 257–71). Tuscaloosa, AL: University of Alabama Press.

Webster, P. R. (1987b). Conceptual bases for creative thinking in music. In J. Peery, I. Peery, & T. Draper (Eds.), *Music and child development* (pp. 158–74). New York: Springer-Verlag.

Wiggins, J. H. (2001). *Teaching for musical understanding.* Boston: McGraw-Hill.

Betty Anne Younker is assistant professor of music education at the University of Michigan in Ann Arbor. Dr. Younker's research areas include philosophy and pedagogy of music education and critical and creative thinking. Her most recent chapter publication, "Critical Thinking," is in the *New Handbook of Research on Music Teaching and Learning* (R. Colwell & C. Richardson, Eds., Oxford University Press). As an educator, Dr. Younker has taught for the last 20 years in public school, studio, and university settings. As a musician, Dr. Younker sings with the Ann Arbor Cantata Singers, plays flute in collaborative projects with a Canadian harpist, and adjudicates and leads clinics with bands.

Related MENC Resources

Composition and Improvisation

Composing and Arranging: Standard 4 Benchmarks, edited by Carolynn A. Lindeman. 2002. #1671.

Composition in the Classroom: A Tool for Teaching, by Jackie Wiggins. 1990. #1006.

Getting Started with Vocal Improvisation, by Patrice D. Madura. 1999. #1638.

Northwestern University Music Education Leadership Seminars

Performing with Understanding: The Challenge of the National Standards for Music Education, edited by Bennett Reimer. 2000. #1672.

World Musics and Music Education: Facing the Issues, edited by Bennett Reimer. 2002. #1512.

For more information on these and other MENC publications, write to MENC Publications Sales, 1806 Robert Fulton Drive, Reston, VA 20191-4348, call 800-828-0229, or visit our Web site at www.menc.org.